Stand Up Paddle
A Paddler's Guide

KANU CULTURE

publications since 1994

published by

BATINI BOOKS Est 1994

Stand Up Paddle
A Paddler's Guide

A Kanu Culture publication,
published by Batini Books,
written and researched by Steve West.

KANU CULTURE
publications since 1994

Disclaimer - Copyright Issues

Apart from any purposes of private study or research as permitted under the copyright act, no part of this publication may be reproduced, stored in a retrieval system, or transmitted in any form or by any means, electronic, mechanical, photocopying, recording or otherwise, for the purpose of financial gain or resale. Ensure bibliographic reference when extracts are used in associated publications. The management of Batini Books, Kanu Culture, along with the authors and editors of this book, shall not accept responsibility for any injury, loss or damage caused to any person acting or failing to act upon information arising from material in this book, whether or not such injury, loss or damage is caused by any negligent act, or omission, default or breach of duty by Batini Books, Kanu Culture or the authors and or editors, except as provided by law.

Publishing Information

© Steve West, Batini Books 2012. **www.kanuculture.com**
Photography Steve and Mandy West unless otherwise indicated.
Additional photography: Dana Edmunds, Daphne Hougard,
Karen Baxter, JOSS, Sue Sheard. Where photographic credit omissions occur, please notify us so as we can rectify during future reprints.

Bibliography

Holmes, Tommy, The Hawaiian Canoe. Honolulu. Editions Limited. 1981.
Toro, Andras. Canoeing: An Olympic Sport. San Francisco. Olympian Graphics. 1986.
West, Steve, Kanu Culture. Volumes 1-10. Australia. Batini Books. 1995 - 2005
West, Steve, A Paddlers Guide to Outrigger Canoeing. Sydney. Kanu Culture Publishing, 2006.
West, Steve, The Art and Skill of Steering. Sydney. Kanu Culture Publishing. 2006.
West, Steve, Level 3 Academy of Surfing Instructors (ASI) Downwind Manual, 2012
West, Steve, Level 1 Coaching Manual. AOCRA. Australia. Batini Books. 2000.
Burch, David. Emergency Navigation. Camden Maine: International Marine, 1986.
Kyselka, Will. An Ocean in Mind. Honolulu: University of Hawai`i Press, 1987.

ISBN 978-0-9574664-0-1

Cover Shot

"Travis Grant is one of the most composed athletes I have come across. I have seen him take wins at SUP events in Hawai`i under huge pressure and fierce competition. However, this shot was taken during a sunrise shoot at the sea cliffs of Hawai`i Kai on the South shore of O`ahu. I appreciate this shot because it shows the composure Travis has in such a dynamic, unpredictable ocean environment. What makes it even more impressive is this was less than 15 hours after Travis had his first big win at the 2011 Battle of the Paddle, Waikiki."

Dana Edmunds - www.danafoto.com

Contents

Mandy West - Grape Bay Bermuda

STEVE WEST
2014 Winner World Paddle Award for Media
2015 Admitted into the World Paddle Academy

British Windsurfing Display Team
UK Board Sailing Open Sea Examiner
Royal Yachting Association Senior Instructor
International Windsurfing Schools Instructor
First windsurfer to sail on the River Nile.
Co-Founder of the UKs Around Hayling Island Race
Level 1 Coaching Principles (Aust)
Level 2 Coaching Principles (Aust)
Level 1 Outrigger Canoeing Coach (Aust)
Elements of Shipboard Safety (Coxswains)
Co National Coaching Director (Aust) with C. Maynard (5yrs)
Co National Coaching Director (Fiji) with C. Philp (5yrs)
Founder of AOCRA Coaching / Author of Manuals
Founded Kanu Culture 1994
Author of 12 Books on the subject of Outrigger Canoeing
Founding member and Vice President Mooloolaba OCC 1990
Former Vice President Australian Outrigger Canoe Racing Association
Former Secretary Australian Outrigger Canoe Racing Association.
Team New Zealand Crew 1998 New Caledonia
Former International Polynesian Canoe Federation Delegate.
2009 AALS (UK) Authored the Good Practice Guide for SUP
2009/10 UK SUP Coaching Development
2010 Team Starboard Racing Team UK (SUP)
2011 Appointed ASI CEO Europe SUP Division
2012 Authored Stand up Paddle - A Paddlers Guide
2014 Authored V1 - A Paddlers Guide
2014 Authored OC1 - A Paddlers Guide
2014 Mistral International VP Mistral Red Dot MD
2015 Authored SUP - Water Safety and Rescue
2015 Winner of World Paddle Awards for Media Lifetime Achievement
2015 Admitted into World Paddle Academy

Of over 15 years of competing in the Hamilton Cup Australia, I finished out of the top 5 crews on but a few occasions, testimony to the men with whom I was fortunate to paddle with.

Winner Masters Division of Moloka`i Hoe 1998/99
Winner Masters Division of Hamilton Cup 1998/99/07
Winner Masters Division 16km Round Hamilton Island 1998/99/07
Winner Cairns To Port Douglas (OC1) 2008 with C. Maynard
Runner up Hauraki Hoe New Zealand 1998/2003
Runner up Catalina Classic 1998 (Mixed Division)

My Thanks To
Tahiti Tourism, Air Pacific
Air Tahiti Nui, Fiji Tourism
Palau Tourism
Marianas Tourism
Hamilton Island Resort
Infront Communications
Susan Boyd, Harvie Allison
Sue Sheard, Chris Maynard
Jim Foti, Todd Bradley
Colin Philp, Jackie Taylor
Kialoa Paddles and to my
beautiful wife Mandy.

Most of my paddling years have been spent either in seat 1, 2, 5 or 6. My favourite if I had to be honest, is seat 5 in big water with a top crew. In 2007 our Mooloolaba Masters crew consisting of Chris Maynard, Danny Sheard, Grant Kenny, 'Lemmo', Darren Mercer and myself won the around Hamilton Race. Sitting in seat 5 behind these guys in the hands of Danny Sheard was an epic experience I will never forget. We were fast, but did not beat the record we set in 1998, with Danny Sheard and Grant Kenny also in that crew.

Have raced in these events either once, twice or on multiple occasions. The Hawaiki Nui Va`a I have raced twice, followed it five times and the toughest by far, especially the 2nd day, 60km iron. Catalina, Moloka`i Hoe, Hawaiki Nui Va`a, Hamilton Cup, Micronesian Cup, Gold Coast Cup, Bay of Islands NZ, Hauraki Hoe NZ, Ouvea to Poindimie New Caledonia, Fiji International and no doubt, some I've forgotten.

Foreword by Travis Grant

Steve West is synonymous with the Pacific-wide sport of outrigger canoeing, not just as a writer, but as a competitor, trainer and mentor. For as long as I remember, Steve's books have been a part of my paddling life. His colourful stories, educational pieces and obvious passion for the sport, have not only influenced myself, but the global 'ohana' of fellow paddlers and readers, a community drawn together by a love of the sport and the ocean around which we live.

Within the pages of, 'Stand Up Paddle – A Paddler's Guide' Steve draws strong parallels between stand up paddle boarding and outrigger canoeing, a background from which many of the sport's leading competitors and ambassadors have emerged.

As a lifelong outrigger competitor, I have no doubt that there is indeed a strong synergy between the two disciplines and this instant appeal is certainly what led me to begin stand up paddle boarding in the first place. In this context, Steve will be recognised as one of the sport's most respected authorities on this subject.

This book exposes the sport in a refreshing new light amidst all the noise and clutter of so many other ideas and beliefs. The contents presented, will not only make a better paddler of you, but will also serve to bring greater depth and meaning to your participation, as could only be expected by a writer and journeyman who has lived and traveled so extensively throughout the Pacific, dedicating a major part of his life, to the art and sport of paddling.

As a lifelong paddler raised on the Gold Coast, Australia, ocean paddle sports have always been a consistent, omnipresent part of my existence. My journey has been influenced by some of the world's most elite waterman and women. Stand up paddle boarding has come along at just the right time in my life, whereby I can explore new possibilities and take my paddling lifestyle further than I could have ever imagined

I am stoked to have been able to race with Steve, as team mates in outrigger canoe crews and shared experiences together in beautiful parts of the world such as the Marquesas Islands (Tahiti) Hamilton Island and Hawai`i. Now, I'm proud to watch, as he pushes himself once again and continues his own journey in being a constant in yet another emerging global paddle sport.

Steve's publications, have provided many years of positive impetus to the sport of outrigger canoeing, assisting the spread of the sport, through his passion and dedication to clarity and presentation of ideas and facts. This publication sets out to do the same in the context of stand up paddle boarding, on a level yet challenged.

'Be inspired by "Stand Up Paddling — A Paddler's Guide" and join us as we ride the oceans of the world together.'

Travis Grant

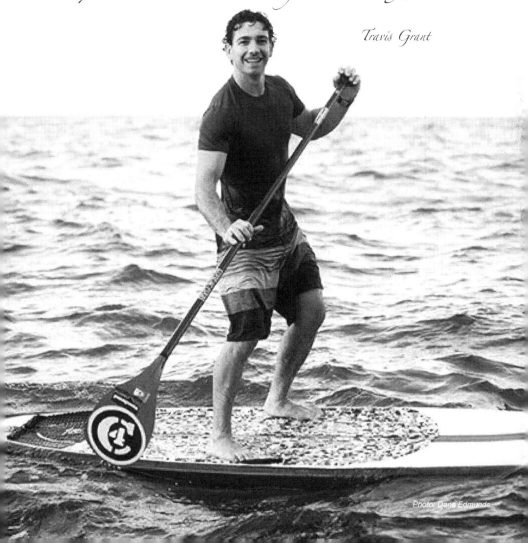

Photo: Dana Edmunds

Preface

"Man is a tool-using animal."

Thomas Carlyle 1795-1881

Taking stock of oneself is tricky at the best of times, but justifying to myself, let alone to you the reader, why five years of my life invested in this publication was worthwhile, is another matter altogether.

In the time it has taken to bash this into shape, several other books have been written on the subject, each author viewing the sport within their own field of interest and expertise, be it surf or river running. For me, it is perhaps no different, for it is the clear and distinct reality through my own particular field of interest and expertise, that stand up paddle boarding has, beyond any reasonable doubt, an overwhelming association and lineage with the 'Sport of Kings' otherwise known by its Eurocentric name, outrigger canoeing.

It is from this premise alone, I felt the initial urge to research the sport. Naturally, an involvement through participation was not only inevitable, but highly desirable, being as my OC paddling buddies were getting involved.

Todd Bradley, someone whom I've raced against, interviewed, hung out with and who has been immensely supportive of my publications in contributing over the years, was one such enigmatic figure who got me thinking about the sport around mid 2000 through his own involvement. Woogie Marsh, Kai Bartlett, Thibert Lussiaa, Aaron Napolean, Sue and Danny Sheard, were all relative early starters, who influenced my interest and then along came Danny Ching, son of Al Ching of Redondo Beach who had contributed for many years to our KANUculture outrigger canoeing publications and remains one of California's respected elders and ambassadors for the sport.

Travis Grant hooked up with Danny to race OC1 craft together in a team format and went on to win and set records for the Catalina to Newport beach race. Today they are at the top of the stand up paddle board race scene and then there's Jamie Mitchell, whom I've interviewed, raced and travelled with as part of an OC6 crew in both Fiji and the Marquesas.

The pattern here, is that we are all part of a very close family of ocean paddlers and while Jamie is uniquely set apart through his dominance of prone paddle boarding, he has always kept an affinity with outrigger

canoeing. He too, has taken a leap of faith into stand up paddle boarding as an extension of all that he knows. What makes their involvement so significant is the fact that many of them have risen quickly through the ranks to become world ranked stand up paddle board competitors.

For my part, the participation of outrigger canoeists is not merely co-incidental, it is highly significant. Regrettably, it is a sport not omnipresent or known much beyond many island shores of the Pacific or Pacific Rim. Consequently, surfing has become the medium by which many manufacturers, the media, the newbie or joe-public, have decided as being the closest, most easily understood summation of the sport with which they can associate its connection. This book challenges this notion head-on and at full speed, while giving lengthy consideration to the technical aspects of the sport.

Throughout Europe the ripple affect is working in a reverse cycle. Those new to stand up paddle boarding, are now being attracted toward outrigger canoeing, seeing the cross-platform benefits to be had in terms of fitness and the learning of paddling and ocean skills. It's because of this, that for me, there's no question that stand up paddle boarding has become the bolt-on link between the two sports, a marriage of bio-mechanics, where each serves the other well within the context of paddle sports. With stand up paddle boarding now emerging I, like many of my contemporaries, feel fortunate to be a part of this emergence, able to take existing skills and transpose them to something so profoundly appealing and broad in its spectrum.

Through over 23 year of travelling, racing, researching, educating, documenting outrigger canoeing across the Pacific and Pacific rim, my life has been a prism of immense dimension. A childhood lived in Africa, the far East, Mauritius and England, I moved to Australia in 1982. I started paddling kayaks at the age of 7, windsurfing at 19, outrigger canoeing at 28, stand up paddle boarding at 45. Through each, I've been fortunate to forge a lifelong career as a competitor, writer and educator.

The University of Hawai`i and University of the South Pacific (Fiji) currently house my publications concerning outrigger canoeing and are recommended by the Lonely Planet Guide Books (Hawai`i). I trust this offering respects the sport in disseminating tribal knowledge as I have come to understand it.

Steve West

1

Introduction
So what's it all about, where's it all going to and how should we define this sport and should we care?

Surfing does not share an association with canoeing, yet stand up paddle boarding does and herein lies the significant difference which assures us, these sports do not in fact share identical roots, far from it. Indeed canoe surfing no doubt existed before surfing in the context of evolution, out of necessity, not so much out of pleasure, but on account of the canoe's utilitarian purpose for fishing, trade, travel and at times, warfare.

Makaha, Hawai`i, OC4. Steerer Mel Pu`u. Crew: Chris Miller, Jimmy Boy Austin, Todd Bradley.

JOSSPhoto

Introduction

If researching, writing and producing a book was easy, then as the expression goes, 'Everyone would be doing it.' The fact is, it's a long journey from conception to completion and where subject matter is dynamic, in a constant state of evolution, by the time information is written down, it's already under threat of extinction. In this context, this is how the production of this book has felt. In the meantime and by comparison, many questionable websites and video clips clog up the web daily and often resound authoritative.

What is unique about the growth of stand up paddle boarding, is perhaps the way in which it has evolved and been served up so readily and so quickly in a manner which on many levels has permitted it to bypass the usual labour pains of birth and evolution itself. The internet has driven its popularity in a manner and on a scale rarely experienced by any other water sport on account of the age we live in and this is in stark contrast to say how surfing, windsurfing or outrigger canoeing experienced growth and evolution.

Outrigger canoeing is genetically linked to stand up paddle boarding, in a way which few participants readily acknowledge, understandable for a sport not so universally known. Consequently, it is erroneously overshadowed by an association with surfing. Australia's Mooloolaba OCC master men's crew whose legacy of Moloka`i wins over the past twenty years, makes the club and some of the crew members, the most successful in the history of the event. 1998 Moloka`i to O`ahu master men's crew.

Photo: Sue Sheard

3

Everyone has something to offer in what can only be very loosely described as part of the pioneering process and all the while one cannot but help get the feeling that unlike so many other past water sport developments, stand up paddle boarding feels very much, manufacturer and media driven, rather than by that of the end-user, to the point where there has been a surplus of everything; boards, paddles, information and the manifestation of many hundreds cashing in on the sport and many teaching newcomers barely knowing more than some of their customers.

On account of stand up paddle boarding seemingly bypassing puberty along with all of its symptoms, in one fell swoop it takes itself very seriously indeed. Its meteoric rise seems unprecedented from conception to full blown going concern. Entrepreneurs, surfing, prone paddle board and windsurfing brands have tooled up through various factories throughout South East Asia and are producing boards of all shapes, colour and materials to be sold in far away lands. Add to this any number of manufacturers pumping out cloned paddles of varying qualities undermining the intellectual effort of many life-style makers and all the while the sport is apparently enjoying its self proclaimed title of, 'The world's fastest growing water sport' once given to windsurfing and even outrigger canoeing, all in the absence of any hard evidence.

The fact remains stand up paddle boarding has a long way to go if it is to stand the test of time. It requires a healthy dose of self examination and cynicism in order to survive, for if it's driven predominantly by manufactures and the media with strategic agendas and alliances where cashing in is the primary driving force of growth, what will happen when the gene pool begins to thin out and the end-user begins to loose interest.

Force feeding the sport to the masses has been easy, given the internets overwhelming ability to promote. But this sudden flurry may encourage shallow roots which could lead to the sport falling over when along comes another or when folk get bored with it and feel somehow that the experience and offerings of the sport simply don't live up to the hype?

Given the current social sound-byte environment we live in, the valued input of genuinely knowledgeable individuals, is for the most part, overwhelmingly outweighed by those who don't, whose opinions subsequently dismiss and bury these knowledgeable few within the virtual world of the internet, providing the perfect, often anonymous platform,

from where 'empty vessels can make most noise'. On the face of it, the critic, as a profession per se, has essentially been replaced by an incessant natter and drone which serves more to confuse, not resolve.

In this publication, I have set out to consider the essence of the sport as that of a paddle sport and therefore the nurturing of paddle and board skills in the absence of surf, because when you get down to facts, if the sport is to enjoy significant and continued growth, then its the realm of inland waterways and calm coastal lagoons and bays where the sport will need to flourish.

Collectively the sum of the whole of all paddle sports added together have been the fastest growth area within water sports world-wide. The introduction of the sit-on-top kayak, first conceived as far back as 1968 in California (not withstanding whatever canoe and kayak cultures had created thousands of years prior) and unleashed in commercial numbers

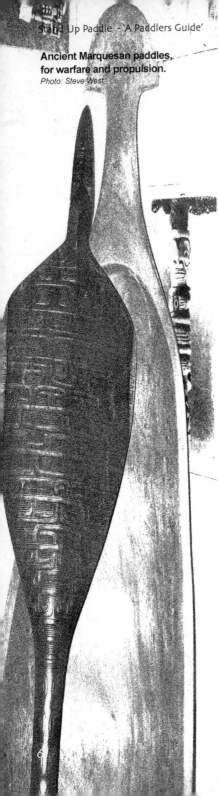

Ancient Marquesan paddles, for warfare and propulsion.
Photo: Steve West

back as far as the late 70s, ultimately led to paddle sports becoming part of hotel chains across the Pacific being that the sit-on-top was stable and did not present issues of entrapment. In this sense, this morphing of ideas, opened up paddle sports to many who had never considered participation until some of the retarding issues had been addressed.

In a sense, I see stand up paddle boarding in a similar vain; a morphing of sports and ideas which has sparked a catalyst of interest and aspiration amongst many thousands of 'wanna-be part of the surfing thing' regardless of where they live, from Colorado to St.Tropez it makes no difference, you can buy your board, paddle and hibiscus patterned board shorts and hey presto, you're part of the surfing culture you always dreamed of. The obvious question has to be, 'But are you really?' or are you merely alluding now to being a part of all that is surfing, but are in fact, closer to all that is paddling? Worse still, are you just a victim of good marketing and aspirational bludgeoning?

Significantly, it's essential we acknowledge the sport as first and foremost as a paddle sport, knowledge without which, would be to miss the fundamental principles by about a million miles. Paddling is an ancient art and skill, specifically canoe paddling, as are the paddles designed for propulsion, though once also for warfare. All that is known of canoe sports and that of ocean dynamics and the interaction

Sunset Harlyn Bay Cornwall

between board, blade, paddler and water, can be drawn upon from the homogenous blending of all that we have learned before.

Paddle boarding stand up style, is not a new sport, simply the melding of the ancient utilitarian skill of canoe paddling and aspects of the more contemporary skills associated with a variety of board sports. From this premise alone, it is important to give respect to an ancient lineage pre-dating naive notions that the sport is contemporary and 'invented' yesterday, when in fact, it is merely a novel innovation manifested by user-innovators which, by its origins and nature, cannot be patented, nor laid claim to by a singular individual. To do so, would be to ignore thousands of years of the evolutionary tree from which this sport has fallen.

Surfing organisations, in an astonishing back-flip and a counter to all that they have ever known or represent, wish now to subjugate this 'new' sport under their authority across the entire globe on account of a unique claim of ownership, through especial knowledge and passion for the ancient art and skill of (canoe) paddling and of flat water environs, racing, adventuring, river-running, yoga-boarding and related skill areas of the sport. This is astonishing, given that these areas of interest are in fact, the antithesis of all that they have known or cared for. Any arguments presented to the contrary are simply impotent and baseless.

While there's some justification in their taking stand up 'paddle surfing' under their governance, even given perhaps a 15% global participation level, does not warrant 100% control. More especially, where surf is absent as a requirement for participation, representing but only a small portion of the sport's current disciplines and where the paddle is the primary means of propulsion, this falls beyond the supposed interests or knowledge of all surfing organisations. Critically, this also falls within the bounds of 'learning' where surf is an absolute non-requirement and where paddling skills and safe practice are.

Claims of ownership of the sport are counter-productive to the greater sum of the whole of the sport's diversities, which will serve to polarise the sport in labelling it as a surf sport by association, alienating the vast majority of would-be participants who have no interest in surf, period.

The Industry, need heed this singularly important reality as the consequences will be omnipresent. What's needed is clear. Stand up paddle boarding, due to its uniqueness and diversity, is beyond the realm of either a surfing or canoe / kayak organisation, requiring recognition in its own right in order to address the sport with parity and without agenda, other than its successful management and growth.

Photo: Steve West Marquesas Islands

8

Photo: Steve West

Voyaging canoe - Nuku Hiva - Marquesas Islands.

From the far reaches of Spain to Australia, USA to South America, the confusion is rife and it has set in motion this very debate, yet few are stopping to ask who should take ownership; not one niche interest group, but one which represents all facets of the sport equally.

When presidents of self proclaimed world governing surfing bodies make statements that surfing and stand up paddle boarding share 'identical roots' let alone the notion that it has been 'a surfing sport since the beginning' I suggest he and others need consult the history books with due haste and diligence, with a view to expanding their knowledge as to how exactly the islands of Oceania were populated and how the resulting cultures of these regions thrived.

Surfing does not share an association with canoeing, yet stand up paddle boarding does and herein lies the significant difference which assures us, these sports do not in fact share identical roots, far from it. Indeed canoe surfing no doubt existed before surfing in the context of evolution.

In addition to all of the hype, let's not forget that in the context of paddle boarding stand up style in the surf, free surfers are for the most part, not happy. To quote Dave Kalama, **'If it's a matter of recognition, let's examine that for a moment. The most I can ever see is an honourable mention at a future, "Stand Up Hall of Fame". We know there will never be an honourable mention at the, "Surfing Hall of Fame", they can't stand us.'**

The canoe and the skills associated with it, existed thousands of years before the surfboard and by default, so too the outrigger canoe. That the art, skills, traditions, synergy, significance and relevance of all that is paddling is all but ignored as an extension of stand up paddle boarding, disrespects the sport at grass roots level, which by consequence, serves to polarise a viewpoint, that this emerging sport, beyond all other considerations, has absolutely no relationship with outrigger canoeing, making it clear, it is not in the interests of surfing organisations to promote such a blatant reality.

If we wish to credit the Waikiki Beach Boys as a point of source, know this. They and their Marquesan and Tahitian ancestors stand today on that beach as a result of their direct association with the outrigger canoe which brought them to these islands and all others in-between and beyond, as a manifestation of all that they knew of maritime architecture, navigation, sailing and canoe paddling. Any association or credit given them from times gone by, to that of stand up paddle boarding, can and must be attributed in part, if not the greater part, to their association with all that they knew and know of the art of paddling and yet it is surfing which is continuously and erroneously promoted as being the central root extension of stand up paddle boarding. Without the paddle, without the knowledge and skills to use it, there is no stand up paddle boarding. More's the pity, indigenous Hawaiians and their kind, struggle to find a voice in what amounts to a veritable sea of Anglo-Polynesian and Eurocentric white noise and ignorance.

'Ironically, stand-up paddling and surfing was founded in laziness. The old Beachboys of Waikiki learned that they could better teach the tourists and take their photos if they could use their surfboards like a platform. By using a paddle they were able to move about more freely and easily, with minimal effort. What started as laziness soon became a tool for training, after they learned it actually improved their core strength and balance while at the same time being a lot of fun. These principles, core to every type of training, and to life.' *C4 Waterman.*

This statement alone reinforces several important truths. Standing and 'paddling' on oversized boards was not 'surfing' it was 'paddling', in essence a utilitarian craft, a moveable platform at first, then a tool for gaining fitness.

If you need further proof, consider outrigger canoe paddle manufacturers now supplying the market and consider the gene pool from where some of the best exponents of the sport now hail from. Respect and recognition of lineage is a requirement for the sports rightful expansion.

Stand up paddle boarding is a paddle sport and while there's no denying in its variant forms it can also be a surf sport, its uniqueness is set apart from conventional surfing through the use of the paddle. The worrying trend in some emerging participating regions, is that there seems a want, to push this sport down the path as being first and foremost a surf sport.

The sport has opened the doors to many different sources of pleasure and is capable of attracting a following from a variety of divergent origins. You can find people who don't care about performance, a fun-loving, new-sensation seeking clientele, people who like to cruise about, right through to racers and fitness fanatics.

The surfing industry have seized upon the idea, that here is an oceanic sport, which can be easily exported to countries and regions of the world without waves. Therein, the sports evangelists can see its development potential. But it's not surfing. Surfing by definition requires surf and as a consequence, it seems incredulous there is a belief their industry can run riot across waveless areas of the world, including the interior landscape of this planet, with blatant disregard for an industry that has long been thriving here in the form of canoe and kayaking, who paradoxically, have now forged an interest in developing instructor training and therefore any exclusivity that surfing organisations may have thought they were going to reap, is no longer so. Fortunately, some new founded companies are centred on a very broad interest of the sport's evolution.

Things are not smooth flowing in this emerging market. On a local level, many shops lack space and so have to settle for a range that is too limited to appropriately meet the needs of new enthusiasts. Many customers don't have enough space at home, let alone space in or on their cars to be able to own a board of a length fit for their needs, but should that limit design?

Retailers and educationalists alike require knowledge and commitment, as much in terms of space as in time and understanding of the discipline. Critically, the end-user will need to know where to take their sport or run the risk of losing interest. Perhaps this publication will be of some assistance in this regard.

SUP Warrior Challenge Waikiki

Photo: Courtesy of Ocean Promotions / Dana Edmunds

2

Evolution of a water sport

First-of-type innovators, innovation communities,
product development and functionally novel innovations.

Prone paddle boarding, legend of the Waikiki Beach Boys,
paddling while standing, stand up paddle boarding lineage,
outrigger canoeing and the stand up
paddle boarding gene pool.

Evolution of a water sport

The evolution of a water sport is an interesting process. In a paper produced by Sonali K. Shah at the University of Illinois, he concluded that users and their communities sphere of networking and interests, fuel the surge in development of most major innovations by as much as 57%, while manufacturers fuel somewhere in the region of 27% of these major innovations, with the balance of 16% being developed by professional athletes (in contrast to recreational users) and joint user-manufacturers.

End-users in the initial phase of a sports development can be considered pioneers. Sonali identified some key structural facets leading to the successful evolution of a sport and to this end he considered snowboarding, windsurfing and skateboarding as focal points. These included;

First-of-Type Innovations

Where users developed and engaged themselves in using existing skills and basic materials to hand to create the innovation.

Innovation Communities

Where a group of like minded people with an interest in the new innovation, operate through open communication and open product design policy. Making the information and innovation(s) available to all, they accelerate the evolutionary process and solution of problems.

Product Development

For product development to occur, there needs to be information regarding the need and use of the item in context, more often than not generated by users and the need for solution information which may be either through specialist manufacturers or individuals. Where information is withheld, manufacturers will hold differing sets of information and consequently differing types of innovations manifest.

The sharing of such information is in a sense what one might call a tribal dissemination of knowledge and in the context of many ocean sports, be it prone paddle boarding, surfing, windsurfing or stand up paddle boarding, the earliest participants and pioneers can certainly be considered as an extended tribal family.

Functionally Novel Innovations

Some user-innovators will often on account of economic reasons, fashion something themselves out of what is already existing, creating what is termed a functionally novel innovation, where an existing item is modified to suit. Such innovations permit the user to advance the performance of existing equipment through modification, elevating their skill levels and enjoyment often allowing them the ability to explore extreme elements of a sport in evolution.

Skateboarding began life with the addition of a handle in the 1900s. Wooden boards, with roller skate wheels and a handle attached for control. More adventurous users either removed the handle or simply continued regardless, developing improved balance and techniques along the way. Had this not of happened, manufacturers may not have had the foresight to consider this handless version. As it happens the end-users did.

Invention or functionally novel innovation

While there have been a number of functionally novel innovations during the early stages of the sport's contemporary evolution, it's fair to say that in truth many of the raw materials were already to hand. It did not take a paradigm shift in thinking to consider the idea of standing on a long board, albeit a sizeable Malibu styled surf board and use of a paddle for propulsion. By comparison, windsurfing required the development of a far greater number of components and had to factor in hydro-dynamics and aero-dynamics and in addition everything had to fit and match, where form and function were paramount, let alone the continued expansionism of the riders' abilities and extremes in which they were performing.

Doubtless, Pacific Islanders, or cultures pre-dating them, such as in Africa where a canoe culture existed (and where surfing was evidenced long before the habitation of the Hawaiian Islands) paddling while standing anything from a raft, to a log or canoe could no doubt of occurred. This was not the genius behind it, this resided in user-innovators having the vision to conceptualise it as a sport, to see all that it could be and of course the potential to commercialise a new idea.

Contemporary evolution of the stand up paddle board, was fundamentally conceived from the long board genre of surfboard - having enough buoyancy to support the rider and provide for a stable platform, sufficiently dry enough to be paddled and therefore move over water not under it. In the context of stand up paddle boarding, if we use the Waikiki Beach Boys utilisation of outrigger canoe paddles to paddle giant sized surf boards of the time (1960s) they are by definition (in contemporary terms at any rate) first-of-type innovators.

If evolution is important, or rather, ownership, we need be careful attributing any one culture with this label. Native Hawaiians did not for example invent surfing, yet the hype suggests they did. It could be argued Anglo-Hawaiians (Californians or Australians for that matter) contributed

towards perfecting it or at least commercialised it to a point of mass appeal. It would be pure folly and optimism to suppose that native Hawaiians, such as the Waikiki Beach Boys 'invented' the idea of paddling while standing on a board, besides the entire meaning of 'invention' per se is really not what happened here, more accurately a functionally novel innovation.

And what of the hasake, a board-boat hybrid of the stand up paddle board family, with alleged Israeli and Arabic roots, possibly dating back as far as the 8th century A.D. There are some striking parallels with the contemporary sport. What sets them apart is information. While the worldwide surge in popularity of the sport continues to grow, with much credit being given to the Hawaiians, this is in stark contrast to that given to the hasake and its origins.

Ultimately, we know that no singular contemporary is laying any claim to invention per se, but more significantly validation, which in turn has led to popularisation, making them first-of-type users, who explored a functionally novel innovation, sparking the imagination of the user-innovators, the collective sphere of the innovative community at large and ultimately the manufacturers and designers themselves.

What is self-evident about the sport and possibly part of what's been wrong with it - or different about it - is that there has not been the same extent of user-innovator input in the typical pioneering spirit as would usually have been expected and maybe that's because there simply hasn't been much delay required in evolving the basic equipment. Manufacturers and a handful of designers, have driven the evolutionary process more than usually expected; seemingly forcing equipment upon us, almost in desperation to dominate the market, so as the input of the user-innovator, as experienced with windsurfing for example, has all but been nullified from the equation.

While the sport may be considered 'new', in but a mere few years, the speed at which product supporting the sport has been produced seems unprecedented, with all manner of existing board sport manufacturers, custom manufacturers and entrepreneurs literally throwing themselves into the market place, reinventing themselves, finding a new lease of life and for many (most) seeing the potential to cash in while the sport is hot. The list is extensive of those striving to emerge as the phoenix rising from the ashes. In China, manufactures are offering to make any shape of board or paddle, branded with whatever logo you fancy, happily pilfering designs and lapping up the sudden rush of blood to our heads.

Meanwhile, at ground level, everyone's an expert, after all the sport is so profoundly easy, what's to know? Indeed many instructors, know little more than their students, in fact less if the student is from a paddling background, the instructor, not.

Such has been the thrust of product into the market, it seems perfectly plausible that there is an over supply, what's certain is the confusion that

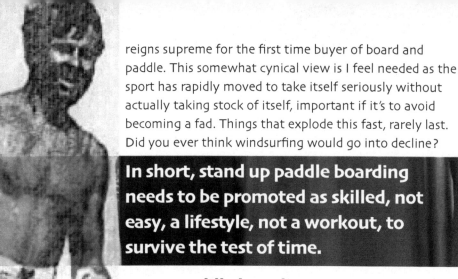

reigns supreme for the first time buyer of board and paddle. This somewhat cynical view is I feel needed as the sport has rapidly moved to take itself seriously without actually taking stock of itself, important if it's to avoid becoming a fad. Things that explode this fast, rarely last. Did you ever think windsurfing would go into decline?

In short, stand up paddle boarding needs to be promoted as skilled, not easy, a lifestyle, not a workout, to survive the test of time.

Prone paddle boarding - a comparison

Certain individuals earn the respect of their peers through their endeavours, often through acts of courage, dedication, athleticism, passion, ingenuity and contribution to a sport, ultimately winning reverence and respect in the same way as a chief or warrior may do, in finally becoming what may be termed as an ambassador for all that is good and noble about the sport, which oddly enough has more to do with the character and integrity of the individual than necessarily the sport itself.

Tom Blake is a good example of such an individual as a result of his contribution to the evolution of prone paddle board design as a stand alone sport in the mid 1920s. Originally practised paddling prone on 100-120lb surf boards of the day and popularised in Hawai`i at the same time as surfing was developing, Tom, like many ocean sports visionaries, designed a craft more specific to being paddled by hand efficiently as a primary design prerequisite rather than surfed.

Tom Blake

In 1928, he arrived at the annual Surfboard Paddling Championships in Waikiki and using his purpose made hollow, prone paddle board which he had designed two years earlier and as such, the first of its kind, he won and caused a stir.

Again in 1929 he won with an improved design and the orders flooded in despite many locals wanting the new design banned, being as it was not a surfboard. In Duke Kahanamoku's biography of 1968 'World of Surfing' he recounts Tom's introduction of his hollow racing paddle board, **'He was the one who first built and introduced the paddle board; a big hollow surfing craft that was simple to paddle and picked up waves easily but was difficult to turn. It had straight rails, a semi pointed tail and laminated wood for the deck. For its purposes it was tops.'**

In 1930, he smashed the race record by almost three minutes paddling his 16', 60lb cigar shaped board. Following the race, a meeting was held, the outcome of which, was that though some wanted to keep the old Hawaiian

styled surfboards, it was conceded that this was the start of a new era in board design, specific to paddling prone using the hands. A year later designers were madly working on new purpose made board designs for prone paddle boarding. The rest is history.

Tom had stirred up a backlash of emotional frailty, sending ripples of discord and confused viewpoints concerning the entire concept of surfboard paddling, which led to discussion of limits of designs being set as a result of the Hawaiian surfing communities wake up call. A subsequent meeting in 1930 of the Outrigger, Queens and Hui Nalu Clubs concluded there would be no future limits whatsoever on the design of prone paddle boards. Blake never competed again at this event out of choice.

Tom's Anglo-American free thinking had served to liberate the sport, indeed helped to define it. Through 1932-1938, hollow boards became popular and with their high volume and buoyancy became the standard rescue device for lifeguards, varying in length from 12-16'.

As a user-innovator, Tom had simply applied his skills of innovation and carpentry to devise a craft better suited to the purpose, which elevated the sports status from merely using what was existing, to fashioning a purpose made craft, not for surfing, but paddling.

When user-innovators, designers and manufacturers moved to design purpose made stand up paddle boards and paddles, the sport was validated and morphed into something separate to the mere act of paddling standing on a make-do surfboard, elevating it into the community at large as a going concern worthy of its own pathway of evolution.

A 1950s postcard depicting 'canoe surfing' in Waikiki.

Waikiki Beach Boy's canoe taking tourists canoe surfing. You can see the steerers paddle at the rear of the canoe as would have been originally used to paddle their long surf boards while taking photographs back in the 60s.
Photo: Steve West

The legend of the Waikiki Beach Boys by Greg Heller

Led by pioneers such as George Freeth and Duke Kahanamoku, turn-of-the-century Waikiki Beach Boys helped revitalise an ancient surfing culture that had languished under oppressive European constraints. Surfing and wa'a (canoe) paddling hadn't completely vanished, but were frowned upon as frivolous and immoral when Europeans took root in Hawai`i during the 1800s. Fortunately, a small band of watermen persevered and went on to see the ailing pastime into the 20th century.

Around 1901, when the first tourist resorts were being completed at Waikiki, these men found their calling. They earned their livelihood from surfing instruction and wa`a rides for tourists. As more resorts were completed and Honolulu tourism started to boom, surfing with the Beach Boys became a major attraction.

Under these conditions, surfing and subsequently wa`a rides would be introduced to the world through the writings of Jack London. In Waikiki with his wife in 1907, London met journalist and organiser Alexander Hume Ford. Ford took London surfing and introduced him to 23-year-old Freeth, the most accomplished surfer of the time. London was so entranced by surfing and Freeth in particular, that he wrote a piece for 'Woman's Home Companion' depicting the 'Royal Sport for the Natural Kings of Earth'.

Canoe surfing has been a part of the Waikiki beach scene for many years. Prior to the 1960s, the Outrigger Canoe Club located on the beachfront, was very

Native American open canoe racing Harper's Weekly (1874) and below, West African dug out canoe where quite possibly, paddling has its origins.

active in providing rides for travellers from all walks of life (becoming the thing to do when in Waikiki) using converted fishing wa`a and some purpose-built surfing canoes. This was to change in the early 1960s when the Outrigger Canoe Club was relocated.

Canoe rides became formalised with hotel beach services cashing-in on and perpetuating them. Along the beachfront, fibreglass surf wa`a await the tourist and vendors shout out to attract a crew to venture out into the Waikiki surf. If nothing else, it is at least a truly Hawaiian experience for the tourist and serves to keep one of the Hawaiian's traditional pastimes alive and well, even though some of the Aloha spirit has long since waned.

The Waikiki Beach Boys association with outrigger canoeing is pivotal to their initial involvement with paddling their surfboards, as this provides a central clue as to the lineage of the sport, not as a surf sport, but as a paddle sport, a fact which seems to have been all but squashed.

The act of paddling while standing

Historically speaking, the act of paddling while standing, is a very ancient skill, used casually and learnt from birth as a utilitarian survival skill, not as a factor of recreation, let alone a sport and used by a wide number of primitive cultures, who stand and paddle all variance of craft from dug-out canoes to bamboo rafts. The act of paddling itself pre-dates surfing by many thousands of years as does the creation of say the raft or the dug out canoe. Growing up in West Africa in both Nigeria and Sierra Leone, seeing Africans standing while paddling their canoes was to witness a mere extension of what they had always done.

How much richer could your participation in this sport be, if you embraced some cultural significance to its existence, in the same way that outrigger canoeing provides?

Not surprisingly a Eurocentric view of the activity is often taken of the sports origins, when in truth the Hawaiian view is flawed when more ancient cultures far from Hawaiian shores have practised variants of the combined skills of paddling while standing; in the same way as Africans were surfing off the coast of West Africa long before Hawai`i had been settled and where a canoeing culture was certainly thriving as part of a coastal and inland water based culture.

Since the birth of modern day surfing and the ambassadorial role of Duke Kahanamoku, along with his brothers and the advent of the Waikiki Beach Boys, the Hawaiian Islands have tended to have a polarising affect on popular opinion which has led to the resounding falsehood that all things surfing or even canoeing orientated, originated from these islands.

Stand up paddle boarding lineage

After making a study of outrigger canoeing over 25 years throughout the Pacific, writing, researching, racing at the highest levels, training, coaching, tapping into the spiritual and cultural significances, I have come to understand the sport as akin to the notion of what 'aloha' translates; an emotional prism of immense breadth and depth. From tree felling ceremonies in Tahiti to canoe blessings and naming ceremonies in Hawai`i, I feel truly honoured to have seen and experienced the sport at its deepest, grass roots level. To all the paddlers I have met, both Melanesian, Polynesian, Micronesian, European and Anglo-Polynesian, I am indebted to their energies, kindness and wisdom. It is through this association and experience that I can see with clarity the synergy between outrigger canoeing and stand up paddle boarding.

Photo: Steve West / Fiji

WAI TUI
FIJI OUTRIGGER
INTERNATIONAL

Mooloolaba OCC
Na Wahine O Ke Kai
(Moloka`i to O`ahu)
2003 Winners.

JOSSPhoto

Danny Ching, one of paddle sports contemporary super athletes, grew up around outrigger canoeing, his father Al, one of California's respected elders of the sport and a once regular contributor to our KANUculture publications, provided a natural lineage. One of the world's best ever OC1 paddlers, his migration into stand up paddling was a natural progression, his ability and body already chiselled and honed through years of outrigger canoe paddling. Of course you cannot be expected to connect the dots if you have no idea of his heritage and so would not stop to consider the significance.

Kaimana

Taking all cultural, geographical, anthropological and historical considerations into account, I am convinced that this so called new sport of, 'stand up' paddle boarding, is to all intents and purposes, an extension of outrigger canoeing and to this end part of what I see as a bolt-on to the canoe culture family.

The fact that the sport is by rights indigenous to the Pacific, fostered by the likes of the Waikiki Beach Boys, who are so intrinsically linked with outrigger canoeing, it is clear that this functionally-novel idea was predominantly a mere extension of all that they knew of paddling and less of what they knew of surfing and so it stands to reason, the sport resonates on a level to which outrigger canoe paddlers already vibrate, as natural to their primal instincts to hold and swing a paddle in their hands sitting, as it is standing.

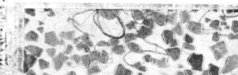

It is in short, a cultural manifestation, through the accumulation of skills already known and embraced as part of an ancient oceanic culture. That some surfers want to claim it as their own is a non-sense, more especially as this was never the initial intent and given the resistance shown by conventional surfers and the acceptance by paddlers, this speaks volumes of the sport's fundamental principles and lineage going back not over 50 years, but over thousands.

Globally if the sport's demographic is targeted correctly, many more thousands of paddlers will be paddling the world's waterways than surfers riding waves, reinforcing the importance of the greater sum of the whole.

Outrigger canoeing

Indigenous to the Pacific, outrigger canoe racing took place in various forms and is believed to be a very ancient competitive sport. There is evidence of it being commonplace in Samoa, birthplace of Polynesian culture, where voyaging canoes departed some 3000 years ago in their exploration and settlement of the Pacific islands.

Outrigger canoeing, in its many variant forms of craft, is omnipresent throughout much of the Pacific and Pacific Rim. It is the national team sport of Hawai`i and the national sport of French Polynesia, a vital and culturally significant sport of the Maori where in Aotearoa (New Zealand) the sport is supported strongly by the Maori Trust and by many other smaller island groups from the

27

Travis Grant, grew up around outrigger canoeing and partnered Danny Ching during several major OC1 change-over races, winning the Catalina Classic race in record time (Catalina - Newport Beach California). Like Danny, his life has been centred on paddle sports and stand up paddle boarding is simply an extension of all that he knows from his paddling. For Danny and Travis their story is not unique as there are many similar examples of long time outrigger canoe paddlers who now embrace the sport and are highly competitive if not already at the pinnacle be it in their respective age groups or divisions - and for others, a means of cross-training and filling in the gaps on days when they just need to do something different.

Cook Islands to Fiji, from Wallis Futuna to Rapa Nui, the sport is far greater than the Eurocentric view of what sport is deemed to be.

Outrigger canoeing is highly structured, organised and unified and forms a significant part of the economy of both Hawai`i and more especially French Polynesia. The first formalised racing began in Hawai`i in 1922 but more strictly during the 1950s. Stand up paddles used today, are essentially

Photo: Dana Edmunds

Photo Steve West

Marquesas Islands. Jamie Mitchell seat two, Travis Grant steering.

extended outrigger canoe paddles with modifications made to the flex properties of the shaft and by no coincidence, the greater percentage of leading stand up paddle makers today, had already built their businesses around the development and supply of paddles to outrigger canoe paddlers of the world and of note include; Kialoa (Dave Chun), Quick Blade (Jim Terrell), ZRE (Bob Zaveral), Pohaku (Todd Bradley) and others.

The synergy between the two sports is palpable on many levels, to the extent that outrigger canoe paddlers of the Pacific have taken to the sport in their thousands on account of the similarity of the bio-mechanics required. Indeed their shift to embrace the sport in Hawai`i, California, Australia, Tahiti and elsewhere has had a major net affect on the sport in their part as user-innovators, first-of-type pioneers of varying disciplines, downwind paddling and racing in particular.

Prone paddle boarding

Surfboard racing pre mid 1920s, was the prequel to prone paddle boarding, with Tom Blake's creation of the first purpose built prone paddle board in 1926. This changed the nature of the craft used by the participants who went on to purchase Tom's new board designs and others which followed on from it. The bio-mechanics of prone paddling went on to evolve with time.

In 2002 when Jamie Mitchell won his first Moloka`i world title, he noted that most Hawaiians and Californians paddled prone, whereas in Australia, paddle boarding was performed mostly kneeling as taught at a young age through surf clubs - a skill which gave the Australians a bio-mechanical advantage over all-comers. Jamie is also a skilled outrigger paddler and has raced with top crews, notably Outrigger Australia. When I interviewed him back in 2005 he said, **'When I had a go at outrigger canoeing, I naturally had good reach, leverage and endurance gained from prone paddle boarding. I have never been a super strong guy, but found that outrigger canoeing improved my strength, which goes to show how paddle sports cross-platform as training mediums for each other. Canoeing and paddle boarding have worked well for me as a combination.'**

Surfing

In some sense, surfing was not the original intent when folk began standing and paddling their surfboards, though of course given the right conditions and skills, paddling onto a wave became a natural extension of this new found novelty. To what extent the paddle was used to execute moves is unclear, but certainly not a mandatory requirement for enjoyment.

With the likes of Laird Hamilton, embracing the sport as a first-of-type user and innovator, he advanced the idea of using the paddle as a critical element to stand up paddle (surfing) as a means to not only paddle out but to drop in earlier on outside wave sections and then to use the paddle to brace, sweep and cut, in order to bring about what were radical moves on over-sized boards. Though he met with criticism, accused of no longer 'surfing', he argued that if he was not (in this variant form) then he no longer knew what defined what was.

Stand up paddle surfing, to the extent it has evolved today, is essentially the sport of surfing evolving now from the inside out rather than the outside in. This is what now makes this branch of the sport unique and segmented from the larger body of interest of the sport; culturally, socially, geographically and philosophically, to which end there is not only division between free surfers but between stand up paddle surfers and everyone else - though some mix between the disciplines. Some of the negative tribal elements of those who primarily surf, have no time for the racing or downwind elements of the sport. They are in short, 'surfers' at heart, not 'paddlers' and herein lies the difference.

Revivalist theories

To suggest stand up paddle boarding is under-going expansionism on account of the activities of revivalists, suggests 'the sport' was a going concern in the first place. At its peak in the dim distant past, no more than the number you could count on one hand were participating. It simply was not a going concern or culturally significant to the extent that outrigger canoe racing had been or even surfing, which was ceased for nearly 50 years on account of missionary intervention.

If you want to know what a true revivalist is, then look no further than the single greatest revivalist in the history of Hawai`i, King David Kalakaua. The intervention of the Boston Missionaries in 1820 led to a ban of outrigger canoe paddling, hula dancing, surfing and pretty much anything else deemed of a lewd nature where being semi-naked, getting wet, or having a good time was a requirement for participation. KIng David, in 1875 reinstated these activities after some 50 years, reviving ancient traditional skills and pastimes. To suggest contemporaries are revivalists of a once proud and omnipresent cultural pastime is grossly inaccurate.

Earliest paddle craft

Transmigration of people, altered climatic conditions, water conditions, raw materials, nature of use, drove the evolution of water craft. Dug-out canoes form the basis of our assumption of the origins of paddling, beginning in Africa. Canoes morphed into many variations, the more complex and accomplished being the double and single outrigger canoes associated strongly with Oceanic cultures. The kayak is a very much later evolution, where a double ended blade is used and the paddler is seated and enclosed. The Cabilito reed boats of Peru, some 2500 years old, need special mention; single person craft used by fishermen who paddle out through the surf using double ended split bamboo paddles.

Stand up paddle boarding.
Prone paddle boarding evolved?

It is perfectly plausible to argue the case, that paddling while standing on a board, employing the use of an extended canoe paddle, is no more than an advancement (variant) of prone paddle boarding.

Prone paddle boarding is inherently uncomfortable, wet and physically brutal; the addition of an extended canoe paddle and in assuming a standing position could be considered an advancement of the sport, bringing with it mechanical and bio-mechanical advantages, together with the addition of some changes of board dimension and deck layout.

If you're looking for a genetic lineage, it would not be unreasonable to consider some of today's modern race boards and downwind boards with the addition of foot operated tiller arm extensions and draw clear and distinct parallels. Add to this the involvement of prone paddle board designers such as Joe Bark and the single most accomplished best ever prone paddle boarder in the history of the sport Jamie 'Mitcho' Mitchell and the associations grow ever more stronger.

Jamie 'Mitcho' Mitchell Moloka'i to O'ahu x 10 winner
Photo: Carol Cunningham

By it's brutal nature and ultimate lack of appeal, prone paddle boarding has always struggled to find popularity and yet because of its adversities, it has forever been considered as one of the toughest tests of the waterman and in many instances an involvement and mastery of the sport led to an ambiance associated with that of a statesman or an ambassador, often partaken by those in later years after a lifetime of surfing, using it as means to remain fit and ensure a continued relationship with the water.

Stand up paddle boarding - novelty to big business

Contemporary wisdom suggests, stand up paddle boarding has its origins in the Hawaiian Islands, combining two traditional Hawaiian sports, notably outrigger canoe paddling (the national team sport of Hawai`i) and surfing. However, we should not get carried away in saying that the sport, 'combines canoe paddling with surfing' as this is an over simplification of the diversity of the sport. More accurately, it simply combines the use of an extended canoe paddle and the use of differing board designs suited to differing niche interests.

In this context, the exploits of various key Hawaiian residents are well documented, though it remains significant how the involvement of these surfing luminaries of the time, some sixty years ago, failed to result in any popular surge of interest; far from it, that is until one notable contemporary in the form of Laird Hamilton, became attracted in the first instance to the physicality and challenge of paddling while standing on a large surfboard and the potential for the conditioning of the body. Beyond these merits, Laird Hamilton and Dave Kalama as user-innovators, set out to challenge themselves in seeking out the full potential of the sport; whether downwind paddling or surfing, which subsequently sparked the imagination of others as if by divine intervention.

The stand up paddle boarding gene pool

One of the reasons that stand up paddle boarding is ripe for growth and ostensibly poised for success is due to the recent massive global spread and growth of paddle sports in general over recent years, between which paddlers more often than not, find appeal and synergy between the varying forms, as either a means of cross training, competition, exploitation of varying water states or seasons, using differing equipment and ultimately making one or more paddle sports primary and secondary interests.

While kayaking has been around for decades, the advent of the sit-on-top kayak, another awkward nomenclature adding a verb by way of a point of difference, has doubtless helped spread the attraction and acceptance of paddle sports globally, the sum total of its 'newbies' equating to paddle sports being the fastest growing segment of water sport for over a decade. If we embrace stand up paddle boarding as a paddle sport, as clearly many already do, including many land-locked inland waterway paddlers, then the sum total of paddle sport participation is once again enjoying another surge on account of this new sport.

Travis Grant Steering, Jamie Mitchell sits seat two from front.

Photo Steve West

Stand up paddle boarding has spread throughout the Pacific and Pacific Rim, bolstered on account of a strong pre-existing paddling culture in this region, emanating from outrigger canoeing and prone paddle boarding, whose participants see the sport for the most part, as a means to cross-training or who have now made it their primary sport.

On account of so many first-of-type and user-innovators having originated from outrigger canoeing and prone paddle boarding backgrounds, it's easy to see how the spread of a community based niche interest and flow of information has now infiltrated stand up paddle boarding.

Outrigger canoe paddlers, already skilled and hardened by years of canoe paddling look at this sport and get it straight away. With over 10,000 paddlers throughout the Hawaiian Islands, 3,000 in Australia, 20,000 throughout French Polynesia, 4,000 in California and various smatterings throughout Canada, America's East Coast and a handful in Europe, these are fertile gene pools from which the sport can and will grow; the more the numbers the greater the percentage conversion, with the possible exception of French Polynesian, where outrigger canoe paddling is a national obsession supported by indigenous participation. The point of this is to make clear that in these regions, stand up paddle boarding is finding its niche very quickly.

Dave Chun founder of Kialoa paddles, began his paddle making career making and developing outrigger canoe paddles and now stand up paddles. Todd Bradley, co-founder of C4 devoted much of his life to outrigger canoeing and the list is extensive; Dave Kalama, Danny Ching, Travis Grant, Kai Bartlett, Aaron Napolean et al.

Consider what promoted the launching of the sport. Laird Hamilton in particular, a tougher and more accomplished waterman you could not meet, began using the sport as an alternative way of conditioning his already hardened body, to prepare for tow in surfing. Stand up paddling for fitness was his primary focus, which quickly changed to seeing the sports potential and by default his interest helped spark a catalyst for the sports growth and today he is an ambassador for the sports virtues, even if he, like so many others, have gained a not unreasonable vested interest in supporting its growth.

Outrigger canoe paddlers are now using the sport as a means of cross training, building core strength and working the stabilising muscles as a vehicle for injury prevention and even prone paddle boarders get it. Jamie Mitchell 10 times world prone paddle board champion (Moloka`i to O`ahu) founded his stand up paddle board school on the Gold Coast Australia and worked with the Academy of Surfing Instructors (ASI) through 2008 to develop the foundation for the world's first instructor training courses, which he then implemented into his school.

For surfers to be attracted to the sport, while this gene pool is also deep and widely spread within and away from the Hawaiian Islands, the sport does provide for them a juxtaposition, that slaps in the face of purity, being that the surfer is essentially a minimalist creature, where less is more and therefore the addition of a paddle one has to ask, must surely add an element of inpurity and a pox on a sport which has been written about since the 60s with divine reverence and spiritual undertones ad infinitum, praised for its minimalistic virtues.

However, when you read through the contest rules of stand up paddle (surfing) the addition of a paddle has seemingly raised this new variant of surfing to something akin to an item of divine intervention and reverence, elevating what was already considered the perfect expression of man's harnessing of nature, for that ultimate free ride, to something greater, or in simple terms, 'performance-centred surfing'.

To quote the rules, '**The paddle allows large boards to be turned with high rates of speed and power. Stand-up paddle surfing is deemed to be, at competition level, a performance-centred branch of surfing, like conventional short boarding.'** Laird Hamilton in Surftime Magazine says, '**The short board revolution has nothing on the SUP. With a SUP you can surf many more kinds of waves with the same amount of pleasure. Its scope of use is ultra wide and we are discovering ways of surfing waves that we didn't know about before'.**

Naturally there are those completely new to water sports, who see the sport as a vehicle for involvement on whatever level they may gravitate towards, be it cruising, adventuring, racing, all the while but one step away from perhaps aspirations of surfing and all that the sport alludes to. That the sport can be practised on most any body of water, within reason, supports the notion that the sport can be omnipresent.

Future evolution

It has to be said, whereas windsurfing, prone paddle boarding and surfing have evolved gracefully in the hands of pioneers who invested intellectual visionary effort, while beating out a chronology of historical precedents, the evolution of stand up paddle boarding it seems, leap-frogged years of evolutionary pain, so much so, that to serve the sport up as a done-deal is almost uninteresting and dull by comparison, though there are a few areas of design still allowing plenty of scope for improvement and advancement, notably ocean downwind and flat water racing boards.

Those marketing the sport, from manufacturer to sponsored participant, and more especially the media and those producing glossy equipment brochures and burgeoning websites, need caution in avoiding pushing this as a surf sport as a primary basis for its raison d'etre as many manufactures would seem to support.

Preaching to the converted will drastically limit the growth of this sport. If you are already a surfer, then you are effectively of that religion, you are by association in the loop, part of a sub-culture, who may or may not warm to the notion of the inclusion of a paddle to your sport. Enticing the surfer, defeats the point of expansionism. The sport must be made appealing to those who have no association with surfing or perhaps any water sport in order for it to truly grow and find its niche.

Anglo-Polynesia Technologica

An entire generation of surfers will debate issues of purity, maintaining a vigilant stand that surfing (without paddle) is the essence and soul of surfing and the inclusion of such is akin to adding preservatives to organic food. Biff is already occurring in the line up as the usual territorial issues overshadowing wave selection begin to bubble to the surface as the sport's numbers increase. Not everyone is stoked about stand up paddle boarding, even the US Coastguard has been quick to address the concerns they have of the sport, it's impact on other water users and the risks posed to the paddler. In essence they don't see this as a surf sport, but as an adventure sport, more akin to kayaking and where it is practised as a surf sport, there are major concerns regarding the compatibility of mixing conventional surfers with paddle-surfers in the same surf zones.

Travis Grant and peers, such as Danny Ching and Jamie Mitchell, represent the all-rounders whose paddling backgrounds raised the bar in recent times, to a level to which many current participants coming in side ways from non-paddling backgrounds would struggle to comprehend the thousands of hours these individuals have pounded out over their lifetimes. Exponentially the list is expanding as Pacific based outrigger canoe paddlers enter the sport from the islands to the Pacific rim. There is however no substitute for raw unadulterated talent as associated with some of the younger prodigy now entering the sport, as true first generation contemporary pioneers, whose physiological maturation process is now running side by side with the maturation processes of the sport itself, in the same way as Robbie Naish and Matt Schweitzer were part of the process of windsurfing's evolutionary process.

3

Devolution of a sport and a cautionary tale of woe

A cautionary tale of why the expansionism of stand up paddle boarding need take heed from lessons hopefully learned from misguided evolutionary pathways and pressures.

KANU
CULTURE
publications since 1994

Mandy West 'splits' sketched by Lisa Vincent 1984

Windsurfing's cautionary tale

User-innovators often create interest in their innovations. Some will move to commercialise their innovation, even patent it, others simply will not. In the absence of any patent, there is freedom to continue to innovate and ultimately create wider variance of equipment.

The patenting of the Windsurfer® by Californians Hoyle Schweitzer and Jim Drake in 1968 and the patent-wrangle which followed, remains as an infamous period of legal bickering in the context of water sports. Ultimately it was challenged from varying sources, with user-innovators such as the United Kingdom's Peter Chilvers of Hayling Island claiming to have invented the concept in 1958, then American inventor Newman Derby's plans were found in 'Popular Science Monthly Magazine' published in 1965 (the design originating from the 1940s) further undermining the Californian's claims and during 1982, the patent ruling was overturned.

This is the scene of what was one of Britain's biggest and most successful annual windsurfing events, a race around Hayling Island co-founded in 1980 by myself and Peter Williams. This is perhaps mid 1980. This scene is no more, more especially in terms of the variance of ages and gender, let alone weight of numbers. At the time, this scene was a global phenomenon, an omnipresent sport which genuinely lived up to all that it was talked up to be.

Photo Courtesy of Dave Hackford Starboard UK

Coincidently at this time I was a professional windsurfer, writer and photographer, having taken up the sport in 1979 and subsequently working from Europe's then largest windsurfing centre on Hayling Island in the United Kingdom. I was required to sail a version of Newman Derby's board which was filmed and presented in court. I was young and just doing what I was asked, but historically, it was an interesting time and experience.

Of course the idea of patenting the concept of stand up paddle boarding, is paradoxically a near impossibility, being that the sport simply melds other existing water sports together. If it could have been, doubtless it would have been if money were to be made from it, but it does illustrate the point that the sport's evolution is merely a functionally novel concept.

The late Jim Drake worked with Starboard for some years designing windsurfers and on occasion designed stand up paddle boards, one of the most successful having been the K15 race board. Hoyle Schweitzer's son Matt Schweitzer, is intrinsically linked with the early days of the Windsurfer® One Design board and together with Robbie Naish in particular, they dominated the early days of racing and went on to pioneer wave sailing in Hawai`i with such names as Larry Stanley, Mike Waltz and others during what was a fascinating period from the mid 70s to the mid 80s. Matt Schweitzer's son Zane Schweitzer, is one of the

Peter Chilvers Hayling Island England 1982 (seated) toasting the news of winning his claim as the 'inventor' of the concept of windsurfing - back dated to 1958.

leading paddle surfing exponents and a world class kiteboarder. The synergy here between all the characters represents a continued lineage of evolution from father to son.

Today it's clear that stand up paddle boarding as an evolving sport, has interesting challenges ahead, not least of which being the simple question of determination of its essence and within this maelstrom of flux, the sport's uniqueness needs to stand its ground in raging against the notion that it is definitively not a surf sport, but ultimately, very much more.

Steve West sails a Darby board specially constructed from the 1965 plans.

The sailboard, 1965 style

'Sailboarding — Exciting new water sport.' That was the headline on an article in an American magazine. 'Popular Science Monthly,' published in 1965. It gave detailed instructions on how to build a sailboard, together

If you're asking yourself why leading windsurfing brands / manufacturers have leapt into the sport, producing massive volumes of boards over an unfathomable range, the answer is simple; the windsurfing industry is in decline, having shot itself in the proverbial foot helped along by magazines and videos having squeezed the sport dry, to a point of leaving only the residue of high wind and wave sailing to the detriment of all other areas of the sport's fundamental appeals. In 2012 windsurfing was briefly dropped as an Olympic sport, replaced by kiteboarding, then reinstated, but for how long?

One of the world's largest windsurfing companies and now subsequently stand up paddle boarding companies, had in 2010 no less than 24 differing models, 16 of which were essentially surf specific and sporting fundamentally impractical volume and hull shapes for being paddled in comfort over even a reasonable distance; 3 were essentially compromise, all-round boards and the balance of 5 specifically designed as efficient paddling hulls. In 2011, another leading windsurfing brand by example had a whopping 30 differing board styles of which a mere 7 were purpose made as paddling-specific boards, possibly 5 others could be considered all-rounders and the balance surf-specific.

This would seem to support the view, they and other prime movers view the sport's appeal as largely that of a surf sport and by association that this is the true nature of the sport, which seems to smack in the face of logic if we accept stand up paddle boarding as a paddle sport. Of course it doesn't help lessen this belief when so many of those involved in the decision making progress, hail from strong surfing or wave sailing backgrounds. When looking at the global picture, the product line is arse about face, where the greater variance of range should consist of boards designed specific to paddling not surfing, catering to the hugely greater demographics of those who live near lakes, rivers, dams, estuaries and flat, sheltered waters?

This advert from 1982 represents all that was great about the sport - fun, laid back, mellow, a fulfilment of one's dreams. Pretty soon after, boards and rigs like this were killed off (and this type of advert aimed at a particular demographic) replaced by hi-tech expensive kit and young lads like this and his mum, were pretty much booted out of the picture all together, replaced by high wind and wave imagery and in so doing the sport slowly but surely, backed itself into a corner. Pure genius. So the question has to be, what of stand up paddle boarding. Will it go the same way, if not already?

The ability to add a sailing rig to some stand up paddle boards, brings back the versatility associated with the bygone days of longboard windsurfing, but is yet to become popular.

What seems self evident, is the continued powerful commercial reality, that the sex appeal and lure of the surfing lifestyle and all that it alludes to, from tropical beaches to azure waters, what you would rather be doing, where you would rather be and who you would rather be doing it with, continues to be a potent selling tool. Better to jam pack your brochures predominantly with photos of waves than flat water imagery if you want to sell the dream.

So much for the counter-culture of the 50s and 60s, where dropping out of society and the capitalist treadmill epitomised the appeal of surfing, where today it could not be any more joined at the hip through commercial and capitalist principles if it tried, indeed they are inseparable through the blur of must have clothing, board and accessory brands all associated with a particular surfer, paddler, wakeboarder, snowboarder, kiteboarder.

Initially many windsurfing shops sold and continue to sell stand up paddle boards, however this now seems somewhat opportunistic folly, but provided a suitable starting point. When we see (some) pro-windsurfers alluding to being converted to stand up paddle boarding, this is more likely due to their sponsor now having branched out into the area, rather than the individual exercising free-will per se.

Though windsurfers stand while sailing, the old school longboard designs and styles of sailing, draw greater comparisons than with most of today's designs and that's about where the similarity ends and fantasy begins.

Windsurfers are by and large speed junkies and I can respect the fact that finding the urge to invest reasonably serious amounts of money in a board and paddle package would smart when faced with the reality that the sport is heavily equipment dependent; there's just too much to be had.

The expansion of windsurfing - the phenomenon

The fledgling sport of windsurfing in the late 70s early 80s enjoyed monumental growth on account of many factors, not least of which, the sport was sincerely promoted on the basis that it was for all-comers, no matter the age or gender and that '**Wherever there was wind and water'**, an involvement was not only possible, but highly desirable.

In a 1984 Windsurfer® brochure - Hoyle Schweitzer says, ' **A futuristic vehicle for your dreams has risen out of the western sea, bringing new dimensions to life itself. How can such a simple, easy-rider device bring so much joy to millions? Because it puts you - with your skills and your dreams and your hidden potential - into a perfect interaction with wind and water. Thus, this one small vehicle brings with it the power to make your visit here on planet earth even more fulfilling.'** Sure sounds what stand up paddle boarding could be, should be and should remain.

Not driven home as a surf sport, but fully embraced as a sailing sport, it promised aspirations of friendships, communing with nature, health and fitness, the buzz of gliding over water and to some considerable extent it conveyed the feeling that we were part of a pioneering spirit – a new frontier in water sports.

The interim years, provided a suitable gestation time for the sport to evolve and flourish, giving rise to the global establishment of International Windsurfing Schools (IWS) by using a systematic, unified methodology, which went on to successfully and safely introduce countless thousands to the new sport that spread like global wild fire to nearly every corner of the planet.

Flat water sailing, regatta racing and freestyle (hotdogging) on the Windsurfer® one-design boards and the like, contributed unprecedented levels of interest and participation in the sport. It sold itself. It made its way onto TV and was regularly demonstrated at boat and trade shows. It captured people's imaginations and the global response was truly staggering as hundreds of thousands (if not millions) took to the sport. Triangular multi coloured sails zig zagged across many varied bodies of water, the sport felt omnipresent genuinely taking the world by storm. By comparison SUP is yet to launch.

Lessons to be learned

Inevitably as windsurfing morphed into adulthood, magazines worldwide lost interest in promoting the mellower nature of the sport. No longer was it about the long board and casual summer days spent clowning around in light winds with friends and family. It had been driven relentlessly through the evolution of equipment and the growing capabilities and demands of the rider who was growing ever more hardcore. It was now a high wind surf sport, first and foremost.

Magazine covers no longer printed dreamy sunsets, silhouetted by triangular sails or bikini clad babes gliding over glassy waters, imagery to which every Tom Dick and Harry related and would rush to pick up at the News Stand. Front covers now jostled to outdo one another, publishing the most outrageous big wave image they could lay their hands on.

Worse still, the elderly, the frail, the more mellow at heart who had purchased their Windsurfers, Windgliders, HiFlys, Bics and Mistrals, were hung out to dry and forgotten; their owners, expendable, pioneering participants no longer relevant to the way forward. Local races died out, social sailing folded, long boards died a natural death, flat water freestyle became a lost art, boards and kit morphed into moss and dust collectors in garages and gardens on a global scale.

It had become in your face niche interest material, which slowly but surely ousted the elderly, kids and thousands who neither related to surf or had an interest in it, let alone lived in close geographical proximity to where conditions permitted this form of hardcore sailing. Laced with idiosyncratic language and new ideologies, the sport had finally reached its apparent zenith, but in doing so, left in its wake any notion of encouraging a truly broad spectrum of participants. In short it has now near disappeared up its own fundamental orifice and everyone within the industry, from the manufacturers, to pro sailors, designers must take their share of the blame.

Pioneering sailors (user-innovators and professionals) and designers had nurtured a uniquely close relationship, constantly refining designs, incorporating new materials as they came to hand, in the push to go faster, higher, tighter, pushing equipment to the point of obsolescence as sailor's abilities demanded more than their gear could deliver.

Mike Waltz's classic 80s line **'Wind and water, natures most powerful elements, to combine them in harmony is the ultimate free ride'** or words to that effect, remain as a poignant, encapsulated notion of the essence of the sport at the time, or at least what it had set out to be.

Kirsty Jones now says of stand up paddling, **'Stand up, is a lot like life: you need balance, focus, inner strength, and the ability to get back up every time to get the best from it.'** It seems waxing lyrical and drawing

As evocative as this imagery (and achievement) may have been at the time, on many levels this aspirational directional shift within the sport, was not a shift into over-drive for the sport to expand and speed up, other than for the creation of hi-tech, high wind equipment, but in many ways the opposite, as this was (and remains) out of the realms of reality or objectivity for thousands of existing or would be windsurfers, which detracted, not attracted participants.

metaphors go hand in hand with a passion for water sports and indeed essential to any marketing spin alluding to aspirational lifestyles and experiences.

A come back

At the end of the first decade of 2000, the windsurfing industry was taking a look at itself, coming to the realisation that long board sailing needed to make a come back, being that entire segments of the global community had been alienated from a sport originally intended for the masses. Having been pushed and promoted to the abyss of extremity, through the mechanism of ego and the media, promoting the sport using aspirational imagery beyond the realms of even the wildest dreams of your average suburbanite, the sport niched itself into decline, while kiteboarding certainly helped nudge the sport closer to the brink.

Sadly, while there has been a brief realisation of what needs to be done to reinvigorate the sport, one wonders if the industry will simply drop the ball altogether and put its efforts into their massive

Photo Mandy West

www.kanuculture.com

Ironically, one way to fast track your entry into the sport if strapped for cash, is to rummage around many a back yard cluttered with 'make-do' stand up paddle boards; long since forgotten; stock Windsurfers, Hi-Flys, Bics, Mistrals and more besides. Retailers may not like this idea, but it provides entry into the sport and advancement to possible buying. Clean the dirt and dust off, throw the dagger board away, take off the straps if attached, add paddle and hey presto, el-cheapo learner board. Invest in a quality paddle.

Photo Mandy West

51

investment within the stand up paddle board market, as many seem to have done, seeing it as a sure thing, rather than a long shot. At days end maybe windsurfing has had its day and stand up paddle boarding may well need to be their saviour.

The warning for stand up paddle boarding

The net point of this comparison? Simply put, stand up paddle boarding is the singular most accelerated water sport of our time, largely because of the intervention of the windsurfing industry (and the internet) who need this sport to work for the sake of their own survival. If the sport is going to be goose-marched down the path of its extremes, promoted and portrayed as a surf sport as a consequence of the media and magazines, led by their editors controlling content and photo editors promoting imagery which serves to alienate the elderly, women or children's involvement, then stand up paddle boarding will be a dead sport floating.

Add to this the machinations of surfing associations who wish to 'govern' in particular and we will already be more than three-quarters of the way to backing the sport into a singular niche - that of surfing. Thankfully, some magazines seem to cover a good deal of content regarding flat water recreational paddling and long may that continue so as the sport can be related to by as broad a cross section of the community as possible. The worrying issue remains, who will win out on the issue of governance and what will that say about each region of the world, where this might vary.

For retailers

'The necessity for analysis and technical know-how on the product and its uses are just as high at the point of sale, as the cost itself of a board. On the other hand, be careful not to slip up on the over technical. This was windsurfing's vice that killed it in its glory days and that could come back to haunt the sport. It remains a simple, accessible sport. The all-round should reign over this discipline. The more any specific products and their technical properties are assimilated, the less likely the sport is to be reduced to a micro-niche of high-performance athletes. Diversification should be achieved through marketing and community development rather than through a myriad of separate technical properties too advanced for the average customer who, up to now, barely knows how to hold a paddle'. *French Editor, Iker Aguirre of boardsource.com*

A night time display we put on using a light from a Navy Destroyer for the locals at one of our local pubs in the UK. This is 1981 and here the idea was to simply show the sport off for its most rudimentary appeal. Triangular coloured sails like this tended to evoke a response in people - taking on an almost iconoclastic form like the paddle.

While this is sound advice, all-round boards are simply not particularly good at any one thing, let alone being paddled in a straight line, which is not very encouraging for the beginner. By all-round are we alluding to it being both a surfboard and a board capable of being paddled efficiently over distance? Once again this further confuses and reinforces the notion of the sport's identity crisis. If I live in Paris, should I be sold the all-round board when all I want to do is paddle on the river?

One very self evident problem at present threatening to meet the needs of the end-user, is that too many beginners, are being sold boards which are too short to be practicable boards capable of being paddled efficiently or travelling any distance, when in truth many could and should be sold boards of 12'6" and upwards.

During the bygone days of windsurfing on longboards over 12', where roof racks were a must, we simply figured out the issue of storage as an extension of participation. In time everything went into miniature, with smaller booms, 2 part masts and ever shorter boards, so as it could all fit neatly into any sized vehicle.

Photo: Chris Smith 'The Telegraph Newspaper"
and Sports Photographer of the Year 1982

Photo Mandy West

This obsession with ensuring that the boards in particular became as short as possible for the sake of convenience, not performance, perhaps helped contribute to the demise of the sport in ridding the waters of longboards.

So too now with stand up paddle boards, retailers are overcoming buyer's objections to the size of the board and the issues of cost, leading to selling boards too short to be of practical purpose for the end-user's needs. Inflatable boards on the other hand, can and do certainly address the issue of storage and transportation, but not always performance. It's imperative to grasp the reality,

Top: Mandy and I in 1980, enjoying the sport at grass roots level. Freestyle was an essential element for the learning of core skills used when wave sailing. The middle image is me sailing an 8' Brian Hinde board given to me by close friend Angus Chater. This image was part of a photo shoot for the UK's Telegraph Newspaper. Some 25 years later we recently tracked down some original Windsurfers, my all time favourite freestyle and good time board by far. This simple, no-frills board design gave me and thousands of others some of the best years of our lives. For cheap, unadulterated fun, nothing came close and yet what you're looking at is essentially no more - save for some isolated areas of the world (USA / Australia) where the design is being reborn and rediscovered.

54

that in the context of developing fast hull shapes for paddling over distance, length is an important part of that requirement and therefore an insistence on a short board by degrees, will diminish this particular area of performance.

With the windsurfing industries considerable history, perhaps their involvement with stand up paddle boarding today, can be hugely positive on account of their resourcefulness and willingness to experiment and take the sport to the masses in a way in which they managed within the context of their primary interest, so long as there is an adherence to a mantra which is inclusive of nurturing all-comers to the sport and not just the elite or extreme athlete.

Photo Steve West
Rider Mandy West

4

Definitions

Forms, functions and nomenclature.

KANU CULTURE
publications since 1994

Stand up paddling any craft still counts, but thankfully the real thing works considerably better than most make-do alternatives. Bermuda fun.

Photo Mandy West
Rider Steve West / Bermuda

Adventures
in Paradise

58

Definition

Contemporary definition of the sport suggests paddlers utilise a purpose made board of adequate volume and stability to support their weight while paddling using an extended canoe paddle to propel the board over water, employing a forward canoeing stroke, combined with directional steering strokes and varying weight placement to control direction.

'A board sport where the primary propulsion, beyond consideration of all other natural factors, is delivered and controlled through the use of an extended canoe styled paddle. It is in summary a paddle sport, in the same way that windsurfing remains at its very core, a sailing sport.'

The niche interest area of stand up paddle-surfing, remains exactly that, a niche interest, of which it has been reinforced by a variety of manufacturers, that some 70-80% of their sales, are in areas of the world where there is no surf and increasingly to inland waterway areas of mainland USA and of course large areas of Europe. When the entire scope and variance of the sport is considered, stand up paddle-surfing is but one of maybe half a dozen areas of specialisation and therefore it is implausible, inaccurate and unrepresentative to generalise that the sport is a 'surf sport'. Furthermore, because the learning phases of stand up paddle boarding, (should) take place on flat calm waters as would the learning phases of windsurfing (in the interests of safety and diligence) stand up paddle-surfing can be considered no more than a niche area of advancement of an individual's interest, as would be wave-sailing be to the windsurfer.

A paddle sport

If a blood analysis were made of the sport's leading paddle designs, typically the primal ooze extracted would confirm an OC positive blood type - a marginally modified and extended outrigger canoe paddle. It's this significant fact which defines this sport. The importance it is given, seems matter of fact, if at all.

While dedicated outrigger canoe paddlers, prone paddlers and surf ski paddlers may devote a lifetime to perfecting paddling techniques and styles incorporating periodisation plans and interval training, stand up paddle boarders have for the most part, not fully embrace the same passion for the act of paddling and perhaps this has been on account of some hesitation to acknowledge it as a paddle sport; by the industry itself, let alone those surfing organisations wishing to take ownership of it, which then filters into mass consciousness. It must be acknowledged however, stand up paddle boarding lends itself to being purely recreational, in the same way as sit on top kayaking, which has found mass appeal.

Stand up paddle boarding deserves to be pushed as a sport in its own right, for all of its variations and appeal to the wider global community, but a part of this process will require a willingness to label it on account of its central propulsive and controlling extension - the paddle.

Stand up paddle surfing rules the airwaves

While the lifestyle paddler is often a humble creature, who very often paddles solo, or as part of a squad or in six person team canoes in the case of outrigger canoeing, with fixed training times, often rigorous and ruthless, there is rare opportunity for instant gratification and short lived highs as associated with the individual surfer, who drops in to ride a wave, attracting attention to themselves wherever possible and in the process providing an immediate, albeit short-lived sense of accomplishment and purpose. While chest-beating is intrinsic to the surfing condition, it is by and large not so to the paddler, whom even after a hard fought race or session embraces the efforts of their peers and of the experience.

Those who paddle-surf, like nothing better than to see photos or clips of themselves or of others, uploading a flood of imagery to forums and social network sites and like petulant children exclaim, 'Check this out' or 'Look at this guy' to the bleating shrill of their peers who respond with such intellectual quips as 'Sick!'.

Regrettably and to the great detriment of the sport's many other varied disciplines, footage depicting more mellow pursuits, are generally not as visually eye-grabbing or it may simply be the case that the participants are devoid of egos requiring attention or approval.

For every paddle-surfing image, there's a thousand other images of folk just enjoying the simple act of stand up paddle boarding in the absence of waves, imagery that is evocative, though not always as provocative.

Nomenclature - what's it matter?

Stand up paddle boarding, is a clumsy mouth-full and sounds more like the result of a work in progress than an intelligible construct to which the world can immediately work with, accept and embrace. So bad is it, that its acronym is used at every opportunity to save on spelling it out.

The genetic lineage the sport shares with outrigger canoeing, Hawai`i's national team sport, is all but ignored yet it is intrinsically linked to the origins of the sport. The surfboard combined with the extended outrigger canoe paddle, two of Hawai`i's indigenous ocean sports, was a natural blend of two skills, that of surfing and paddling, yet alarmingly, the paddling (canoeing) element in this marriage of Hawaiian sports has been overshadowed on account of surfing's global appeal and recognition and outrigger canoeing's relative obscurity.

The current nomenclature took its name from another ocean sport simply by adding a verb intransitive, justifiable on the grounds that paddle boarding, is a uniquely different sport, having been named and formed some eighty years prior. Confusingly, to 'stand up' implies one is in the process of 'standing up' and once 'stood up' one is said to be 'standing'. Prone paddle boarding, seems clear enough, but It's a shame SUP was not named in a manner more encompassing, simple and to the point, perhaps, 'board paddling' as an all encompassing generic term and 'paddle surfing' in relation to the activity performed in the surf. Naturally, paddle boarding sounds very much better, whether prone, kneeling or standing up using a paddle. Even 'upright paddle boarding' has been used and a list of others.

Coming back to the premise that stand up paddle boarding is in fact, first and foremost a paddle sport, maybe this simple, clear distinction would help anyone attempting to market the sport to the world. By giving it a definitive identity, that of a paddle sport in the same way as windsurfing was a sailing sport first and foremost, then just maybe the collective masses may begin to tune in and warm to the fundamental principals of the sport. That the board often continues to be seen as more important than the paddle, reassures us that the sport has been taken over by those who do not hail from a paddling background, who just don't get it, be they retailers, promoters, manufactures and 'wannabe' governing bodies, who need to wake up to the fact, that it's the paddle that's the most important item together with the skills to use it.

Avancement or impurity?

(or simply an alternative . . .)

Photo Steve West / Portugal

Free surfing and surfing with the inclusion of a paddle require mutually exclusive skill sets. Surfers should not be so quick to think that paddling and the skills associated with it are fundamentally easy and without a right of passage and neither should a paddler think the same of surfing. Lack of mutual respect and consideration at this fundamental grass roots level is causing friction, a clashing of egos and jingoism of the worst kind. Dedicated stand up paddle surfers, will always consider themselves 'surfers' first, paddlers second (if at all) in being part of a tribal extension of surfing, while all other stand up paddle board disciplines generally lead the participant to consider themselves 'paddlers', to which end the sum total participation level is estimated as being in the region of 80%.

Synergy

Photo Mandy West
Paddler Steve West

If you are genuinely serious about becoming a top level stand up paddle board race contender, or wishing to broaden your paddling horizons, then you could invest in an OC1 and put in the miles, as nothing trains you better, which goes along the same principal, if you want to learn how to tear it up on the waves, then you should invest time free-surfing in the absence of a paddle. This practice follows the evolutionary principles associated with spending time at the source as a right of passage, followed by a migration outwards. This is how true waterman and women evolve, through a willingness to embrace the notion of variance through cross-platforming their training regimes and skill sets. Surfers who come to this sport with no paddling skills, would benefit substantially through this mechanism.

Armed with the possible paradigm shift in thinking, the industry should promote and market the sport for what it is, a uniquely varied paddle sport, requiring a structured approach to learning. Paddle sports universally appeal to a much wider audience than that of surf sports regardless of the stoke you personally may feel when surfing and the reasons for this are not hard to grasp. In the first place, there is by far a greater abundance of relatively flat, surf-less water, both coastal and inland on this third rock from the sun of ours.

In terms of weight of numbers the world over, canoeing and kayaking in it's different guises, are cumulatively more omnipresent and accessible than surfing could ever dream of being - ironically, the commercial nature of surfing, within the clothing and accessory areas are the envy of all, where on account of aspirational imagery and marketing, some 70% of end-buyers of surf clothing, neither surf, let alone live near a beach.

Comments on the hype

Thumbing my way through stand up paddle board product brochures, magazines and burgeoning websites in preparedness for this publication, provided a portal into the mindset of those driving the sport; how they perceive its very nature and ultimate appeal. Page after page, aspirational imagery, methodically chosen to inspire one's imagination, hints at the seemingly endless experiences the sport will provide. Spiced with many of the usual cliches; I will be good looking, athletic; a maverick journeyman who will find my spiritual high place whether on a lake, river, dam or fjord, shore break, point break, reef break or idyllic tropical lagoon.

Technically simplistic with the bare minimum of equipment, participation will seemingly elevate your average suburbanite to quasi-waterman status faster than you can say, 'SUP'. For all the undeniable merits of this new sport and the consequential myriad of appeal to which the sport alludes, there lurks the possibility, some fundamental core identity issues may well be stunting its otherwise predicted meteoric rise and that's not to say that it hasn't boomed quickly in some key areas of the Pacific and Pacific Rim.

Mass appeal will ignite when imaginations are inspired to bring about a response to act and get involved. Part of the success of this process will evolve as a result of embracing and promoting the sport as a unique paddle sport, with the stand alone identity it deserves. Appropriate teaching strategies promoting skills development; while acknowledging much of what needs to be learned; balance and ocean knowledge, can only be learned by time on the water, time which becomes a habit, which becomes a lifestyle, where ultimately your reactions become instinctual, accomplishments matter of fact, but the thrill never diminishing.

Forms and disciplines

The transportable nature of the boards, their shallow draft and manner of propulsion using a simple extended canoe paddle, allows for the sport to be performed wherever there is a body of water, whether fresh water or salt and all its varieties in-between. As a consequence the sport is likely to find mass appeal wherever there is water and a will to participate and to date this is proving to be the case.

The following stand up paddle boarding activities and consequently the evolution of related equipment to suit, have evolved to some extent through user-innovators living in varied geographical proximities influenced by the nature of the body of water type close to hand, melded with pre-existing paddling or surfing skills or first-time-user experience.

Recreation

Flat water paddling and cruising in sheltered areas utilising appropriate equipment. This represents the entry level to the sport for most, possessing little or no water sports experience. This is where educators are predominantly focused and where potential for mass-appeal exists.

Adventuring

Adventure / recreational paddling centred on localised paddling or travel between destinations, whether on inland waterways or the ocean, which can include shorter half day excursions or longer, including camping.

Racing

Flat water distance, flat water sprint, ins and outs through the surf using specialised boards for differing water conditions.

Downwind

Downwind paddling between two points on any body of water, where the emphasis is generally on speed, chasing waves and swell at the upper end of which are hard core athletes who thrive on extremes of nature.

River running

A form of white water kayaking involving use of specialised boards and safety equipment; helmets, body armour, leashes. A branch of the sport which evolved (unexpectedly) in the hands of inland waterway paddlers in the USA; a classic user-innovator evolutionary shift in thinking away from the original first-time-users centred their interests upon as an ocean sport.

Yoga boarding

Where the board is used as a floating platform from which to practise yoga exercises, meditation and core exercises.

Paddle surfing

Surfing within a surf zone, paddle-surfing has been deemed by some as a form of high-performance variation of surfing akin to short board surfing on account of the paddle providing the rider added power and control in executing radical turns on stand up paddle boards, purpose made for the task using many varied designs as associated with surfing.

Lifestyles

Inevitably, as this image depicts, perhaps this is really what it's all about, for most people. The pure and simple pleasure found in the utilisation of a simplistic device which at its core, is fundamentally primitive, being little more than a rudimentary platform, propelled by means of an ancient paddle form, using simple bio-mechanical movements and muscle power in order to squeeze just that little bit more out of life and a relationship with water.

River Thames London - Blue Chip Sessions

5

Stand up paddle evolution

The evolution of the stand up paddle has taken a linear pathway from outrigger canoe paddle, to the humble oar, back inevitably into the hands of the outrigger canoe paddle maker, acknowledgement of which has been largely over-shadowed by a flood of many ill-conceived water whackers.

KANU
CULTURE
publications since 1994

Duke Kahanmoku

John Zapotocky
Photo C4 Waterman

Paddle evolution

When famous names such as Duke Kahanamoku and other Waikiki Beach Boys began stand up paddling, they simply used outrigger canoe paddles of the time, long enough to be used stood up on a surfboard. Another famous Waikiki Beach Boy, Bobby Achoy and father John Achoy would use modified oars, from row boats.

John Zapotocky, originally from Pennsylvania, having moved to Hawai`i, participated in stand up paddling for some fifty five years as a result of encouragement from 'The Duke' (Duke Kahanamoku) after having seen him out paddling on his surfboard. Asking what was it all about, he took to the water using a paddle having already been surfing for ten years prior. He went on to import river canoe paddles from Calhoun City, Mississippi from the Caviness Woodworking Co., which still operates today, specifically the 'Featherbrand'. He had them make a dozen at a time and sent to Hawai`i - the company had no idea what they were being used for. Ironically, Zapotocky retired from stand up paddle boarding around about the time it was popularised and commercialised in 2000.

'Caviness Woodworking Company, Inc. is a family owned and operated manufacturing company which produces boat paddles and oars for the marine, fishing tackle, canoeing, kayak and whitewater rafting industries all over the world. The

company was founded in the late 1940s by the late James T. "Jimmy" Caviness and became incorporated in September of 1954. Initially, the company made wooden furniture parts and

brooms as well as paddles and oars. With the enormous amount of fishing habitat in North Mississippi, which includes Grenada, Sardis, Enid and Arkabutla Reservoirs and their tributaries, Mr. Jimmy Caviness saw the need for good-quality, low-cost paddles. He retired in 1972 at the age of sixty eight. Over the past 50 years, Caviness Woodworking Company, Inc. has grown from a "backyard" operation into the world's largest manufacturer of paddles and oars.'

When Laird Hamilton and Dave Kalama improvised outrigger canoe paddles for their long boards in the mid 90s and Laird finally turned to Dave and said, **'I'm going to get a proper paddle made for this,'** that became an epiphany in elevating what was essentially a novelty, to serious intent, in standing up on a board and paddling. Paradoxically, it took notable contemporary characters in the surfing / waterman community to acknowledge the potential. In one fell-swoop, the sport was made credible.

Despite John Zapotocky's half century commitment to the sport, significantly he had no interest in advancing or promoting the sport, just simple pleasure through participation in his bubble of eccentricity, yet

today, he's an accidental legend, a 'hall of famer' and rightly so, not for his achievements per se, but through his own personal vision and commitment to a concept few embraced or took seriously.

In contrast and almost within an instant, with notable figures now acting as a catalyst, we were at the bottom of the hill in so far as product development was concerned. The need for the use of the paddle in context (paddling standing up) had been elevated from novelty to serious intent and what was required was a solution, to which end the notion of simply extending an outrigger canoe paddle, omnipresent throughout the Hawaiian islands, presented as the obvious solution as it had been in the early days of the Waikiki Beach Boys original involvement.

It should be noted outrigger canoe paddles even during the 70s were very much longer than they are today, averaging 5' (60") from tip to top - they had no grip.

Laird contacted Malama Paddles on Maui, maker of custom hand made outrigger canoe paddles and had a purpose made extended outrigger canoe paddle made. This in essence was a functionally novel innovation which simply required an outrigger canoe paddle's shaft to be extended.

Over time it became inevitable that other leading outrigger canoe paddle makers began to see their role in evolving stand up paddle design. By 2004, leading outrigger canoe paddle maker Kialoa, had begun their move into the sport - indeed I recall Dave

Chun telling me in Hilo Hawai`i in 2004 at the International Va'a Federation World Sprints, that he was making some carbon stand up paddles for Laird.

Though this was the catalyst for outrigger canoe paddle manufacturers to tap into a new market, there was now to be a period of time in testing and experimentation. Indeed even the end-user was not sure about the exact dimensions or properties the paddle should take. How tall, how big should the blade be, how much flex? All these questions would need to evolve over time and continue to evolve.

Outrigger canoe paddles had undergone a great deal of evolution through the 80s and into the 90s as the sport evolved into something more hi-tech rather than hung up on notions of traditions. Many of the design ideas were feeding in from the influx of user innovators from the East Coast of America and Canada in particular, where canoe river racing (C1s, C2s) had been evolving without restriction for years.

Designers and makers such as Bob Zaveral (ZRE) and his super lightweight carbon paddles, Black Bart, Brad Gillespie, Sawyer, Jim Terrell (Quick Blade) and Kialoa through Meg and Dave Chun were all significant players in paddle evolution, responding to the demands of users who were bringing in new paddling techniques and ideas from other paddle sports in particular, in the quest to go faster and further.

Though Kialoa began their paddling making exploits in Hawai`i servicing the outrigger canoeing market, they ultimately moved to Oregon frustrated by a lack of reliable source of timber suited to paddle making. Kialoa stands out as the paddle of choice for many top Hawaiian outrigger crews, which by osmosis spread to areas such as Canada, Australia and mainland USA.

Careful strategic marketing, by sponsoring and working with paddlers in the same way as a surfboard shaper would work with professional surfers, Kialoa paddle designs evolved, to produce a product of outstanding form and function, more especially through the creation of its hybrid (carbon/timber paddles) which they pioneered to perfection.

In terms of carbon made paddles, Bob Zaveral (ZRE) has always been ahead of his time, a pioneer and one of the longest involved in the manufacturer (1973) of carbon canoe paddles and continues to make paddles at the very pinnacle of their type to which many aspire.

Many paddle makers servicing the outrigger canoeing market and indeed the river paddling fraternity, have moved towards the making of stand up paddles, some by chance, some by association, either asked directly by users, or by way of seeing monetary potential. What we have now is paddle makers jumping in to add these paddles to their product lines to service, in particular, existing customers whose interests have gravitated towards the sport as could be expected.

Todd Bradley's involvement is not insignificant in this regard. An enigmatic, highly driven modern day visionary, he thrives on advancement and in breaking things down in order to squeeze the greatest potential out of the sports he's been involved with, outrigger canoeing and now stand up paddling in particular, as co-founder of C4 Waterman. As a world class outrigger canoe steerer, not content with steering paddles on the market, Todd designed and made his own during the 90s, the result of which created a shift in thinking, not only in the way steering paddles were designed and made (incorporating carbon laminates between layups and carbon on the blades) but how canoes were steered. Kialoa adopted a Bradley model and later went on to work with Jim Foti, legendary steerer for Lanikai.

Todd's paddles produced under the label 'Pohaku' (stone, rock, strong) are paddles which ooze with intellectual consideration of all the dynamics at play. As it was with Todd's input into the evolution of outrigger canoe steering paddles, so too he has had input into the design considerations of stand up paddles.

Jim Terrell (Quick Blades) made his name paddling and racing C1's. He moved into canoe paddle making, progressing into making OC paddles and now for stand up paddling. This has been a typical evolutionary process for many canoe paddle makers. Jim brings with him a science orientated view of paddle dynamics and as a high level paddler himself his knowledge as an end-user and manufacturer permits him to evolve his paddles quickly to suit ever evolving paddling techniques and demands.

The stand up paddle board industry owes a debt of gratitude to these outrigger canoe paddle designers and manufacturers. The shame of it is, that for all of their intellectual wisdom and pioneering initiatives they have carved out over time and to all of those end-user pioneers who worked in conjunction with them, they are rarely afforded the respect

All carbon ZRE paddles 1997 Team Hawai`i Masters / Hamilton Island Australia.

they deserve, manifested today in the form of large companies often churning out ill-conceived after-thoughts masquerading as poor excuses for a means of propulsion and even worse, producing unintelligible marketing babble-speak, alluding to having us believe they know what they are talking about, after investing but a mere nano-second in consideration into all that a paddle should be.

The function, importance and significance of the paddle has rarely been so misunderstood in the context of a paddle sport on account of the rush to produce and sell.

1990s Kialoa timber paddles for the OC market.

Tahiti Hoe Paddles
Point Venus Tahiti

6

The paddle

The singular most important item you will own as part of your
acknowledgment of the sport as a 'paddle' board sport,
is your paddle, to which end it should add to your
experience of the sport never limit it.

"As a quiver of arrows is to the archer,
so too the paddler should aim to possess a quiver
of paddles for varying boards and purposes"

Photo Steve West
Paddle carver Huahine
French Polynesia

The paddle

'A man feels at home with a paddle in his hand, as natural and indigenous as with a bow or a spear. When he swings through the stroke and moves forward, he sets in motion long forgotten reflexes, stirs up ancient sensations deep within his subconscious.' *Sigurd Olson.*

It seems incredulous that the design and performance merits of the paddle in the context of many paddle sports, are considered secondary to those of the craft you are paddling; regrettably no more so has this been true of stand up paddling. From a paddler's perspective, a good paddle should be an essential, not an after thought, which is often how retailers approach customer sales to the extent of making it often the last consideration, not the primary.

Typically, the would be paddler enters the store and enquires about the sport and by the end of the buying-selling process, all the money has gone into the board and accessories with just a few pennies left for a cheap stick to paddle it with (it may even be so bad as to be free). The fact remains, when the budget is tight, the novice purchaser should be frugal regarding the board purchased, setting aside money for a quality paddle, for reasons which are practical and sound beyond rationale argument to the contrary.

In short, I make no apology for stating that there should be, 'no such thing as a novice paddle', it is a myth of biblical proportion, the end product of which is more often than not, a fraud and a fake, which hinders, impedes and sabotages the very core foundations of all that is spoken of learning. Novice and expert alike, require the best possible paddle design in order to have any chance of executing sound, efficient, injury free paddling technique together with all other associated benefits.

A quality paddle's long list of virtues, far outweigh its one and only vice, that of cost. Put another way, a quality paddle should possess all of the qualities which lead to optimising performance and enjoyment. Most cheap (novice) paddles, have but one virtue, cheapness, which manifests as a vice.

'Ownership of an expensive, quality paddle is not a right of passage into the realms of being an advanced paddler, they are available to all comers of any standard and are in every sense, easier to use than the lifeless, heavy, industrial dross, which more often than not, end up in the hands of the novice as the result of sound advice.'

The simple fact of the matter remains, being that the paddle is your primary means of propulsion, it has the capacity to injure, limit your physical abilities, reduce your endurance, paddling enjoyment, your craft's performance, all on account of being utterly inefficient and or inappropriate.

Many retailers tend to ensure the bulk of their customer's money is spent on their new board, giving only secondary consideration to the paddle, to the extent that it takes on an almost optional extra persona, far from being portrayed as a vital component. Those that don't should be praised.

Wherever you see 'Free paddle with every board', you can rest assured, here's a retailer or indeed a manufacturer, who perceives the paddle as a secondary consideration, an optional extra, a rudimentary accessory, a necessary evil, which because of its cost, may hinder the

end-user in buying a board (or least a more expensive board over the cheaper option) and you can bet your rotator-cuff that this 'free' paddle will possess all the subtle refinements of a meat-axe, reinforcing the sellers conviction, the paddle is the least important item?

The paddle maker

There are often strong cultural affinities between the end-user (the paddler) and the paddle maker / designer in terms of geographical proximity and consequently the style and nature of paddle the manufacturer has built their reputation upon, often relating directly to the predominant nature of the body of water close to hand - that is to say if they are coastal or inland based.

The finest paddle makers for the most part, function as lifestyle firms, employing only small numbers of employees, generating a modest income creating paddles for innovative users, allowing them to continue innovating and advancing their own skills within their sport.

If outrigger canoe and river paddles had not evolved to the extent they have today or the sharing of ideas between users, stand up paddles would more than likely be heavy, low tech slabs of wood by comparison, limiting the sport's appeal and multi-facetted nature. In many ways, outrigger

canoeing throughout the Pacific, did for paddles, what the windsurfing industry did for the evolution of wet suits, roto-moulding, sail and mast design and more besides. This is not to take anything away from river canoe paddle designers and manufacturers - however, outrigger canoeists, unquestionably pushed the envelope in so far as ocean canoe paddle designs are concerned, exclusive of any other ocean canoe paddle sport.

While some paddle makers attempt to cater for every conceivable scenario of budget, age, size and circumstance, this does not necessarily mean that all paddles are OK. They are not.

A windsurfer knows the value of a good rig, the primary means of propulsion and control. A tennis player knows the value of a good racket and the violin player the need of a good bow.

A paddler, novice or otherwise, who fails to place importance on the virtues of a good paddle (or be taught this consideration) need consider what in part, makes for a good paddler, the answer to which is surely a good paddle and the way in which the paddler uses

Photo Mandy West

79

it. The craft you are in, or on, has no relationship in regards to your paddling ability as such.

Don't ever fall into this trap, or be told by an 'experienced' paddler, your best friend, your salesman, or some random internet rant that a 'paddle is a paddle' and not to waste time or money on a good one. Frankly you can never own enough or try enough. Every self respecting paddler of worth should make it their quest to accumulate a quiver of choice and buy the best they can afford.

The art of paddling is a dynamic experience. The nuances of your paddling skills blended with the nuances of your board, will change over time and so you must strive to adopt and embrace new paddle designs with differing characteristics and qualities in your quest to constantly improve your paddling experience.

Even with the march of progress, whether all wood, carbon or a mix of materials, a well crafted paddle is the pinnacle of art, form and function. Its simple form evokes in the paddler an empathy for what it represents; a way of propelling yourself over the water, symbolising freedom from constraint, recreation, a good time and ultimately what you would rather be doing.

In ancient times throughout the Pacific, the paddle was in the context of warfare, both a means of propulsion and a weapon. The blade face was often used to shield and protect the warrior's face and body from thrown objects. The blade edge was used to chop down and cut at their opponents, while the shaft was often used as a staff or long-bo as used in martial arts. Some designs from around the Pacific could have doubled as spears, with razor-sharp blade tips and edges.

With the passing of time, the form of the paddle has narrowed down to one primary concern, efficiency as a tool for propulsion over water. In this respect, the changes have been enormous and exhaustive in every single facet of their creation. Once carved from a single solid slab of timber, today's paddles are manufactured in a wide range of materials, all offering differing levels of performance and feel.

Without exception, high performance paddles used today are only vaguely traditional in design and very much different with regards to the materials used. Many contemporary design elements are due to the advancement of Native American open canoe (river) paddle designs fostered by Euro-American and European racers and shapers.

Photo Steve West.
Samoan paddles.
Captain Cook Museum Auckland
Aotearoa (New Zealand)

Opposing viewpoints

'Thousands of budget paddles are on the water each week and work fine.'

This somewhat depends upon the definition of 'just fine'. One can presume this means 'adequate'. The sole reason that thousands of budget paddles exist, is due to the unfortunate reality that they exist in the first place. These are churned out for the most part, by non-specialist paddle makers (fabricators) who no doubt genuinely feel they are catering to the apparent overwhelming global demand (by the end-user) for budget orientated, cheap paddles.

For the most part, cheap boards are few and far between, yet the market place is literally flooded with cheap paddles. A paddle, in the context of paddle sports, is a moving-part. It is if you like a mechanical component, a product of engineering, unlike the board, which by comparison is relatively inert. The paddle in the context of all paddle sports is an extension of you and the bio-mechanical forces you deliver to it, which subsequently moves and controls the board under your feet.

Much of this demand for cheap paddles is in actuality, directly pushed by board manufactures / retailers, who, when faced with having to sell an often unfathomably expensive board, use the free of charge paddle / cheap stick, as the dealmaker, the clincher that hints you are being done a favour. The fact of the matter is, it's not much of a favour.

I can think of few other sports, where an item of equipment, so profoundly central to the sport itself, is all but reduced to being the lowest common denominator in the buying process, often actively encouraged and supported by those claiming to be in a position of expertise. By comparison, no self respecting outrigger canoeist would use an aluminium shafted paddle, with a plastic pizza scoop blade riveted to the lower shaft, nor surf ski paddler either, as they value the nature of a good paddle and its a given within the paddling community at large, that investment very early on, if not from the very outset in a quality paddle, is essential. You are investing in a paddle sport even at a recreational level.

'There's no point having a budget board and using an expensive carbon blade as it won't add to the SUP experience.'

This statement is actually the wrong way around, as there's actually every point to be made for paddling a cheap board around with an expensive paddle. The implication here also, is that carbon is the key to a good paddle. It's not the singular defining quality of a good paddle - far from it. Many carbon paddles are heavy and of poor design.

Let's be absolutely clear. Budget means cheap and by association inferior in design, quality, materials and performance, so long as you understand this concept then you can be clear about what you're investing in. Worse than this, a poorly performing paddle will in every sense, negatively affect the beginners rate of learning and subsequently their experience.

To suggest that investing in a carbon (lightweight) blade will not add to the stand up paddling experience, is to completely ignore the fact that this is a paddle sport. What exactly is the first time experience we are looking to create? One would assume a positive, encouraging one, which in the first instance has most beginners learning new paddling skills, balance and board skills. A heavy, poorly designed paddle with ineffectual blade design, will bring about the onset of early fatigue and work against the paddler on every level, to the point where their experience may be so negative, they quit in the steep part of the learning curve.

I once encountered an Italian chap on the river Thames in London. He owned a carbon paddle which he had paid a substantial amount of money for. It was unbelievably heavy and had a massive blade shaped like a pizza scoop. I leant him my 20oz carbon fibre vacuum bagged paddle costing only a little more than he had paid. His eyes lit up and off he went! He could not stop raving about the difference, said he was about to give the sport away, but now he had a revelation and vowed to upgrade that very day. That's the level of experience I speak of.

With regards to price point versus performance with specific comparison between board and paddle, there is by and large, a gapping trench between the two. Comparatively, an expensive board, rarely amounts to being twice the board in terms of performance in relation to its cheaper counterpart. Yet, a paddle perhaps twice or greater than the cost of an inferior paddle, more often than not, exceeds twice the level of build quality, performance, resale value, improved enjoyment, reduced fatigue, added time on the water, design merits and ergonomics. The added cost is justified and not a complex equation to fathom.

Paddle anatomy

Every paddle is composed of a basic anatomy. Understanding these parts will provide you with better understanding of their construction while the paddle's measurements will arm you with knowledge of how they affect your relationship with the paddle, bio-mechanically speaking.

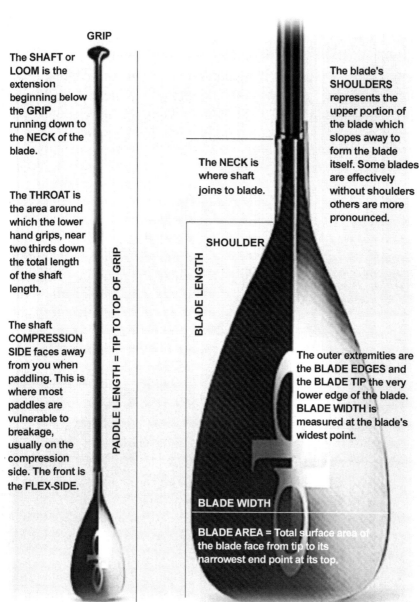

GRIP

The **SHAFT** or **LOOM** is the extension beginning below the **GRIP** running down to the **NECK** of the blade.

The **THROAT** is the area around which the lower hand grips, near two thirds down the total length of the shaft length.

The shaft **COMPRESSION SIDE** faces away from you when paddling. This is where most paddles are vulnerable to breakage, usually on the compression side. The front is the **FLEX-SIDE**.

PADDLE LENGTH = TIP TO TOP OF GRIP

The **NECK** is where shaft joins to blade.

The blade's **SHOULDERS** represents the upper portion of the blade which slopes away to form the blade itself. Some blades are effectively without shoulders others are more pronounced.

SHOULDER

BLADE LENGTH

The outer extremities are the **BLADE EDGES** and the **BLADE TIP** the very lower edge of the blade. **BLADE WIDTH** is measured at the blade's widest point.

BLADE WIDTH

BLADE AREA = Total surface area of the blade face from tip to its narrowest end point at its top.

TIP

Form and function, two of the world's leading canoe and now SU-paddle designs by Bob Zaveral ZRE (Zaveral Racing Equipment USA) and a Kialoa paddle by Dave and Meg Chun of Bend Oregon USA. Other high end makers include Jim Terrell's Quick Blade paddles and Todd Bradley's Pohaku paddles, who now heads the C4 paddle range amongst other things. These mentioned represent some of those who have been leading the charge in ocean canoe sports for some years now. ZRE paddles continue to be hand-made, as are Kialoa's top line paddles.

Shoulders

While some blades have very pronounced shoulders, which tuck in and away from the edges up towards the neck of the blade (where it joins the shaft) many lack these curved shoulders. Shoulder-less Tahitian teardrop shaped paddles, have dominated the outrigger canoeing market for many years since the Tahitians introduced them to outrigger canoeing. Paradoxically, pronounced shoulders were a manifestation of high end open canoe racing in the USA.

Pronounced shoulders allow you to drive the paddle closer to the edge of the board and even under the hull to some degree so as some surface tension can be broken between hull and water. Often associated with low aspect paddles, they tend to offer improved levels of balance permitting the greater part of the blade area to be concentrated in a more uniformed area or block rather than a rapid diminishment toward the blades upper limits.

The C4 X-Wing has shoulders which taper inward from its square running edges, the ZRE has very pronounced shoulders, while the Kialoa paddle is essentially 'shoulder-less', its edges tapering continuously to the neck.

A paddles vital statistics

Paddle length measured blade tip to top of grip. **Blade height** measured blade tip to neck. **Blade width** measured at its maximum edge to edge width. **Blade area** being the sum total of area from tip to shoulder or neck depending on blade shape. **Grip circumference** taken around the throat and the overall **paddle weight** are all major considerations.

How a paddle should feel

Even before venturing onto the water, it's possible to determine at least some basic tactile virtues inherent in any paddle you choose to pick up. Above all, it must feel comfortable in the hands, at the grip (handle) and where the lower hand wraps around the shaft (throat). Avoid paddles which are excessively blade heavy so as the paddle should balance in your hand at around one-third the way up the shaft. Even before price is a consideration (don't ask) just go through a variety in your hands and essentially pick out the ones which feel best to you and then enquire about the price. This simple test will provide fuel for thought versus cost.

Paddle grips

The grip should not be so big that your hand struggles to fit comfortably nor too small that you have to grip tightly to maintain control of it. Make sure it moulds to your palm and fingers. If you are going to be paddling any distance, a poorly shaped grip can bruise the palm. Ensure your fingers can wrap over and establish firm control without unnecessary squeezing.

From left; Palm or Pear Grip, Hammerhead or J-Grip and a T- Grip. The Palm Grip (above right) has been popular for river cruising and canoeing for its level of comfort. Some include a recessed section for the fingers to fit into, which greatly improves control in rough water and high winds. Badly designed Palm Grips can cause your palm to slip on occasion which can lead to a bashing in the face, literally. Ensure you affix with the finger recess forwards!

Grip circumference

The circumference of the shaft at the throat is important for both comfort and control of the blade. It is fair to say that most adult men's grips are larger in diameter than women's and junior's. Many paddles come standard, with no allowance for women or juniors with the possible exception of a few manufacturers, who are now catering to this need.

If the circumference of the throat of the shaft is too small, your hand cannot relax, often having to squeeze continually and firmly to maintain control, resulting in tight (cramping) forearms - add foam wrap around to resolve - too large and you will loose control over the blade and struggle to maintain any level of power or control.

Many elbow injuries can manifest from incorrect throat diameters and shapes, where the paddler is failing to paddle with a relaxed grip. It is a mistaken belief that the shaft should be squeezed as such. At the initial entry, yes, but thereafter the hand can relax as pull generated, will keep the shaft pressured into the lower three fingers in particular.

Rounded shafts vs oval

The shape of the shaft makes a big difference in terms of comfort, control and how the paddle feels in the hand. The vast majority are near perfectly cylindrical (round) and for the most part this is probably down to ease of manufacturer when in actuality, an oval shape tends to be more ergonomic and better suited to the shape of the closed hand. The oval shaft is generally stronger in engineering terms. Importantly, it prevents the shaft

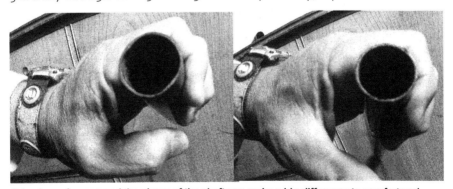

Grip circumference and the shape of the shaft can make a big difference to comfort and control, especially if your hands are wet. The oval shaft can sit in the nape of your fingers without rolling off-axis. Ultimately it comes down to personal preference, but it is yet another factor to consider regarding the paddle's overall design merits.

A mix of shaft cut-offs showing a wide range of variance from ovals to circular.

rolling off-axis and permits the shaft to rest between finger and palm without unnecessary pressure having to be applied. The lower three fingers should not have to squeeze hard, but should be partially relaxed, the pull should provide enough pressure to prevent the hand slipping.

Blade performance

Blades can be assessed on five performance criteria; **entry, catch, grip, exit** and to a lesser extent **recovery**. This directly translates into the various phases of the paddle stroke. The rigidity of the blade and the degree of flex where the neck joins the shaft and the flex properties of the shaft, are all critical factors in ensuring the blade can perform within its limits of design.

Entry / catch

As the blade enters the water, it should do so in a way that minimises energy waste; seen as splash and excessive bubbles of air around the blade. Clean entry is vital in order to establish a sound 'catch'. Air tends to be dragged down with the blade when entered into the water, as a pocket of air on the front face, where low pressure exists and water implodes and as bubbles of air on the front (power) face. This greatly reduces the blades ability to 'anchor' as it leads to cavitation and blade slippage. While the paddler is largely responsible for clean placement, blade design can either hinder or assist in this respect. Developing a smooth entry technique is for the most part essential, though there are arguments for 'hard' (dirty) paddle entry on occasion ie when paddling upwind in rough waters.

88

Waterline

Flat blade creates
turbulent flow
behind blade.
Generating little
forward force.

Curved blade keeps
a laminar flow
around the back.
A strong forward
force is created.

Slice

Curved blade tips can assist with vertical blade entry in minimising take down of air. However if the paddle is swung in more side on, a straight tip may work better.

Grip / catch / blade size

The blade must grip the water so an effective pull can be generated, leading to the analogy of the blade acting as an anchor in being stationary as the board is pulled up to its level over the water. Importantly, 'stationary' is not a relative term. Regardless of blade area, so long as the blade is stationary during the pull (power) phase, blade area only need be of sufficient size to achieve this important 'moment'.

Additionally, regardless of blade area, if insufficient compression (power) is given to the blade, it will slip backwards on account of uncompressed 'soft' water spilling from its edges. Blade area therefore, needs to be proportionate to the paddler's strength, body mass, paddling style (fast or slow stroke rating) and of enough area to offset these loads by way of resistance.

Blade areas have greatly reduced in canoe sports from the mid 90s, moving away from the 'bigger must be better' theory as experienced with the evolution of outrigger canoe paddles. Surface areas beyond an optimum size, simply add extra weight and ineffectual surface area which translates into unnecessary resistance and drag, particularly during the exit phase of the stroke.

For cleaner entry so as to limit air take-down on the back face of the paddle, slicing the blade inwards and downwards should be a natural continuation of your recovery (swing through).

89

Blade area measurements, only provide part of the puzzle as makers often use differing formulas and points of measurement. Blade width is often used as the predominant point of reference for blade size. Outrigger canoe paddles, with shorter lever arms (shaft) fall between 10" to 8" while SU-paddles now vary from around 9.5" down to 7". The longer lever arm, makes it desirable to lessen blade size and there is a clear shift now towards ever decreasing blade width and area. Oversized blade areas, can lead to a variety of body stresses and injuries, ranging from haemorrhoids and tearing of minor core-muscle groups in particular.

Smaller blade areas have led to more aggressive paddling techniques and styles, with higher stroke rates and greater emphasis on power at the front of the stroke. Compression of the water against the blade face is critical to maximising the benefits inherent in smaller blades. Some paddlers as they age, may move back to wider, larger blade areas to accommodate a slower stroke rate.

Concave (scooped) paddles

The inclusion of a concave on the power-face may improve grip at the catch and power phase of the stroke giving the paddler the sensation of loading up the blade.

While many paddle makers strive for some degree of concave, too much will have negative results, so as at the end of the stroke, rather than water spilling from the blade face in a clean even flow, it will tend to hold water during the exit phase of the stroke.

The net consequence is excessive drag at the exit phase leading to early fatigue, slower stroke rates and often a 'pull-down' effect acting on the

A deep concave blade 'scooping'.

The 6.95" C4 X-Wing blade. The power face features a strong dihedral for even water shedding and mild concave to improve grip. Moving away from the OC tear drop shapes this is an SU-Paddle built from the ground up.

board. Blade designs with any amount of concave must be released very early at the hip and 'lifted' to allow the water to spill from the face of the blade. Only a marginal degree of concave is required to make a significant improvement in grip.

In a sense, the urge to add (excessive) concave to the blades power-face, works on a sort of primitive fuzzy logic, which only considers the stroke from the point of view of catch and the power-phase (pulling) but fails to consider, quality of entry and the exit phase, where a flatter blade face in this regard, is generally far superior offering up much less drag.

The idea is borrowed from kayak paddles which bio-mechanically require a completely differing entry, power and exit phase and consists of a definite pull and push phase which sweeps for the most part away from the side of the craft, unlike canoe paddling or stand up paddling technique, which relies predominantly on pull, not push and parallel travel along the rail.

From the learner's point of view, scooped blades are problematic in that they hold water during the power phase, but at the end of stroke the blade remains loaded which can pull the paddler off balance (backwards). The overall feel is heaviness associated with excess drag and therefore counter-productive to learning.

High aspect blade
A high aspect blade by ratio, is relatively long in relation to its width (long and narrow) and may lack shoulders which merely curve away to meet the neck. As a result of their shape, they tend to have a relatively high centre of effort. The C4 X-Wing 6.95" paddle can be considered high aspect, but differs in featuring straight long edges, giving the blade good balance but also include very definitive shoulders as with the ZRE blades.

In terms of 'feel' the high aspect paddle with its higher centre of effort, is often preferred by taller paddlers in rough water, being that you don't always need to bury it fully to reap the benefits of grip. In terms of feel, the high aspect paddle is less forgiving with regards to poor paddling technique, especially when pushing forwards

Taller paddlers may benefit from a high aspect paddle in off-setting their own high CG.

91

It's not just the area of mass of the blade which is significant, it's also what's missing. If you look at the white space beyond the blade area, this tells you something about the balance of the blade in relation to how it will remain vertical. Note where the widest point of the blade is on each of these blades. Extended wide spots create a larger 'sweet-spot' in which the blade can find bite and balance and remain vertical for longer.

The Nitro Werner is an example of a high aspect blade, with minimal shoulders. The Kialoa, is a conventional tear-drop shape without defined shoulders. The deeply curved shoulders of the ZRE and C4, permit the blade to travel close and neatly under the hull of the board, closing the gap between blade and board and assist in breaking hull surface tension.

Each provides differing levels of feel and performance. Blades which provide a narrow 'band width' of balance (centre of effort) low down, which diminishes rapidly towards the neck of the blade are prone to 'falling over' at the vertical 'moment' when some delay is required in order to lengthen the drive time of the blade, hence why we are seeing evidence of some blade templates evolving away from conventional tear drop shapes for SU-paddles.

with the top arm during the power-phase (which you shouldn't). It can very easily trip over itself, the top portion of the blade travelling over the tip, which acts as the fulcrum point. Being that there is considerably less surface area in the upper portion of the blade, there is less resistance (counter-resisting water pressure) and so the upper portion of the blade, wants to move faster (easier) through the water than the lower portion of the blade, which tends to remain anchored.

Low aspect blade

A low aspect paddle tends to be rounder or more squat in shape (more equilateral) and has its maximum width somewhat higher up towards the mid section of the blade's height. These blades tend to have more pronounced, curved shoulders leading up to the neck of the shaft and require careful, deeper placement, though the low aspect paddle can be a little more forgiving than the high aspect paddle, being that the bulk of the blades area is often spread over a greater area of its overall length.

Flutter

This is a characteristic associated with the blades tendency to

On the left, a flat faced Kialoa blade. On the right a ZRE Power Surge, with dihedral running from the neck progressively diminishing towards the tip. These dihedrals or splines, add some degree of balance to the blade, permitting water to leave the blade surface in near equal proportions toward the end of the stroke as the power diminishes. With the evolution of smaller blade areas, splines have slowly been omitted or diminished, as faster, more aggressive paddling techniques have evolved, requiring paddlers increase compression of the water against the blade face at the catch phase. Smaller, flat faced blades demand an aggressive catch and do not always suit the entry level paddler as flutter will occur if not used in this manner.

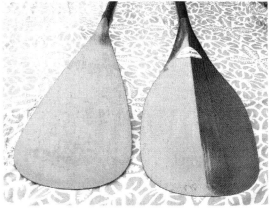

'flutter' (oscillate) side to side as you make the pull. It can be associated with the blade area (resistance) being excessive for the paddler relative to their strength, technique or body mass. It can also be associated with poor blade design, which either encourages water run-off or may morph under load, causing water to leave the blade edges under varying degrees of pressure as the pull is made.

Essentially flutter results as water, under pressure, leaves the blade face at random points along its edges, causing shifts in the forces (resistance) acting against the blade during the power phase.

The inclusion of a spline or raised dihedral from the neck to a quarter or two thirds down the centre of the power face of the blade, can provide some balance and reduce this tendency, but relates more towards taming this behaviour at the end of the stroke as the power band diminishes and

the water begins to naturally leave the blade face. Paddles with small blade areas will often tend to suffer less from flutter, but demand a more aggressive, explosive catch and power phase in order to compress the water against the blade, to prevent this behaviour, along with blade slippage. With diminishing blade areas over recent times, the spline has disappeared or diminished from paddle design but a remnant of it is still often added in the very top quarter of the blade to improve stability.

Exit

When you remove the blade from the water, your aim is to minimise energy loss from yourself and the paddle. This is achieved by exiting the blade from the water at the earliest opportunity after the power-phase of the stroke, even if some of the propulsive power is lost from the end of the stroke.

If you pull the blade too far past your body, it slows your potential stroke rate and uses unnecessary energy, as the critical and most powerful part of your stroke has already been made. Once the blade passes your hip, your pull becomes a push; a much less effective use of both blade and body.

The larger the surface area of the blade, the greater the drag or resistance at exit part of the stroke. The solution for this is to reduce the surface area of the blade, particularly its length and to design a paddle that does not hold water at the end of the stroke as associated with heavily concave blade shapes.

A short blade length; measured from blade tip to the neck, will mean that there is less blade to be buried deeply below the water surface. It can therefore be exited and re-entered with smaller movements and with less energy expenditure. A relatively flat blade surface will also improve exit of the paddle from the water, encouraging water to flow from its surface.

Recovery

An efficient recovery achieved by rotation and swing through of the paddler to the set up phase of the stroke, is often argued around issues of weight and the degree of flex inherent in the paddle shaft.

Weight - because it is said the paddle is carried through to the entry, the lighter the better. Flex - because if the paddle shaft is too stiff, it will lack recoil and will make for a discouraging sensation, affecting the paddler's rhythm. This is counter argued by the virtues of having a super stiff shaft so as no energy is lost in the power-phase.

These issues have little to do with blade shape. What can be said is the more aerodynamic and smaller the blade, the less affected by wind it will be in the recovery phase.

(See section on Flex Appeal).

Contemporary blade templates, have evolved primarily through the intervention of individuals not of a canoe based culture and for the purposes of paddling while seated. Speculatively, if we consider ancient cultures such as the Congolese fisherman of Central Africa, who still use paddles without grips, blades still long and narrow as used for day to day stand up paddling of their dug-out canoes, should we consider a total rethink of the paddle for the purposes of paddling while standing?

Timber paddle construction

It's easy to forget that not everyone, everywhere is as affluent as the next person or culture. This is especially true throughout the Pacific islands. In some remote parts of the world such as the islands of French Polynesia, the art of paddle making is revered. Limited to tropical timbers and an economy that must allow anyone to be able to afford it, the paddle is considered more of a consumable item, than a permanent fixture. As such, this keeps the flow of ideas constant and dynamic.

Here the premise is that the paddle must blend with the paddler's technique not the other way around. They are, in short, demanding of, not subservient to the paddle or the paddle maker.

While there are certainly some laminated hand made timber paddles available, they remain in the minority. In actuality, in a Western economy,

Photo Steve West
Tahiti Hoe - Tahiti

because of the time required and the quality of timbers needed to make a hand crafted timber paddle, they should cost as much as, if not more than a carbon paddle, however the general perspective is often that the timber paddle is inferior.

A timber paddle feels very different to a synthetic paddle. There's the weight. They are generally always heavier. There's the flex, being always more flexible through the shaft and they will in time literally wear out if used for long enough, through continual crushing of the fibres along the compression side of the shaft resulting in a breakage. This being said, you cannot replace the natural, organic feel of timber, its beauty or forgiving nature, its lesser environmental impact and the support of the artisans' skills.

Laminations

Traditional paddles were simply carved from solid lengths of timber. Contemporary paddles use a well known manufacturing procedure known as laminating. The laminating or layering together of woods by gluing them, adds to the uniform strength of the paddle. Another advantage is the creation of a lighter paddle by combining light and heavy timbers, rather than just being limited to one type for strength (usually heavy).

Weight versus strength is the eternal quest, as strong as possible, as light as possible. These requirements are in the hands of the craftsperson, whose skill resides in the considered selection of the timber and meticulous laminating methods, determining the paddle's durability. In this process, the quality of the water-proof glue is essential for ensuring the longevity of the paddle. The quality of the join or laminating performed by the craftsperson is also critical.

Assessing a timber paddles construction

Thin glue lines between laminates indicates a strong finish. Wide gaps between laminates indicates the timbers have not been butted up hard against each other during curing. Adhesion between timbers is essential. The greater the number of laminations, the stronger the paddle will be.

Check for wood defects such as knots, resin pockets, short grain shakes and warping. All of these will cause weak spots which will be prone to breakage. Look for a well-made, long tapering splice on the shaft. This will ensure good shaft strength in a uniform length from the neck to the grip.

Check the quality of the varnish and the lay-up of the glass or carbon on the blade or between laminates. Check for air pockets. Pay close attention to the edging and blade tip regarding the seal and finish. Is the edging synthetic or fibreglassed hardwood and is it sufficient protection for the blade to withstand impact.

Hardwoods - Softwoods

Hardwoods include all the broad-leafed groups of tree species; eucalypts, oaks, etc. Softwoods include all the cone bearing species (conifers) pine, spruce and fir trees. Hardwoods are not necessarily hard, nor softwoods, soft. These general terms are biological classifications and are given to describe the general qualities of the wood and in particular its resistance to

Adjustable Alloy Shaft - Moulded Plastic Blade 8.5" Blade Width

Carbon / Fibreglass Womens Paddle 7" Blade Width

Carbon / Wood (hybrid) 8" Blade Width

Carbon / Kevlar 9.5" Blade Width

Carbon 9.5" Blade Width

impact. However, do not put too much faith in this, as balsa wood, one of the softest and lightest of timbers, is classified as a hardwood. Many paddle manufacturers use a combination of hard and soft woods, primarily to keep the weight to a minimum while relying on the strength of the lamination and the use of hardwoods to provide strength.

Wood composite paddles - hybrids

Advances in materials and construction techniques led to the development of hybrid paddles, which use a mix of timber and synthetic materials. Wood composites are similar to traditional all wood paddles in that both have timber blades and sometimes shafts. Where the two construction methods differ is in the use of reinforcing composite skins such as fibreglass, kevlar, or carbon fibre on the blade. The combination of the lightweight core and composite skin allows the builders to use lightweight woods, usually balsa or foam as the core of the blade. The combination of a light weight core and composite skin produces paddles which are lighter, stronger and more durable than traditional wood paddles.

Outrigger canoe paddle manufacturers were motivated to start building wood composites because of requests from sponsored athletes, who wanted something light and durable. They felt strongly about developing something with paddle makers as a surfer works with a shaper.

(Left) The Naish range of paddles for 2011, typified a spread of paddles suiting budget and purpose. (1)The adjustable alloy / moulded plastic bladed paddle, represents a basic design, catering for use by multiple-persons in being adjustable, less centred on performance paddling, but merely a means to an end in providing propulsion. (2) The carbon / fibreglass paddle with a mere 7" blade, has been specifically designed for women, a concept first created by Kialoa paddles within their range of OC paddles where female participation is high. Certainly many women and junior age paddlers benefit from smaller blade areas, narrower grip circumference and overall reduced weight in improving levels of manageability. (3) The hybrid carbon / wood paddle offers a hint of organic quality with the use of a bamboo laminate over foam which can be less damaging to your board rails. In performance terms, a similar vacuum bagged well made all carbon paddle, would have an even lighter blade weight. The difference in balance is what would separate these paddles and whether you preferred some blade weight rather than next to none and therefore a factor of control. (4) The carbon / kevlar paddle provides some level of compromise, being that kevlar would permit increased shaft flex and therefore recoil (or 'reflex' as Naish like to call it) and no doubt there may be some cost saving. The swallow shaped blade is a curious addition. Certain ancient paddle designs within Oceania had sometimes the inclusion of this divot. It could be purely a novelty, on the other hand it may well provide some measured improvement in reducing flutter and improving blade stability, however I would be inclined to believe that if it improved performance, specialist paddle makers would long ago have evolved such a design. (5) The final all carbon paddle at 9.5" wide, has a sizeable blade area.

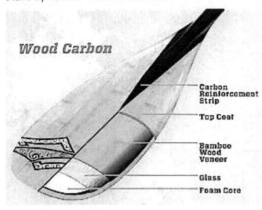

Wood Carbon

Carbon Reinforcement Strip

Top Coat

Bamboo Wood Veneer

Glass

Foam Core

A good example of a hybrid paddle construction as produced by Naish with carbon shaft and laminated timber (bamboo) foam core blade. The aim is to produce a very lightweight blade, ideally lighter than the total weight of the shaft in creating a 'blade-light' paddle which is strong and easy to wield around.

Dave Chun of Kialoa was instrumental in the perfecting of hybrid paddles beginning with 'Dave's 99 Hybrid' outrigger canoe paddle, in production of June 2001. Hybrid paddles provided the missing link between, too soft and too stiff, in terms of paddle feel, combining a super stiff blade face and neck area with a laminated timber shaft, providing a comfortable level of flex at a weight with enough inertia to be neither too light, nor too heavy.

Hybrid paddles provided weight reductions of up to 25% when compared to similar size wood paddles. While hybrid paddles aren't as light as a full carbon paddle, they are right in the middle. The extra weight can be user friendly into the wind. They have just enough weight to keep them on track. The carbons sometimes fly around. Paddlers often guess the weight of their wood composites as much lower than they actually are.

With its composite skin and synthetic edge around the blade, wood composite paddles are generally more durable than all wood paddles. The use of epoxy resins and aerospace skin allows the paddle manufacturers to utilise high performance technology from other applications such as auto racing, airplane and space travel. It can take up to 40% more time and twice the material to build a hybrid paddle.

Static load testing by Kialoa yielded data which suggested that their Hybrid paddles are up to 25% stronger under compression loads than their all-wood paddles. While it is difficult to translate this data into real world paddling, in the test environment, wood composites proved to be stronger than traditional paddles.

For all of the merits associated with hybrid paddles, Kialoa's range of stand up paddles, has predominantly stuck to carbon as the preferred material, on account of using the best material for the task and building the paddles down to a weight and up to a suitable level of shaft stiffness and durability.

Carbon paddles

The benefits of an all carbon paddle are simply stiffness and lightness. Stiffness does not mean strong per se, as hollow carbon shafts certainly crack, then snap if impacted badly. For the most part, top level stand up paddle boarders use these in preference to any other paddle material and most specialist paddle makers use carbon or carbon / fibreglass blends exclusively for all of their top of the line paddles.

It must be said that there are many sub-standard carbon paddles on the market, more often than not manufactured in the Far East, often heavy or technically impaired through shape or mismatch of material components (blade / shaft fitment). This is in contrast of the few, who genuinely value the importance of a good stick, opting for the best materials, techniques and designs, including vacuum bagging and pre-impregnated (pre-preg) materials and manufacturing techniques, used to give the paddle optimum strength, minimal weight (residual material content) and optimum behavioural qualities.

A heavy carbon fibre paddle, is contrary to the benefits which carbon provides - high strength to weight ratio. Parting with money on a heavy carbon paddle, defeats the purpose.

Carbon paddles began their push into paddle sports in a meaningful way during the mid 1980s. The introduction of carbon paddles to outrigger canoeing came about through paddlers who predominantly trained and raced in flat water conditions by virtue of where they lived, notably East Coast USA and Canada. Many hailed from river canoeing backgrounds.

Finding their way to Hawai`i by the mid 90s, carbon paddles found favour with solo outrigger canoe paddlers for open ocean paddling, initially through ZRE paddles (introduced by Todd Bradley and Walter Guild). Tested by top OC6 crews they were ultimately rejected on the basis of being too stiff, too light and fragile compared to a 'woodie' or 'hybrid' but continued to find favour with OC1 and OC2 paddlers, where relative loads are less.

CRFT - super charged plastic

This is becoming the latest material to find its way into paddle manufacture and used more especially for blade construction. Far from being a new technology, it has been used for the past twenty five years in aerospace and defence applications. One of the early pioneers of this technology in paddle making has been Kialoa.

Known as, super-charged plastic, CRFT is extremely stiff, impact and corrosion resistant, impervious to water and most chemicals, yet it's 40-60% lighter and significantly less expensive to work with than competing materials. What's more, it doesn't produce any volatile organic compounds like the ones given off in the production of fibreglass products.

Weight issues

There is a universal obsession with weight or the lack thereof in the context of paddles, though this idea seems to be alluding much of the stand up paddle board market. Some argue against super-light paddles believing the lack of weight, leads to a lack of swing-weight or inertia during the recovery phase of the stroke. In the context of stand up paddling, it has to be said, the lighter the better so long as the weight distribution is correct. Significantly, the world over is festooned with brochures and catalogues, in which paddle makers provide all the information you may need about their paddle, but stop short at telling you how much they weigh. The advice here is to ensure you find out what they do weigh and begin making comparisons. Light could currently be considered less than 25oz, super light less than 20oz.

Swing weight

When a degree of flex exists in the shaft of the paddle, recoil at the exit phase actually assists the blade with its travel forwards during the recovery phase. The paddle should not so much be carried through to the set-up and entry, but in part thrown in a controlled manner through the rotation of the wrist, the outward movement of the elbow and the roll of the shoulder, the blade 'feathered' so as it can fly-through the recovery phase. In flight, it is near weightless.

The weight inherent in the blade, when swung through the recovery portion of the stroke (ie when moving the blade once exited back to placement in the water) will have greater or lesser degrees of noticeable swing weight. This must not be so much as to be fatiguing nor so light, that the blade must be carried and controlled entirely due to a lack of inertia. In windy conditions in particular a super light blade can fly away on you - especially upwind or cross-wind.

Typically, hybrid paddles are blade light, the blade weighing less than the shaft and certainly all carbon bladed paddles should be so. Traditional wood paddles tend to be blade heavy, unless they have a small blade surface area. Blade light paddles have a quick, balanced feel to them.

Much like a golf club the distribution of weight within the club as in the paddle is critical to its feel, especially during the recovery phase of the stroke. Ideally the blade's total weight should be less than that of the shaft, not the other way around. Of two paddles of equal weight, a paddle with the heavier blade will feel heavier. Having the bulk of the paddles weight spread the length of the shaft will provide a lighter more pleasing swing weight to the paddle.

The argument that light has to be superior, always, though discounted by many of the world's best canoe paddlers, who genuinely prefer some noticeable weight to give the paddle a degree of inertia during the recovery phase, the much longer recovery required of the stand up paddle alters the rationale, where light seems best, always.

KANU CULTURE

Flex appeal

It was concluded towards the end of the 1990s, that the ideal ocean racing outrigger canoe paddle should have a super stiff blade and neck area to prevent flex and morphing of the blade shape and that the shaft should have a degree of inherent flex. Hence the creation of wood composite hybrid paddles and the evolution of incorporating (varying) flex within carbon shafts using differing cloth weight and / or the blending with kevlar or fibreglass. The same logic applies to stand up paddles, however the potential for flex is much greater due to the longer shaft (lever-arm). Zero shaft flex is considered a negative, giving the paddle a lifeless feeling, lacking recoil at the exit phase of the stroke when load is released from the blade.

There are two critical stress areas where flex can occur on a paddle, at the neck and further up the shaft, particularly just below the point where the lower hand grips around the throat of the shaft. If the neck and shaft flex as you apply pressure during your pull, it's like compressing a spring and this energy will remain stored in the paddle, until you release it when the pull is relaxed and the blade exited.

Essentially the paddle has redirected and reduced the effects of torque at the most powerful and efficient phase of the stroke, absorbing the pressure applied so as the pull up to the blade is delayed, the energy stored, being released at the exit phase, resulting in excessive recoil of the shaft.

Blades which warp under load, folding away at the edges, allow water to spill away from the blade face resulting in a loss of power. If there is bend where the neck joins the shaft, water spills away from the blade tip and again this results in diminished grip and therefore power. You can pick up a paddle and access these qualities often just by pressuring it around these key areas. Any of these traits result in an ineffectual blade regardless of how good the shape, weight or price may be to your way of thinking.

On the cautionary side, if the shaft cannot flex, then your body's joints, first your wrist, then elbow and shoulder, can be stressed and injured. You may find you can offset the strain of a stiffer shaft by reducing blade size. It's easy to identify the problem, when you begin to feel soreness in your joints which may take some time to set in. For ultra distance paddling especially, you will want a paddle which stresses the body as little as possible which

Pressure

The blade has two faces, the FRONT FACE and BACK FACE. The front face also known as the POWER FACE is the side of the blade which is compressed against the water (high pressure) and the reverse side the back-face (low pressure). The skill of the designer is to find a balance between ensuring clean entry, maximum grip, clean low-drag exit and low swing weight recovery.

The relationship you form with your paddle must be so as you are totally at ease with the nuances of how it feels in the water and the air as you wield it from side to side as an extension of yourself. It cannot be overstated that this is central to your full appreciation and connection with the sport itself.

KANU CULTURE

publications since 1994

Weild

Photo Sue Sheard

will require some degree of shaft flex and maybe even some blade slippage.

A small degree of flex or spring in the shaft is generally preferred. At the exit phase of the stroke, the release of this tension is simply known as recoil; the shaft recoiling at the exit phase of the stroke, relative to how much it has flexed under load during the power phase of the stroke (Hook's Law). Super stiff shafts increase the chance of shoulder injuries and without any recoil whatsoever, the paddle tends to feel lifeless and the stroke discouraging. This has erroneously been referred to by some manufactures as reflex (associated with physiological / nerve responses) which puts into question whether they really understand what's going on here. The only time you would want excessive amounts of flex, is perhaps in the case of someone who has pre-existing joint injuries.

Some marginal flex gives the paddler a more encouraging, relaxing feel to the paddle stroke. Advances in synthetic materials and construction, now allows for varying amounts of flex to be incorporated.

Flex test a paddle's shaft by placing the blade on the ground (protecting the tip) and apply pressure to the shaft mid way up to see how it responds.

Flex

107

While it's acceptable to build in some flex to the shaft, flex at the neck is a design disaster. Additionally, a flexing blade creates an inefficient shape on the blade face which allows water to slip away and creates a fluctuation in the pressure and vacuum ratio between the front and rear faces of the blade. This adds to a blades inclination to flutter and results in what can be termed, soft recoil.

Confusingly and in an attempt to cover every conceivable budget, colour ways and preference, some stand up paddle board manufactures in particular (less so the smaller life-style specialist paddle maker) have gone stark raving mad in producing an unfathomable variety of paddles, using every known material possible to the point of blurring any real notion of what actually makes any sense. The most worrying aspect of this mix of materials, is that some simply do not work well in combination especially when mixing for example a stiff carbon shaft with a fibreglass blade which subsequently warps under load.

While some shaft flex is required in order to cushion the paddlers joints, provide some recoil at the exit phase of the stroke, too much flex, as seen here, results in dramatic power loss, as the power band becomes very much delayed, as the shaft bends as the blade takes up the load. The mass (weight) of the paddler and their strength to weight ratio can be a critical factor in determining just how much shaft flex is optimum for the individual. Largely it's a question of personal preference. Over distance you want a shaft that will absorb some of the strain to help lessen the net load on the joints and muscles, but no so much as your stroke becomes ineffectual.

Some of the combinations being used include;

Shaft	Blade	Blade Core
Carbon	Carbon Laminate	Foam
Carbon/Kevlar	Carbon/Kevlar/Laminate	Foam
Carbon/Kevlar	Carbon Laminate	Foam
Carbon	Wood Laminate	Foam
Carbon	Fibreglass	None
Fiberglass	Fibreglass	Foam
Alloy	Moulded Plastic	None
Timber	Laminated Timber	None
Carbon	CRFT	Foam/None
Fibreglass	CRFT	Foam/None

What's going on here has everything to do with making paddles within budget, whilst attempting to retain some level of quality in performance, let alone credibility, when of course in reality, something has to give. In the context of purchasing an inexpensive paddle then you're probably going to end up with the alloy/plastic/fibreglass model.

Selecting a paddle to purchase

When selecting a paddle, you need to take into account your individual requirements which are determined by your physical attributes, your paddling style, your board and in what conditions you will paddle. Budgeting for the paddle before the board may seem like fuzzy-logic, but be assured, it's sound advice. Paddles are designed for racing, river running, cruising, general recreation and surf.

A poor paddle design or even a good one not suited to you, will mean that you will fail to reach your full potential. Remember, your paddle is what provides the essential link between your energy expenditure and the effectiveness of your stroke. Many paddlers are using paddles completely unsuited to their physical and technical needs.

Many first timers, get their introduction to the sport with such abominations.

A novice should not necessarily have an inferior paddle to that of an experienced paddler, yet this seems to be what is advocated. While a novice would genuinely struggle with a radical board design there is no question a novice will struggle with a poorly designed paddle. In short, there is no such thing, as stressed already, as a novice or beginner paddle, only a cheap one.

An experienced paddler may get the best out of a poorly designed paddle. The novice will struggle to make any meaningful headway with the same paddle. Anything labelled 'novice', 'beginner' or 'entry level' in relation to paddle design is usually cheaper and less performance orientated than it's more expensive counterpart. As a beginner paddler you have to ask yourself, does this matter to you. It should.

When it comes to purchasing a paddle, no matter what you read or what you are told about its design merits, performance or 'feel' there's only one way to know if it suits and that's try before you buy.

If the retailer wants you to buy from his store then they need to have demonstration models available. If they or the paddle maker cannot devise a cost effective scheme to allow for this and make excuses as to why you cannot try a particular model prior to making a purchasing decision, then they are letting their customers down by not trying hard enough. They very probably get to try before they buy, why shouldn't you.

What paddle length from tip to grip

This singular topic seems to have evolved into something of a dark-art, which has slipped into the abyss of myth, nonsense and half truths. The most critical tip that can be given; paddle with an overly long paddle and you'll be on the pathway to injury, the most serious of which, is rotator-cuff injury. It may not happen immediately, but given time and the on set of wear and tear, it will. What you need to know is, what is it that defines an overly-long paddle. Simply put, if mid-way through your stroke, your top hand is significantly above the level of your head and your elbow higher than the level of your shoulder, you're already there.

Rotator-cuff injury

Rotator cuff injury and inflammation is one of the most common causes of shoulder pain. There are three common conditions that can affect the rotator cuff: **rotator cuff tendonitis, impingement syndrome** and a **rotator cuff tear.** Of these, tendonitis is the most common form of paddling related rotator cuff injury.

Most people with rotator cuff problems can be successfully treated by a combination of rest, painkillers, anti-inflammatories, physiotherapy and steroid injection or surgery. Regardless, once you have problems with your rotator cuff, it sets in motion the potential for a life long issue as a paddler, with the worst of outcomes being that you can't.

What is the rotator cuff?

The rotator cuff is a group of four muscles that are positioned around the shoulder joint. The muscles are named: **supraspinatus, infraspinatus subscapularis** and **teres minor.**

The rotator cuff muscles work as a unit. They help to stabilise the shoulder joint and also help with shoulder joint movement. The four tendons of the rotator cuff muscles join together to form one larger tendon, called the rotator cuff tendon. This tendon attaches to the head of the humerus (the

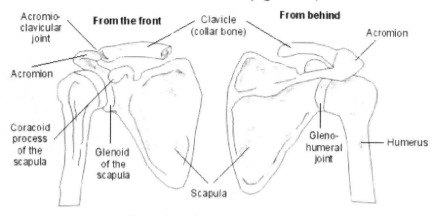

Bones of the shoulder (right side)

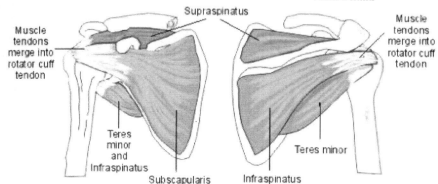

Muscles of the rotator cuff

bony surface at the top of the upper arm bone). There is a space underneath the acromion of the scapula, called the subacromial space. The rotator cuff tendon passes through this point.

What causes rotator cuff tendonitis?

When your arm hangs by your side, you can be assumed to be in neutral. As you progressively raise your arm, the head of the **humerus**, rotates within the **glenoid cavity** of the **scapula** (upper shoulder) and as it does so, it progressively closes the space within the cavity. When your arm is fully raised, this space is minimal. Exerting downward force when the arm is raised high (elbow above the level of the shoulder) can lead to excessive wear and tear on the tendons or the thin sheath which covers the head of the humerus and the glenoid cavity, leading to inflammation.

And that's why you don't want your elbow working above the level of your shoulder.

Rotator cuff tendonitis is caused therefore, by irritation and inflammation of the tendons of the rotator cuff muscles. It tends to have an acute (sudden) onset. It is most commonly caused by undue over-head use of the arm affecting athletes involved in throwing or paddling activities. Sometimes the rotator cuff tendons can become calcified. This is when calcium is deposited in the tendons due to long-standing inflammation. This is called, calcific tendonitis.

What are the symptoms of rotator cuff tendonitis?

The main symptoms are an acute (sudden) onset of pain and painful movement of the shoulder. Pain is worst when you use your arm for activities above your shoulder level. This means that the pain can affect your ability to lift your arm up marginally or above the level of your shoulder.

Impingement syndrome

In impingement syndrome, the rotator cuff tendon gets trapped in the subacromial space. The tendon is repeatedly scraped against the shoulder blade which can eventually lead to fraying of the tendon. This means that the tendon weakens and is more likely to tear. Impingement syndrome can occur because of long-standing wear and tear. It can also happen due to problems with the bone of the acromion. These can include arthritis and bony spurs (protrusions). It can also be a genetic issue, where the paddler has a very narrow subacromial space and therefore greater chance of this injury manifesting. The onset may be slower.

Determine the position of your lower hand first

Importantly, ensure your grip on the lower shaft is near optimum as best suggested by Jim Terrell (Quick Blade) who advocates, raising the paddle level and above head, arms bent at 90 degrees, equally spaced, to determine the relative position of your lower hand. For me personally, its this, less one full hand span back towards the grip. If you don't get this sorted first then, all other factors will impact upon establishing an optimum paddle length. Commonly paddlers hold the paddle too far up to be able to deliver adequate control or power to the blade.

This is a marginally wider hand span width than you would use when paddling seated using an outrigger canoe paddle, which is closer to shoulder width apart. Importantly this will be part way to ensuring that your lower hand is far enough down the shaft, so it can deliver a substantial amount of power and control to the blade through the lower hand, rather than a complete reliance on leverage by being too far up the shaft, putting more emphasis on the upper hand for drive.

The further up your lower hand travels, the longer the lever arm; the distance between your lower hand and the centre of effort on the blade.

Having your lower hand too far up the shaft, will bring about a greater reliance on using leverage (pushing forwards with the top arm) as the primary means in generating force to the blade. If the paddle were being

Elbows at 90 degrees - then one hand span back up the shaft seems about right for most.

There are a number of factors affecting your optimum paddle length, not least of which being the thickness of your board as in this example.

used as a 'first class lever' that would be fine, but it's not, being as the paddler should aim to find a balance in using power generated through pulling from the throat of the shaft through rotation (torque) around the spine and pushing downwards and transversely with the top arm.

Deciding upon a paddle length from tip to grip, is critical in terms of your ability to manage the paddle, apply power to the blade and to avoid shoulder injury in particular. Unfortunately, it is not a perfect science and the best offering at this point has (vaguely) been 6-8" above head height for paddle surfing, 8-10" for cruising and 10-12" for racing. The rationale for selecting a paddle length on this basis, is simply provided as a starting point, but is far from definitive or accurate on a case by case basis.

This wide range of variance, is significant enough to be wary and make you realise that there seems to be some degree of 'rule of thumb' for all people and only two differing conditions of use. One urban myth, suggests a 'Shaka' height above head height (around 6") which defies any rationale explanation.

In brief

When Cruising you will tend to adopt a more upright 'relaxed' stance, which lends itself to a longer paddle length.

When racing you will tend to want to get over the stroke more which tends to suggest a shorter length paddle, though race boards are generally thicker so this means, 'shorter' relative to the boards thickness.

When surfing your regular or Goofy foot lowered centre of gravity stance and thinner board thickness, lends itself to the shortest paddle possible.

When downwinding, high stroke rates, lowered centre of gravity, will warrant the shorter paddle. The rougher it gets, the truer this becomes.

The primary problem with vague measurements is that they fail to account for the length of the paddler's arms. Two paddlers of equal height can and will for the most part have differing arm lengths. Does that mean they have the same paddle lengths regardless. Additionally, board thickness varies, especially between boards for surf and those for racing, varying by up to and over 3" thickness, which puts you 3" higher or lower relative to the water (blade entry).

Form

KANU CULTURE

Reach

Top arm elbow and shoulder in alignment

In this image, the elbow of the top arm is still level with the shoulder so as downward pressure exerted protects the rotator cuff. The top hand is above the level of the head, however this is due to the paddler lowering their centre of gravity in wanting to exert greater downward force, direct power to the blade face and torsional rotation. Under cruising conditions a more upright stance would be assumed and the grip and top arm more in alignment with the forehead / eyes.

The most plausible selection of an appropriate paddle length is as follows: When paddling on flat water and exercising good technique and form at about 60-70% effort, when the blade is fully immersed, just below the level of the neck and at the mid-point of the power phase, when shaft is vertical and hands are 'hand-over-hand' (stacked) your top hand, should be near level with forehead or eyes, so as your arm is not working 'over-head' (ie elbow above shoulder height).

This may sound simplistic – but it does ultimately take into account board thickness and the paddler's physical and bio-mechanical make up. Where the activity requires a lowering of the body (surf, downwind, river) paddles can be further shortened to suit.

Cutting your paddle to length can be permanent in the case of cutting it too short. Using a good quality adjustable paddle can assist with determining length between varying board thicknesses.

Take measurements (Tip to Grip)

Ensure you use a tape measure and make a note of your preferred paddle lengths between boards and disciplines i.e 78" for surf, 82" for racing etc.

An optimum paddle length will deliver

Higher potential stroke rates, as paddle can be turned-over quicker. Shorter recovery times as recovery distance is shortened. Greater ease of handling. Reduced weight and windage. Faster switch speeds right and left. Reduced chance of shoulder injury. Improved ease of handling, less chance of pulling too far past the body-line. Improved blade control and power delivery. Just short enough, so as you have to drop the shoulder to find the water.

Negatives Might Include

Reduced potential reach out front. Some reduced leverage.

When you consider the benefits associated with the optimum (shorter) paddle length versus the negatives, it brings home the need to paddle with as short a paddle length that you can comfortably manage without sacrificing significant loss of reach or leverage in particular.

What should be noted is that the leverage potential of a longer paddle is only as practical to the degree to which the paddler's strength and total arm span can make use of that leverage. Taller paddlers with greater arm spans and strength to match can perhaps make use of the leverage gains inherent in a longer paddle, but the principals remain the same.

What can be said with certainty is that the majority of paddlers at this point in the sport's evolution are using paddles way too long to be efficient The benefits of a shorter paddle far outweigh the longer. This is the same evolutionary pattern which outrigger canoe paddles went through, except it took about 50 years or so to figure it out. It also took the same amount of time to figure out that a bigger blade does not equate to more power.

In this image, paddling a conventional all-round board of around 4.25" thickness, I'm using a short paddle suited to surfing not cruising. Top hand is near level with forehead, top arm elbow bent and angled downwards, hand-over-hand, the initial 'compression' downwards to generate lift is now being converted to pull by simply rotating around the spine, to keep the blade 'vertical' for a delayed period to generate lateral pull.

Vertical Shaft

An (overly) longer paddle length will deliver

Greater reach out front. Greater leverage potential. Promote a more upright paddling stance.

Negatives Might Include

Slower potential stroke rate. Longer recovery times (greater recovery distance travelled). Diminished ease of handling. Increased weight. Increased windage. Reduced switch speeds either side of the board. Increased risk of shoulder injury. Reduced ease of handling in surf conditions. A hinderance when surfing. Increased chance of pulling too far past the body-line. Marginal loss of potential blade control. Marginal loss of power delivery to the blade. Paddling behind the stroke not over it.

'Wherever we go in the world, the most common sight we see is people using paddles that are way too tall for them. Aside from squandering the mechanical advantage of the proper and efficient paddle stroke, using too tall a paddle sets you up for some sort of repetitive stress harm to your shoulders.' *Dave Parmenter C4*

Shaft types

Paddle shafts fall into three basic categories; straight, single bend, double-bend and all variations in-between.

Straight shaft

For the most part, straight shafted paddles are reserved for recreational Canadian canoeing, never used by outrigger paddlers (though by steerers for canoe surfing on occasions)

Single bend

The single bend shaft paddle was originally developed in 1948 for open canoe racing, made popular by Eugene Jensen in 1971 and introduced into outrigger racing at the 1978 Moloka`i to O`ahu race by a mainland American team. For stand up paddlers the preference is for the single-bend paddle, which is not surprising being that the bulk of early development, originated with outrigger canoe paddle makers and paddlers.

Benefits of the single bend shaft 3 - 12 Degrees

Blade maintains less of an angle during latter part of stroke. Thrust is maintained over a greater distance. Tendency to lift water at exit phase of the stroke is reduced. The blade reaches further forward on entry. The blade has a natural tendency to 'feather' on exit. Of note, some new generation SU-paddles have blade angles as low as 3 degrees, claiming to reduce air-transfer time - but encourage high lift exits, reduced reach, loss of 'lift' at the entry of the blade and premature stalling of the blade face.

Double bends

Unlike the single-bend paddle shaft where the bend originates at the neck of the paddle, the double-bend shaft has a bend in both the upper and lower shaft. This additional bend in the upper shaft can be used by the paddler to gain extra leverage during the power-phase of the stroke and requires a modification to the single-bend paddling technique.

Double-bend paddles are yet to be embraced by stand up paddlers, but I dare say they will in time become more common place as they have some important mechanical advantages so long as they are coupled with correct paddling technique - well known and embraced by va`a hoe (outrigger canoe paddlers) of French Polynesia.

The single bent shaft paddle. What many paddlers fail to understand, is that this offset blade angle, with appropriate technique, will generate 'lift' as the first of a set of forces acting on the board as the paddle is 'pushed' downwards at the entry phase.

12'6

Benefits of the double-bend shaft paddle

The upper angle brings the grip back towards the driving hand, so that the paddler's shoulder and arm extension is lessened reducing fatigue. The lower shaft angles towards the paddler so that the wrist is naturally aligned with the shaft at an angle reducing wrist strain. The paddler can use the additional 'crank' for added leverage.

Double bend paddle specific to outrigger canoe paddling come in two distinct types and in time it will be interesting to see how paddle manufacturers approach the design. Those few double bend stand up paddles currently

It's all well and good to identify and discuss the 'Tahitian' stroke, but what you probably don't know is that they have a preference for double bend paddles and have modified their technique to suit. Ten years of travelling and racing in Tahiti taught me this. Consequently, emulating the stroke is not a simple issue as it is a highly evolved 'style'. Below: young Taj Marsh paddles with a double-bend.

Tahitian

on the market, often incorporate the 'curved' shaft option (right) which suggests they are not recognising the mechanical advantage inherent in adding a definitive fulcrum point.

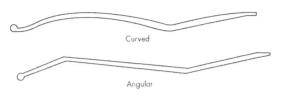

Curved

Angular

The curious issue here is whether this developed from different approaches to construction or genuine thought regarding performance. The top paddle, is essentially a series of 'curves' and more often than not, laminated in a 'jig'; timbers bent and glued to conform to the jig's shape. Conversely, the double bend below it, is far more angular and often made as a straight shaft, then the last third or so of the shaft is 'scarfed' - cut diagonally, reversed and laminated back on to be angled away. This is common to Tahitian paddles.

The soft 'S' curved double bend, provides less mechanical advantage as the fulcrum point is less centred than with the more angular shaft. Tahitian paddlers use this mechanical advantage by pushing forward with the top arm when the blade is vertical, during the power phase, and their concern

is far from one of ergonomics, which seems to be the primary selling point for many manufacturers. A soft curve, permits shifting forces of leverage and of a fulcrum point, making for a less decisive, balanced, advantageous cranking mechanism.

Alternate realities

Taking shaft design to another level, Sawyer Paddles in the USA designed the Sawyer Ergo Quad canoe paddle, well over fifteen years ago, which featured a staggering 4 bends in total. Werner in 2010 presented this similar design in a stand up paddle, which begs the question 'Why?', when the Sawyer Ergo Quad never took off in significant numbers at it's time of release or indeed since.

The point being, advancement from straight shaft, to single bend (blade offset from shaft), double bend (blade offset from shaft and crank in top quarter of shaft) and other variations on a theme, are all created in an attempt to improve specific levels of comfort, reach, blade control and / or power delivery to the blade.

Werner's bent shaft paddle, has 3 bends in total with the blade's attachment running straight as a continuation of the shaft. While it may provide some extra reach and comfort benefits in terms of wrist alignment, it does not increase catch or make for a more powerful forward stroke as suggested. The fact remains, single bend shafts remain the most practical over a range of paddling scenarios and for the entry level paddler, being the easiest to learn sound paddling technique.

By and large each succeeds on one level or another, but to assume they are definitively better in all things, than all other shaft designs, would be to disregard the overwhelming reality that most paddlers prefer a single-bend paddle for ease of use.

Sawyer's Ergo Quad canoe paddle (below) is well over 15 years old and includes 4 bends, hence the 'Quad'. Despite being radical for its time, it certainly did not revolutionise paddler perceptions. The Sawyer adjustable Venom, now features an even more angular replication.

What is misleading are statements (marketing babble) regarding the bent shaft such as, 'the bend in the shaft increases catch' is a blunder of epic proportions. Catch, is the point at which the blade is fully immersed, primed and ready for the power phase to begin and is not a factor of the degree of bend in the shaft or extent of reach, indeed it is primarily a factor of clean entry and a well designed blade. To also suggest that you can, 'get more power from the forward stroke' on account of greater reach, is also incorrect and misleading. Power (force) is delivered by the paddler in the form of leverage and torque. Greater reach, simply makes for a longer stroke and in no way does it have an affect on power per se.

Adjustable paddles

If you purchase an adjustable paddle you could perhaps avoid the try before you buy phase, though these can be expensive, a little heavier and not always as reliable as a cut down fixed paddle, but they certainly have their place being that the paddle can be shared with others and an excellent option for commercial ventures, families and for using the one paddle between surf and cruising.

The shaft is adjustable in length through a variety of release, slide and lock systems. While these are extremely practical from the viewpoint of the paddles extent of use between a wide number of individuals of differing heights as may be encountered by hire and school operations, the compromising factor is by and large weight, being generally 'heavy' even by heavy standards. (Note: Many adjustable paddles do not cater for paddlers much over 6' in height).

With the exception of but a few, most adjustable paddles don't take themselves very seriously from a design perspective; that is to say, for the most part, they are budget orientated in terms of materials used, being that they are not considered high end use focused for surf or racing for example. However some manufacturers have certainly made the effort to provide as a high end a paddle as possible in an adjustable format. Where you can afford to, purchase as light a design as possible and take into consideration how the mechanism for adjustment works.

Some systems rely upon mechanical hinged pin systems, others upon a twist grip system which acts as a vice to tighten the male and female parts of the shaft. When sand enters any of the components, adjustment and / or locking or release can be a problem and therefore you must keep all

Practicality

The adjustable paddle is a brilliant concept if they weren't for the most part so 'industrial' and heavy. There are few genuinely good designs available at a reasonable price. Some fill with water and sink, most whistle a lovely tune as the wind blows over the adjustment holes, most are heavy, the adjustment clip bangs the hand each time you change sides, sand is its natural enemy and if that's not bad enough, invariably the alloy shaft has a pliable blade lovingly shoved on for good measure. Schools are crying out for affordable, quality adjustable paddles as are families, but currently the better ones aren't cheap - but on the plus side you are getting maybe 5 paddles in one.

components free of sand. A build up of salt crystals can also be a problem and therefore rinsing with fresh water is recommended after use and certainly prior to storage for any period of time.

Break-apart paddles (2 and 3 part)

Break apart paddles are nothing new and have certainly been common place within kayaking and surf ski paddling, where transportation of a long double ended paddle has been problematic. Whilst the adjustable paddle exists for the purpose of use by multiple users of differing heights, the break-apart paddle exists for the purpose of ease of transportation. Unlike the adjustable paddle, some break-apart paddles are of a very high quality, intended to be high performance.

Footnotes:

Optimum blade size / area

A blade's total area need only be as large as is necessary for it to 'anchor' itself and remain stationary for long enough for you to pull (rotate) yourself up level with it. A blade area larger than this will sap your energy and make greater demands upon your energy levels at the exit, recovery, set up and entry phases. In this context the vast majority of paddlers are using paddles of a blade area larger than required.

Slippage

Slippage is said to exist when the blade moves through the water. This can be on account of a variety of issues. Some elite ultra-distance paddlers actively seek out a blade which offers slippage, in order to decrease the load for each stroke taken. As a point of interest, water is 700 times more dense than air. Tahitian OC crews are known for starting a race with wider / larger blade areas, changing down to smaller blade areas over the course of the race as their energy levels are sapped in being able to manage the larger blade area over time. Typically for sprint racing, blade slippage is undesirable.

While blade slippage may occur when the load (pressure) exceeds the blade's capacity to deal with it, hence moving backwards, there are many other complex factors to consider. Poor blade shape, flex of the neck area where blade meets the shaft, poor technique (entry) leading to poor catch and therefore cavitation (slippage). Another factor is simply the paddler's speed and strength and the lack thereof.

Counter-intuitively, the learner paddler who has neither the speed, strength or technical know how to perhaps effectively achieve excellence of entry or catch, can benefit from a blade offering a larger blade area for added 'purchase'. As paddlers advance in terms of speed, strength and technical ability, it's common for them to down-size blade area to a point which is optimum to a variety of paddling conditions.

Small blade areas

When using a small blade area, the aim is as for the larger blade area. You are looking to compress the water against the blade face with enough force so as water is effectively under sufficient pressure that it 'hardens'. This will hold true given all other factors are optimum (entry, catch, blade shape, body mass etc).

During the mid nineties, Kialoa produced a very small blade area paddle called the 'Helium' for downwind solo OC paddlers (now in its SUP range). This was in response to downwind paddlers demands for higher than average stroke rates as they achieved higher than average speeds assisted by wind / wave power. Downwind paddling is aerobically demanding, but punctuated by high anaerobic stints between waves / swells (in the trough) where you may be 'priming' the board to break free from opposing revolving water particles.

Downwind blade size / areas

There are differing schools of thought on blade sizes for downwind paddling and this centres on two approaches to the art. While the visual narrative of a paddle 'being like gears on a bike theory' is interesting it is somewhat counter-intuitive in part. When going with the flow (downwind) resistance is more easily over-come and higher speeds achieved, not primarily by pulling harder, but paddling faster, utilising the kinetic energy reserved within wind and waves. This places higher aerobic demands on the paddler. In flat water where there is no assistance, the larger blade is required to make up for this lack.

The skill in being proficient as a downwind paddler is in connecting the dots in staying in the steep and fast sections of the waves, while maintaining a high average speed avoiding stalling between sets. To this end there are two types of basic approaches;

Big Blade Area

Powerful, moderate stroke rates, punctuated with short increases of stroke rates in pushing onto or over the waves in front, a technique suited generally to larger, stronger paddlers, with slow twitch muscle.

Small Blade Area

Higher stroke rates maintained even at times when nearing top speed, or when decelerating and looking to accelerate onto or over the back of the wave in front. This generally suits the smaller / lighter, fast twitch muscle paddler, who may be described as a 'workaholic'.

Paddle length

Optimum paddle length first and foremost will be in direct relation to how thick your board is, followed by how low your relative centre of gravity will be throughout the session, the lower your CG (brought about by crouching) the shorter your paddle will need to be.

International Va'a Federation World Sprints Hilo Hawai`i 2004. Should stand up paddle boarding have the same extent of cultural resonance and significance and if so would it enhance your experience. As much as the canoe is significant to the cultures of Oceania, it is the paddle which provides the iconoclastic symbolism of propulsion.
Photo: Steve West

KANU CULTURE
publications since 1995

Low CG paddling include surfing, down winding, river running whilst **moderate** might be longer flat water races, sprinting, moderate downwind conditions, moderate river flow conditions and **higher CG paddling** includes cruising, learning and general low output recreational sessions.

Calculating blade area.

The simplest way might be to trace out the shape on a piece of graph paper, then add up the area of all the squares. Graph paper gridded off in mm and cm would be easiest. There are also plinimeters used by professionals to measure area. A third way probably accurate enough for paddles, is to weigh a piece of cardboard with a known area, eg 100 sq cm = x grams, then trace out the blade shape onto the cardboard, cut out and weigh that. Apply the conversion factor and you'll have a value for the blade area.

7

Board design and factors serving to shape them

Race board specifications, race types and stand alone
cultural groups and why board specifications serve to stifle
the designer not necessarily liberate them or the sport.

Australian, Ryan Down, in 2006, maker of original timber designed hollow paddle and surfboards adapted one of his boards with the addition of an outrigger assembly which he added for longer paddling sessions on the river for fitness and strength training. 'In the surf its pretty dangerous with the outrigger, but the added stability for distance paddling works well.' Classic user-innovator behaviour. Take what you've got and modify it.

Photo: Steve West - Mooloolaba Australia

Board evolution

In respect of stand up paddle surf boards, this is an area of the sport that was given the most immediate attention, extracting what is already known of surf board design and where parallels of design run close.

The future evolution of the stand up paddle board, is truly wide open, more especially in the area of downwind ocean race boards, flat water race boards, adventure boards and river boards.

Without putting too fine a point on this, stand up paddle surf boards are, after a basic recreational board, the least challenging of the scope of designs being considered, simply because what needs to be known, already is.

What can and will be applied to paddle-surf boards will come from all that is known of surfing and herein lies the synergy. In contrast, all that is known of prone paddle board design, will no doubt provide much of the ooze from which open ocean race

paddle board designers will feed upon and flat water race boards will no doubt look to kayak and canoe designers in the future.

Designers who have devoted a lifetime to surfboard design, have for the most part struggled to come to terms with the overwhelming complexities of trying to design boards specific to paddling and therefore of greater dimension and where the paddle is the primary means of propulsion. In fairness it's a paradigm shift for the surfboard designer to stray into such territory and many have struggled to get it right and many still do.

Some of the more successful designers of boards made specifically for paddling, have emerged from prone paddle boarding backgrounds drawing upon what is known of larger volumed designs, designed to perform at relatively slow speeds within very similar power bands, where the board is driven by the arms and hands in often identical water conditions from glassy to choppy, through the surf and back, or downwinding. Essentially it' all about specificity.

What is extraordinary about the sport of stand up paddle boarding with regards to the evolution of equipment, is that so much is now known through similar ocean sports, that a melding of all these ideas can now be drawn upon for each of the disciplines to advance the sport and the end-user's enjoyment.

While in the past a 57% input by the end users may have been applicable to design, this is doubtful in the context of stand up paddling, as one has the feeling that much of the innovative pioneering process has been bypassed more especially in areas such as paddle surf board design, where there may well be less innovation when compared to open ocean and flat water race boards, where truly radical innovations will occur and are already happening.

But more importantly, there is a sense that this sport, rather than being something radically new, is merely a variation upon a theme, being that board designs are not so different that a lineage cannot be traced back and this is certainly true of paddle designs.

As is turns out, this has been a huge windfall for existing manufacturers already tooled up and involved in sports such as windsurfing, surfing, prone paddle boarding or the manufacture of outrigger canoe paddles. The synergy is so tightly interwoven, that there is less than six degrees of separation to the point that in one fell swoop, the possible tedium of head scratching for new ideas within their core business has been revived by something which has fallen from the sky almost by divine intervention, along the same evolutionary tree, but that's not to say it's a risk free venture - what is?

As already stated, the sport of windsurfing, invented itself out of nothing over some thirty years or so. The development of the paddle board is by comparison a relative no-brainer. The homogenous melding of all that is known of prone paddle board, surfboard, windsurfer design and outrigger canoe paddle design and the bio-mechanical skills required of each sport, are being exploited and cross-platformed, jettisoning the evolution of the stand up paddle board, paddle and participants, on an out of control sleigh-ride of unprecedented speed to a point where evolution and the notion of a pioneering spirit have all but been obliterated; no disrespect to those contemporaries involved - there are a few exceptional pioneering figures.

It would indeed be easy to be cynical and say that in actuality, most stand up paddle board designs are merely overblown long boards and where's the advancement in that you ask? Well the fact is, you can of course readily lay your hands on suitable craft to stand and paddle; old long board windsurfers, giant sized long surf boards, maybe the odd paddle board. Indeed, not only is it possible, but if you're on a budget, it could well be

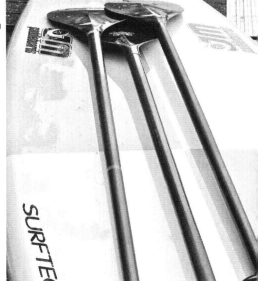

highly desirable, more especially if performance per se is not your primary concern, merely an alternative means of gaining a good workout.

Worryingly, many larger manufacturers, seem hell bent on flooding their range with surf orientated boards, further congesting the world's already overly subscribed to popular and accessible (and less accessible) surf breaks, which suggests overt optimism that the current global surfing population can be convinced to make a paradigm shift into paddle surfing or indeed total newbies to the surfing experience should use the mechanism of stand up paddle surfing as a right of passage.

Optimism indeed, when surely the purer intent and long term view, should be in the getting of customers and participants from canoeing and kayaking backgrounds, (or no water sport background whatsoever) which constitutes a very much larger, global gene pool already familiar with the appeal and skills of paddling, who would welcome a wide range of choice, not such a narrow one. In this context, the stand up paddler (not paddle-surfer) is being treated as secondary to the sport itself.

I have suggested, much of the pioneering grass roots evolution of this sport has been bypassed, being that manufacturers have to a much greater extent than most any other water sport before it, force fed the sport and product development and choice upon us. How they want us to react, think and purchase and what we the end-user want, seems in a state of flux, if not to some degree diametrically opposed at this point.

The gold rush

If you've ever been part of a new and growing sport, driven by aspirations of what 'can be' and what you would 'rather be' doing to the point of obsession, chances are you were very well by default, a pioneer, whose raw enthusiasm no doubt contributed, no matter how small, to the sum of the whole as the sport matured and developed into its full blown form.

Be it skateboarding, windsurfing, surfing, outrigger canoeing, prone paddle boarding or surf ski paddling, they all began as a result of vision, more powerful than your basic idea, because a vision embraces an almost dreamlike, hypnotic state which drives the user-innovator beyond the simple premise of a singular idea. It is in short, an emotional prism into which you dive, open to all and every possibility.

Whether a pioneering spirit is a product of your nature or as a result of your nurturing, one thing is for sure in the early days of most all equipment dependant sports, they begin life in rudimentary form, fashioned from whatever happens to be lying around the back yard or cluttering up the garage. For the most part, others devoid of such spirit, right you off as crazy, usually your parents.

In the very early 80s, pioneering windsurfers such as Mike Waltz, Larry Stanley, Matt Schwietzer and others set aside their longboard Windsurfer Rockets, frustrated with their lack of manoeuvrability and bone shattering landings, grabbed their surfboards and hurriedly converted them into wave-boards, merely by adding a single set of foot straps and a fin box to the deck.

2006 Mooloolaba Australia and here we are 'pioneering' the sport in Australia, which seems a ridiculously short time ago. Note the wooden paddles which would soon be replaced by carbon sticks. This is 'Woogie' Marsh in the foreground, a world class OC paddler and Moloka'i Hoe winner and Chris D'Aboitz of Noosa in the background. Through our working and paddling OCs together, Woogie convinced me this was the way forward.

If six degrees of separation is a maxim used in relation to our genetic lineage, it's true to say, at that exact point in time, the degrees of separation between a pure surfboard and a wave board were minimal. They were in short, one and the same thing.

Stand up paddle boarding at its most basic level and by some vague comparison of that moment in time, could perhaps draw some parallels, in that without modification, using a large surfboard was an obvious solution. In time, the need to create purpose made boards emerged thereby validating the sport and naturally, purpose made paddles a paramount concern, as oars and open canoe paddles were hardly the way forward.

www.kanuculture.com

Noosa's Australian pioneers, Chris D'Aboitz, 'Woogie' Marsh and 2006 World Longboard Champion Josh Constable. *Photo: Steve West 2006*

From the mid 90s to the end of 2000, the sport was embryonic at best. In outrigger canoeing circles, stand up paddle boarding was unheard of within the very inner circle from where the sport was ready to attract willing takers.

By 2005, living in Australia and being heavily involved with outrigger canoeing and a variety of publications, I wrote my first article about the sport. Long time friends such as Hawaii's Todd Bradley had begun ramping up for the take off of this new sport with the creation of C4 Waterman. In Australia, outrigger canoe paddler and friend Sue Sheard and later 'Woogie' Marsh, had Mandy and I hooked in just one short session.

By mid 2005, outrigger canoe paddlers in Hawai`i, California and Australia were having their interest spiked by this new paddle sport and at that point it seems there was a collision of commercial need and consumer interest to exploit this new activity to the limits.

2006 World Longboard Champion, Australian
Josh Constable. Mooloolaba Australia.
Photo: Steve West 2006

In 2006 when buying our first boards, the choice was limited. We settled for the largest of the NSP boards, which oddly enough had been selling as a surfboard (Longboard) yet in the brochure when we viewed the board's description, it had been crossed out in pen and handwritten was, 'SUP Board' which was indicative of the way things were going, with some surfboard manufacturers re-branding their larger boards as SUP boards. I wanted a board which we could paddle with ease and catch the odd wave. A cheap entry level non-specialised board to abuse in the early phases was ideal. If you're a strong paddler you will soon discover this board style however doesn't deliver when it comes to noticeable gains in board speed relative to effort.

What looked somewhat ridiculous standing on the shoreline watching, made perfect sense from the moment I stood on the board and took my first stroke. What followed over the past 5 years from 2005-2010 would seem to be the single biggest, short lived explosion of any water sport I can remember; short lived, because I believe the sport has already peaked once but will peak a few more times yet as it hits differing parts of the world.

Within the space of a mere five years or so, the range of boards and paddles is quite staggering. The pioneering quest seems to have been fast tracked by a simple process of osmosis. Stand up paddle boarding has supped from the plethora of existing equipment to hand. Tooling up for many existing surfboard, windsurfing or paddle board makers has, it seems, been a relatively simple process; good for them and perhaps even better for the participant.

Fiji 2007
Photo: Steve West

Contemporary innovative board paddlers in Hawai`i simply used longboards (Malibu style 'Tongue Depressors') and extended outrigger canoe paddles, already available. In a matter of a few days, paddles were lengthened to accommodate paddling in a standing position. The design and manufacturer of specific stand up paddle boards came later, first custom made the old way, shaped from a foam blank and glassed, then mass produced in epoxy in far away places such as Thailand and China, though custom made boards are still in demand in the Hawaiian Islands.

On a budget?

So here's a suggestion for the would-be stand up paddler thinking of venturing into the sport, who may be on a budget or simply needing an effective workout-platform (if you only own a short board). Coming back to my premise that pioneering waterman often look around for what is already to hand lying in the back yard or garage, it occurs to me that there

Mandy paddles a Mistral Shredder

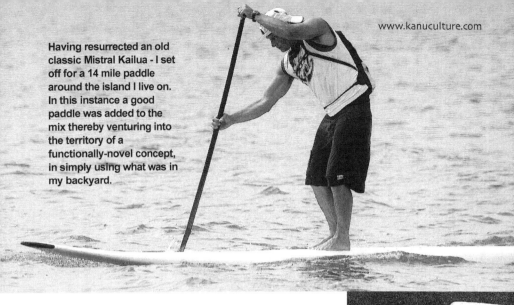

Having resurrected an old classic Mistral Kailua - I set off for a 14 mile paddle around the island I live on. In this instance a good paddle was added to the mix thereby venturing into the territory of a functionally-novel concept, in simply using what was in my backyard.

are already many potential stand up paddle boards, in varying states of neglect or otherwise, long since stowed away and forgotten, in the form of windsurfers in all shapes and sizes, many eminently suited to the task of providing a perfectly sound learning platform.

I realise some folk have already figured this out, but I wonder why this has not been promoted more widely, except for the obvious, that manufacturers for one, may not want you to think outside the loop and magazines by their need to generate advertising from such manufactures, would reserve judgement promoting this idea.

Such is the synergy between the boards produced, Naish, Starboard, Mistral and others have produced stand up paddle boards which can be converted into windsurfers having a mast step fitment point on the board, a no-brainer means of adding versatility to the product, for companies already involved in the windsurfing industry more especially, thereby nurturing current interests and cross-platforming neatly within the niche.

Board dimension

For many years, the windsurfing industry was only concerned with length - then volume measured in square litres became the yardstick, on account of an indication of how much buoyancy the board possessed in order to cope with the riders weight (gravity) - boards were termed 'sinkers' which essentially only 'floated' when at speed, hence the need to indicate board volume.

Stand up paddle board designs are now beginning to indicate vol / metric sizes in the same manner. What you need concern yourself with, is the distribution of this volume.

Starting at around the 10' mark, we have boards often termed 'all-rounders'. Below 10' boards for adults begin to lean towards being surf specific orientated. Boards between 9.6" - 10'6" represent the majority of sales globally as first time entry level platforms.

The more folk who get involved within the sport, regardless of how they start out by way of innovation will still contribute to participation numbers. Like the early days of windsurfing, where equipment was cheap and low-tech, there has been universal agreement that stand up paddling board equipment went hi-tech and expensive in one fell-swoop, making it almost unattractive, let alone affordable to the person thinking of involvement. For a sport tagged as 'easy' bragging minimal equipment needs, with few or no moving parts, the cost was and still is to some considerable extent, out of alignment with this minimalistic simplicity.

Using a cheap, readily available old windsurfer for example will still permit you to master the basics of paddling technique and balance, regardless of what you may be told. The body can be conditioned and strengthened, and once you have developed skills and a vision

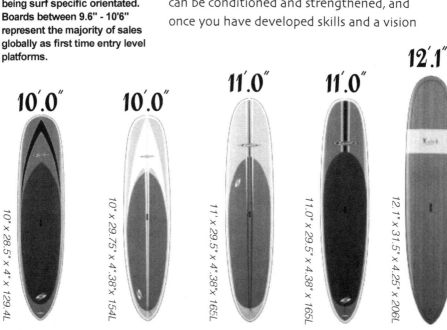

10'.0"

10" x 28.5" x 4" x 129.4L

10'.0"

10' x 29.75" x 4.38" x 154L

11'.0"

11' x 29.5" x 4.38"x 165L

11'.0"

11.0" x 29.5" x 4.38"x 165L

12'.1"

12.1" x 31.5" x 4.25" x 206L

for which discipline you wish to pursue; surf or distance for example, you can tap into the innovations and designs specifically suited to that discipline as produced by manufactures, where the interplay between equipment and technique becomes more critical.

Perhaps by way of sympathetic response to this, or a sudden epiphany, some manufacturers now acknowledge that what they thought was reasonable by way of cost as an entry-level board, has proven to be unpalatable to many newcomers.

While a response to address this issue is a good thing, there is still merit in recycling old styled longboard windsurfers, costing your average newcomer next to nothing; their initial investment being in a good quality paddle as against over purchasing on the board and buying a cheap stick to paddle it with. End users by their simple innovation and thinking outside of the loop, can enter the sport economically, while boosting participant numbers which will lead to what all manufacturers and retailers want, increased sales of boards and all associated equipment.

The all-rounder basic stand up paddle board

Stand up paddle boarding is promoted as 'easy' though this is dependant on a number of external factors; board design parameters, whether rigid or inflatable, paddle design used, paddler ability, nature of the water and prevailing weather conditions.

The classic longboard surfboard, remains the most universal shape, used by schools and sold to many first timers providing an ideal platform for low performance paddling, paddle-surfing in shallow plunging waves, gentle cruising and exploration in calm, sheltered waters and as a core workout board.

Marketed as all-round workhorses, these boards are essentially a compromise design, offering a stable learning platform for the beginner of various body weights and vary in length generally between 10'-12' x 28"-36" wide. These boards are functional but nevertheless a compromise the moment you aspire to wanting more. In essence this style of board is not high performance per se, but serves the purpose of recreational entry into the sport. For the most part stability is the key design element, not performance.

12'6"

12.6" x 30.0" x 6.18" x 255L

12'6"

12.6" x 29.0" x 6.5" x 233L

The original 11-12' tongue depressor styled boards sold in their thousands representing the bottom of the curve of stand up paddle board evolution and many were raced; essentially over-blown surfboards by any reasonable argument. However, this was quickly addressed as paddlers wanted to go faster and designer / manufacturers wanted to establish themselves through the kudos of making a faster purpose made race board, the pinnacle of which today, has become the elite 12'6" racing division of the Battle of the Paddle styled races, though it has to be said not everyone is happy how this has seemingly been 'forced' upon a sport in its infancy.

Events shaping our race boards

Ocean paddle sports around the world nuture the creation of events, which lead to specification rulings, which create divisions. Manufacturers subsequently design and produce craft within the limitations of these respective divisions and in so doing, the kudos of winning these divisions, leads to sales - a very simple formula.

In terms of stand up paddle board racing, two events now dominate the race board designers' thoughts; the Battle of the Paddle (BoP) races and the Moloka`i to O`ahu annual race together with other prestigious downwind races more especially throughout the Hawaiian islands.

You could think that's a simple enough formula for weeding out the gene pool of equipment, not withstanding the athletes ability, but there is a dark side to specification rulings, creating divisions in more ways than one. Historically there has been controversy over who gets to determine these factors, as rules set benchmarks for the parameters in which the designers can function.

Such rules either liberate the designers creativity or stifle it, not to mention the evolution of the sport itself. Most importantly, the moment a designer / manufacturer gets involved in the determination of board specification rulings, you can assume there will be an agenda to ensure their needs are served - they are hardly going to create design rulings which are contrary to their own designs?

Board specification rulings influencing designs

A few historical notes of interest.

1. 'Stock' as an off the shelf concept, is directly taken from long established prone paddle board rulings, where 12' (stock boards) and under must conform also to a weight ruling. Open board designs of 12' and over are designated as unlimited / unrestricted. Some boards exceed 20' in length and have the inclusion of tiller-arm steering.

2. California introduced a 14' stock, prone paddle board division during the early part of 2000 in response to end-users demand for the longer board which then became a regular part of production by the likes of Jo Bark et al. Stock 14' as it applies to stand up paddle boards was simply adopted from existing prone paddle board designs of the time, not by divine intervention as an optimum length, but simply by osmosis.

3. By no fluke, 12'6" was also a popular open prone paddle board length and so too, it evolved into a stock stand up paddle board length, which by no-coincidence was the maximum length of foam blank produced by Clark Foam (until it recently closed its doors).

The evolution of the 14' race board represents in some sense the board which should very probably be the 'preferred' board of choice for most racing circumstances and from the viewpoint of performance in both flat water and downwind conditions. However, they aren't as easy to lug around and airlines don't care much for them, so many travelling racers become limited to travelling with a 12'6" board. The 14' board bridges that gap between trying to squeeze the absolute best out a 12'6" board and delivers a leap in performance on account of the increased length at the water line and a greater range of 'sweet spot'. For deep water, long distance downwind races, the Moloka'i race in particular is the one race which has most inspired this design, in which there is no 12'6" division as such and would / should not be the board of choice for such a task.

14'

14'

14' x 28.0" x 7.30" x 285L

14′

14' x 29.25" x 5.2" x 235L Expedition Board

14′

14" x 29 x 6.65 x 259L

Joe Barks 14' Expedition board is a great example of a board designed for the simple pleasure of travelling distance in comfort, with very simple lines it would make for an excellent first time board for the paddler who wants to 'paddle' and breaks the stereotype entry level belief in purchasing a 10' all rounder as a first time board. The quicker you can figure out what you want to do with your board, the less boards you will have to buy to get there.

4. The 12′6″ stand up paddle board division was made popular in the context of racing through the existence of the Battle of the Paddle races - not because the boards are inherently versatile and / or good in the context of being raced and or paddled, but moreover, because they were what had been easy to fast track into production and flood the market being easier to transport and cheaper to manufacture.

5. Stock should in fact be 'stock standard' as it comes off the shelf, though it should be noted, boards raced by pro riders are rarely 'off the shelf' and therefore the term is misleading.

6. The 32 mile open ocean Moloka`i to O`ahu race does not offer a 12′6″ division on account of this board length being essentially unsuitable, even if feasible. 14′ is the most popular division.

8. The Battle of the Paddle races favour the 12′6″ elite division where paddlers must paddle through shore break, around markers and back through the surf. There are however other divisions.

Within the field of racing 'signature' models are now omnipresent in the 12′6″ and 14′ designs.

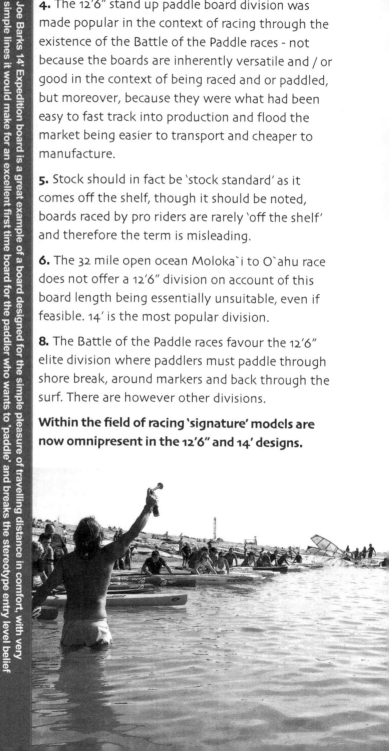

A note concerning water line length (foot print)

Design rulings haven't altered much since racing first began, however in respect of the central issue of board length, the current rulings in the context of racing, could possibly be considered over-simplified on the basis that a 'length over-all' (LOA) is being applied when more significantly, 'length at the water' (LWL) could also be factored into the mix.

Simply put, if you're going to bring length into rulings on account of a determination of performance, potential hull speed, equality and fairness, length at the waterline should be a factor of these design requirements.

As an example, the Hawaiian Canoe Racing Association (HCRA) specifies that; **'the maximum length of a canoe that will be allowed to compete in the Hawaiian Canoe Racing Association sanctioned or sponsored races will be 45 feet in overall length, which means from end of hull to end of hull, or end of manu to end of manu, or any combination thereof that represents the longest measured length. This length is to be determined by the use of a plumb bob or the establishment of a right angle from a level base line. Overall length – 45 feet . . . the maximum length at the water (LWL) will be 39 feet 0 inches plus a 5% allowance for design error, etc. This water line is to be determined by the use of the methods used to establish the measurement by the Committee.'**

While LOA gives us a maxim, LWL gives us a footprint length, which in some sense reflects the degree of 'rocker', which by use of a formula applied to displacement and semi-displacement hulls, determines 'potential' hull speed. What this means to the sport, is that a 16' board may only have a 12'6" waterline length. If that's a critical element as applied to some canoeing and sailing craft, why not stand up paddle board designs - more especially in the context flat water racing / sprinting?

Three lengths dictate the machinations of our designers - 12'6", 14' and unlimited. Adding in a LWL ruling, may liberate imaginations, while addressing the issue in a more scientific, rationale basis than the current singular design parameter.

A note concerning future rulings

You, me, us and them, as so called pioneers and custodians of the sport's future, need be actively concerned about the future of race rulings or suffer the consequences. There should from the outset, be a universal philosophical agreement, that any design rulings are at the very core, a poor rationale for the development and evolution of the stand up paddle board. As I once famously or infamously wrote in the context of the evolution of the outrigger canoe,

> **"During the thousands of years of architectural evolution of the va'a, the Polynesians weren't limited by specifications of length, width, curvatures and weight and only the village idiot would have suggested such an imposition."**

Imposition of design rules, is central to the Eurocentric condition. Mathematical limits are established, which inevitably lead to a retardation of design through the safeguarding of fairness across socio-economic status or perhaps levels of sponsorship. But we could argue fairness on the basis of genetics, physiology, life circumstances and ultimately age, of which I once heard at the University of Hawai`i at a seminar in 1995, **"Old paddlers don't retire, they simply create new age divisions."**

Only in 2004, we had our first stand up paddle entrant in the Moloka`i to O`ahu race. In 2008 our first BoP races commenced, now in 2012, we're already thinking, not of relaxing the rules, but tightening them. In 2008 when a saw was being taken to boards in shortening them to 'regulation length' did it not cross anyone's mind that the water line length was the primary significant issue, if concerned about fairness in having a longer or shorter board than the next person.

As already buried within this body of work, flat water sprint racing is the 'anal-end' of all paddle sports, where rule makers and designers revel in an orgy of micro-management in dealing with constants. In contrast, open ocean paddle sports or indeed surf sports, work more at an intuitive level, where there are no constants, where nature works as your self governing process on any given day, in self regulating what will or will not work.

Races which take place through any shore-break, will always present a self governing limitation on board design, with or without the intervention of rule makers. Try taking a 16' board out through a sizeable shore-break and you'll get the picture, because for any given day, only a limited number of board designs will be 'ideal'. BoP races may be very good for the industry and hoopla, but one wonders if the rulings aren't polarising the sport so early on in its evolution, when many believe, the 14' board would offer a far greater freedom of design for the designer, pleasure for the rider and suitability for a wider range of abilities and rider weights.

With regards the transportability issue, are we seriously going to accept that designs be limited by what has manifested into a convenient central issue? The length versus transportation versus evolution debate should be booted into touch. We either want evolution or we don't. Explain how canoe, kayak and surfski paddlers manage? 100, 43' canoes make it to Molokai`i every year and around the world, many canoe and kayak events exceed 200 entrants. Passion, dedication and a willingness to make it happen regardless I would suggest.

While one-design racing is the fairest ruling to determine the best paddler, it's about as popular as a crack in your shaft, as it flies in the face of commercial interests - and right now everyone wants a slice of the action. Unlimited design restraints (divisions) must always be considered the dog off the leash end of the sport's evolution. With no road blocks or road signs, designers are free to deliver the best of the best, for whatever circumstance and you the buyer, the paddler, should take full advantage of this and guard this fundamental principal vigourously.

Significantly and ironic to this concern, no one has yet gone so far as to specifically determine what 'is', or 'is not', a stand up paddle board in the context of what could be deemed 'within the spirit of the sport.' Right now, a kayak could be paddled in the unlimited class without protest and here we are worried about length, beam and weight issues.

Above: Starboards 2012 BOP 12'6" and 14' boards. In the context of future flat water sprint racing in particular, if water line length is a factor of speed (which it is) this may need to be considered. The major beneficiaries of using LWL rules are the designers, who can free up their minds. Paddlers benefit by improvements in performance and the level playing field that is being pursued.

Even 14' should be considered 'short' in the context of being able to provide glide over flat water. In a sense we may need to alter our perspectives of what defines a long stand up paddle board. For downwind paddling the rules change somewhat, where you want rocker to conform to wave form and a moveable footprint which 'rocks' back and forth but are ultimately seeking 'planing speeds' on a very reduced rear hull section, so there seems no need for LWL rulings.

Below: C2 racing in a 100km river race Australia. Limits on LWL apply to all manner of craft.

Here's the WPA rulings in 2011 by way of an example.

SUP UNLIMITED CLASS No length, weight or design limits
SUP 14 Ft CLASS 14' ft maximum, no weight or design limits
SUP 12'6" CLASS 12'6" ft maximum, no weight or design limits
SUP Surfboard CLASS 12'2" ft maximum, no weight limit, board must be a surfboard style in shape with the minimum dimensions, nose 17" wide(12" back from nose), 14" tail (12" up from the tail) and maximum thickness of 5".

Further to this it is recommended if only 1 class of board is to be used, the following boards should be used in relation to the distance; 12'6" from 4-6 miles. 14' from 7-9 miles. Unlimited 9 + miles.

Events shaping stand up paddle surfboards

From the viewpoint of paddle-surfing, board designs are influenced by professional riders' wants, forged by creating an association with differing shapers and manufacturers. The range of wave size, form and demand of riders varies so widely, it has manifested a range of boards unfathomably diverse. Pro tours certainly provide a wide source of opportunity for designers to experiment, which doesn't always translate well down the line for the 'average' rider, but has its value in testing the limits as with any form of competitive based sport.

Board designer Dave Parmenter comments, **'Properly designed paddle boards are not over-size long boards, nor are they blown-up short boards. They are stand-up surfboards - a wholly new, rapidly-evolving class of surf craft, one that borrows design components from all the existing types of surf riding craft and combines them in a finely-tuned matrix that allows the progressive paddle surfer to lean on the paddle and push the board into places and angles no big board has ever been.'**

Regions and philosophies shaping our boards

Geographical regions of the world who share a unique perspective and philosophical view of the sport (and of life) are shaping boards to suit and no better example of this are the Lake Tahoe Boards of California. In an area of outstanding beauty, where a strong artistic community, mixed with those who share a close and binding connection with the land and the lake itself, this company has forged its products around the very lake which it resides.

Rubicon Specs:
12' long. 29" wide and 37 lbs

Dog pad ready. SUP
with your best buddy.

Comfy deck pads.

Soft carry handle.
Easy for one person
to load and unload.

8" dry hatch. Good
for cell phones, cameras,
GPS, etc.

Displacement hull for great
secondary stability as well
as primary. This is a fast SUP

Bungees on back for gear storage.
Go for an overnighter!

Lake Tahoe Boards

As their website says,

'...we're the only company specifically building boards for flat-water touring, whether it's on calmer ocean waters, harbours, lakes or rivers..'

and credit where it's due, they have set themselves aside, using the mechanism of a strong philosophical belief to guide them through the rhetoric of so many others attempting to promise and deliver everything for all waters.

Inflatable boards

As a solution to overseas travel, easy storage and the like, the iSUP solves many consumer issues. In terms of high performance usage, reinforcing the point that stand up paddling is first and foremost a paddle sport, whitewater kayakers throughout mainland America, have, by pure ingenuity, seized upon what they recognise as their chance to make their mark on the sport by taking it to another place beyond paddling on calm inland waterways.

Armed with paddling skills and knowledge of river flow dynamics, pioneering professional level white water kayakers have been taking to the rivers, to put into practice, a whole new branch of the sport, unsuspected by the ocean watermen of Hawai`i who naturally had their sights set on the sports potential as a coastal ocean sport.

When Hawaiian company C4 started out, they figured naturally the sport was going to be largely coastal based, with strong leanings towards the surf, that is until they began getting inquiries for boards purpose made for

"Vail, Colorado 2011 – Against a backdrop of snow-capped mountains and a bluebird sky the confluence of surf and river culture met here today during the second annual Stand Up Paddle Surf Sprint competition at the Tenth Annual Teva Mountain Games. Sponsored by Maui Jim and presented by C4 Waterman, the SUP Sprint is a three-mile long time trial pitting competitors against the clock and their ability to balance and paddling hard while navigating the challenging rapids of snowmelt-swollen Gore Creek. This is just the second year stand up paddling has been a competitive event at Teva Mountain Games, the Olympics of outdoor adventure sports."

river running deep within mainland America. Here was a bunch of paddlers who could see the potential and they didn't want to miss out. The end result was the development of the inflatable iSUP boards - the rest is now history. Not all boards for river running are inflatable, but from it has spurned a range of accessories and innovation.

Late in 2008 Dave Parmenter of C4 commented, **'We've noticed that most of the interest in stand up paddle is coming from inland locations. In places where there's kayaking and canoes in lakes and rivers. All that kind of inland thing is huge. 80% of our boards are for that area. It's really taking off in the United States.'**

Mariko Strickland charging down river on a C4 inflatable board, specifically designed for river and rapids conditions.

Dan Gavere has been pioneering SUP as an extreme white water sport through his aspirational exploits.

It seems that while it is acknowledged that stand up paddle boarding brings together canoeing and board skills, whitewater inland waterman have seen that it's perfectly possible to surf and ride fast moving water, drop off of waterfalls and in short put themselves into challenging, if not a little dangerous but exciting situations in much the same way as they have in kayaks.

There's already a USA 'Whitewater Standup Paddling National Championship' and kayakers claim, that running steep fast moving rivers is more difficult and dangerous than surfing ocean swells, demanding skills and knowledge of river safety and rescue along with mandatory additional equipment; helmet, shin pads, rescue vest. Already paddle and board makers are moving on designing equipment specific to river running.

Whereas aspirational imagery first manifested from the shores of Hawai`i, now we are seeing images of paddlers meandering their way down the inland rivers and ravines of North America, Canada and remote parts of South America and wherever someone with enough journeyman spirit and money (or sponsorship) can take them, for that shot of fame, for being the first.

"Shaped by Tahitian master wood carver, Maui Hucke, this trophy was created for the Heemoana Va'a race along the coastline of Tahiti in 2002, which begins through the reef pass at Teahupoo. Carved from coconut wood, this striking iconoclastic form represents the outrigger canoe (va`a) paddler, not the stand up paddler, yet the form draws powerful similarities to which the stand up paddle boarder can relate."

So predictable is the synergy between the human spirit of adventure and the manufacturers willingness to explore the possibilities, that wherever there's a stretch of water, preferably in the most remote place unimaginable, in waters as inhospitable to match, then we can assume this is fair game.

And the point of all this, is simply to promote and spark the imagination in us all no matter where we live, a catalyst to lure us into an association with a sport, so far reaching that we want to be part of all that it represents and all the time there's no escaping its roots back to the islands of the Pacific, the sound of ukuleles, the smell of coconut oil and the imagery of blue skies and peeling waves. **'It's a link to surfing and the surf lifestyle that everyone wants to be part of'.** *Jimmy Lewis*

'While whitewater paddle boarding per se may not reach massive numbers, the number of inland recreational lake, river and dam participant numbers is set to be huge, with whitewater paddlers no doubt creating that aspirational edge for the inland paddler and thereby fuelling the fire in the same way perhaps, as big wave paddle surfers, serve to spark the imagination of many ocean participants. Inland retailers, see the same potential as seen on the coastal belts, for paddle boarding to be an important cross-training and full-body fitness workout for all manner of athletes.' *Lee Hart - Colorado*

Yoga boarding - yoga on water (YOW)

As if to reinforce the notion that the ingenuity of the human race knows no bounds, who would have thought that yoga boarding would have manifested from the roller coaster evolution of stand up paddle boarding. It does beg the question, why wasn't this being done years ago, even in the absence of stand up paddle boarding? After all, the paddle in this instance, is almost surplus to requirements. In an Industry news release written By Mike Mooers San Francisco Feb 9 2011, he outlines the development and release of a range of boards specific to the purpose.

'Boga Yoga stand up paddle boards, designed specifically for SUP fitness and yoga on water (YOW), is the first ever SUP board designed to meet the needs of this new – and rapidly growing – market. As stand up paddle boarding continues as the world's fastest growing aquatic sport, traditional activities such as yoga and fitness classes have merged with it to create exciting new disciplines.'

'**Currently classes are forced to use standard SUP boards which were designed for surfing and paddling, not fitness and yoga,**' said David Meyler, founder and president of Boga Paddleboards. '**For the new board Boga worked closely with instructors active in the SUP community to design a board that handled the unique needs associated with these activities. We managed to design a winning board shape that has strong stability and balance while retaining Boga's leading-edge paddling and glide characteristics.**'

With their background designing specific stand up paddle boards for racers, surfers and athletes, the Boga team leveraged their performance-specific design experience. Features on the new board include a unique and highly supportive Aqua Stable Bottom (ASB) shape, an integrated PVC-free Yoga pad, secure paddle stash system and a fitness resistance kit.

As respected Northern California SUP racer and fitness instructor, Jennifer Fuller, notes, '**The current growth of fitness and yoga on SUP boards is off the charts, and growing worldwide. The combination of the benefits of these traditional exercises, along with the benefits of SUP, creates a unique, fun core workout that hooks my clients instantly. Having a board designed specifically for my needs will grow my client base and provide a much better platform that caters to our class and fitness routines.**'

Boga Paddleboards - 11.4ft
Board Name - BOGA YOGA

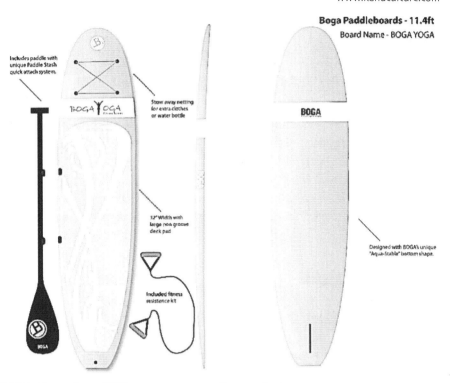

Includes paddle with unique Paddle Stash quick attach system.

Stow away netting for extra clothes or water bottle

32" Width with large non groove deck pad

Included fitness resistence kit

Designed with BOGA's unique "Aqua-Stable" bottom shape.

Pictured here, Certified yoga and SUP instructor Heather George.

'SUP yoga, will lift your mood, your body and your well being.'

Moloka`i styled point to point downwind boards

These boards fall into a similar category as big wave guns. Their shape is what may be termed as 'cigar shaped' and follow a similar plan form to that of Tom Blake's 16ft prone paddle board design dating back to the 1920s.

Specialised downwind boards follow a very different mindset for the designer in that they are looking at the board from the point of view of a high speed missile rather than a wallowing beast struggling to win out over the tedium of pushing against water, but require plenty of wind and wave action to do so. These boards are attempting to break free of the limitations of drag, so as to rise and lift on account of planing on top of the water's surface in what amounts to a sleigh ride powered by wind, water and muscle power. Ultimately control at speed becomes the critical factor.

The Moloka`i to O`ahu race is an epic and historically significant event for a variety of ocean craft; outrigger canoeing, surf ski, prone paddle board and now stand up paddle boarding, raced between these two Hawaiian islands across the deep blue abyss of the Kaiwi Channel, where average winds nudge 20 knots and seas of 8' over the 30 mile plus stretch.

Here the wind alters from being on your quarter (over your right hand shoulder) or essentially down wind. Importantly the maxim here for the designer and therefore the manufacturer has been for many years now, 'Win here and you're guaranteed sales'. There are better direct downwind runs it has to be said; Maui to Moloka`i or even the Maliko Gultch run along the coastline of Maui, which just happens to be where some of the finest downwind boards are conceived, tested and races now staged.

The undisputed pioneer and primary designer of such boards is Mark Raaphorst of Sandwich Island Constructions (SIC) Maui, who has essentially been unchallenged in this specialist design field on account of its niche interest and the apparent shyness of the world's primary mass producers to enter this sphere with any significant gusto or commitment, leaving it to SIC to produce and create the fastest stand up paddle boards on the planet. High tech, expensive, exotic they are intoxicating and offer the downwind paddler, the pinnacle of form and function.

Unlimited boards, of 16 - 17' dominate downwind distance line honours in the Hawaiian islands and that's not to say you can't have a lot of fun and cover a good deal of ground on a 14' board. You can. But credit where it is due, these boards represent a leap frog in thinking and technology far and above the run of the mill boards meeting the domain of any compromise. In a league of their own, they are purpose made to do one thing well - put a smile on your face within an area of the sport which could be argued as the pinnacle of the sport in bringing all the best elements and skills together.

Contrary to the belief these boards need 'big water' to be manageable and go fast, this simply isn't the case, being as the added water line length, hull form and shape delivers in a hugely wide variance of conditions from moderate to extreme.

The rules of the Moloka`i race state, **'Competitors can choose to race on either a traditional paddle board or on a stand up paddle board, entering as a solo paddler or as a 2 or 3 person team. Solo paddlers can choose to paddle in either the unlimited class (no size limit and with a**

Mark Raaphorst stands with an F17 SIC Board. Paddle it, hang it on your wall, these boards are in every sense iconoclastic and masterpieces of form and function.

This branch of the sport and the boards which it manifests, is a sport within a sport - a niche interest appealing to speed junkies, adventurists, the maverick free thinkers and endurance paddlers who truly embrace the art and discipline of paddling in harmony in big winds and a running sea in the absence of road signs and rules, etiquette or waiting in the line up.

When it comes down to it, few people ever consider the downside of paddle surfing. Some who have, have moved to make downwind paddling their primary sport in combining all that they like best in expressing themselves, whilst surfing wave after wave in a syncopated percussion.

A 1980s advertisement for Mistral boards. These plan-form shapes draw strong parallels with the design of many stand up paddle board shapes today.

Below Mark Raaphorst with an F16' downwind board, the lines of which, hark back to the classic lines associated with that of Tom Blake and Joe Quigg boards. Ironically, these designs are not for the most part, embraced by 'The Industry' who are collectively busy feeding the 12'6" and 14' end of the market, over looking what is argued as being the zenith of the sport in harnessing nature's most powerful elements in harmony, even beyond that of stand up paddle surfing. Mass appeal it seems is limited and may stay that way if the industry decides it remain so.

162

movable rudder system) or stock class (12 feet or under for paddle board or 14 foot or under for stand up paddle board with fixed rudder).'

The most popular board designs used, are the rudderless 14' boards, not on account of being the best design to use per se, but due to external factors, of cost, ease of transportation and storage, while also complying more conveniently with manufacturers' commercial needs.

'Battle of the Paddle' styled boards

Battle of the Paddle (BoP) races, have contributed greatly in bringing the sport to the masses, through high levels of exposure and participation levels. They are in short an exercise in marketing brilliance, ensuring a captivated audience with thrills and spills which create a circus-like atmosphere, with the actors acting out their respective parts on the stage, the beach festooned with paraphernalia, sponsors and promoters swimming in a veritable orgy of back slapping hysteria. While the paddlers may feel at the centre of the attention, a podium finish in any one of a wide range of divisions, assures exposure and sales for sponsors and brands.

Out of this mele, the 12'6" 'race board' was born and currently represents the 'Elite' board division - 14' and unlimited divisions are also catered for. Why 12'6" should singularly be considered 'Elite' seems less than 100% tenable. Logic suggests, they represent the cheaper end of the market, the race board most easily transported and mirror manufacturer aims. Contextually, the 12'6" board fails to suit either the physicality or anotomical mass of many of our larger and finest ocean paddlers, even if they themselves are 'Elite' by any measure; a clear enough visual narrative of the ruling's fundamental weakness and inaccurate nomenclature.

Travis Grant practicing BoP skills in home waters - Gold Coast Australia (The Goldie)

These races, as big a spectacle as they are, are something of a lottery, in avoiding flying boards, falling paddlers, rogue waves and the like and does not find appeal with all. While unquesionably serving the industry well on one level, they run the risk of polarising manufactures efforts into producing one board type.

Mark Raaphorst SIC Maui comments; **'The popularity of the 12'6" class grew in part through the Battle of the Paddle (BoP) events, beginning in 2008. The 12'6" length is an evolution from prone paddle boards. This "stock" length became popular based on the availability of the largest polyurethane Clark Foam blank at the time. Manufacturing technologies have changed considerably since then, but the concept to have an affordable, easily produced and common length board for competition has not. Race conditions around the world can range from flat with no wind and no surf to head-on breaking surf with / without wind depending on where you live and race. Our experiences in the California and Waikiki BoP events taught us that a 12'6" competition board had to be versatile.'**

A cultural divide

The Moloka`i races and races like them, remain the absolute testing ground in the context of what ocean paddlers would refer to as 'Elite' where absolutes can be tested to the limit and where constants and limits don't count for much. If you think this isn't so, consider which paddlers we ultimately venerate the most.

In time, a cultural divide will begin to crack wide apart, if not already, between those whose primary interest is open water (downwind) paddling, BoP racing, flat water sprint / marathon or white water - not unsurprising, given as it's fundamental to all canoe and kayak sports and largely dictated by geographical proximity to varying water types, climates, prevailing conditions, historical, cultural and governance influences.

The trickle affect from BoP races

So what have these races manifested and how might this be relevant to Ma and Pa, little Johnny or anyone else a thousand miles removed from the mindset of competition and owning a board whose design parameters are centred around one specific style of racing.

Well the good news is, there have been big gains in overall board designs in terms of improved hull speeds, deck layouts and the micro-management of the basic principles of hydro-dynamic efficiency; in some designs at any rate. It has to be said, many boards are beginning to look a lot like the next and one could assume this to be a natural consequence of a melding of minds all arriving at similar ideas. The top-sides of these boards may appear different, until you flip them over, because it's the underside which really counts. While some are doubtless leading the way, others could be said to be wake-riding others' greater understanding of the principles and are therefore more inclined to imitate, than risk being original.

Some of these design principles have now led to boards with bows, very much thicker board depth, specialist race fins, greater attention to the board's overall 'sweet-spot', the inclusion of better placed carry handles, even side straps and a reduction in weight through improved manufacturing techniques.

If there is one concern, it's the conflicting requirement that the board must perform well as a flat water board, while also being able to be paddled out through breaking waves and capable of being surfed back to the beach, which in many ways provides a design paradox, but overall the gains have been of great value to the sport in focusing designers attention away from surf per se, giving emphasis on creating a better board for paddling, something which for a considerable time during the sport's brief evolution was missing.

The Emergence of 12'6" and 14" iSUP racing boards

During 2012 and moving into 2013, we are witnessing the emergence of inflatable iSUP race boards.

Mistral has produced a 12'6" and 14' race board with which it hopes to spurn 'one design racing' harking back to its windsurfing roots. In many respects, if the technology can create lightweight, transportable, performance orientated race boards, then one design racing is certainly a possibility.

"Mistral firmly believes that the future of SUP lies in inflatable long boards. For this reason Mistral has founded a New Mistral Class Organization for SUP. Mistral is now the first brand in the World of SUP with their own Class SUP Organization, taking this sport into the 21st century, The Mistral M1 International One Design Class (MIOC)."

Their philosophy is very clear in making the sport accessible for all firmly believing iSUP boards as the means by which to reach the masses through all ages and gender.

River paddlers have already prospered because of iSUP technology, it's reasonable to assume that soon all other areas of interest will be catered for.

The 'Flat Earth Society'

Moving forwards, a radical rethink regarding the design of boards for flat water racing and sprints is required. Flat planing hulls, are about as inefficient a design as you could create for such an environment and puts into question here, whether designers are keeping pace with the evolving needs and skill levels of the riders.

One gets the feeling, that many so called new designs, remain dull and simply not radicle enough to break away from the mundane, consequently they are failing to challenge paddlers to advance their skill levels. For the most part they remain 'Ironing board' flat.

Stable (flat) is being marketed as 'fast' not because this is a hydrodynamical truth, but because a relaxed 'stable' paddler can apply more blade pressure than an anxious unstable one. Increased skill levels now demand faster, more inherently unstable displacement hull designs, as part of the evolutionary process and acknowledgement of the sport's progression.

Future rulings

Weight limits on account of fairness and affordability, seems a moot point. OC1 rulings (mid 90s) attempted this idea, but it was dismissed as paddlers wanted 'light' and the sport expanded in part, as a consequence. Safe limits of build strength are a self governing process. Board breaks, orders stop. **Width restrictions are and should be a self governing process of ability versus stability**. Rounded displaced hulls are the way forward for speed on flat water, coupled with added length, not merely narrowness. Paddler skill levels and wants should be our yardstick for extremes of designs, not mediocrity.

From a paddling performance perspective, 14' boards are ultimately 'better' and representative of a board size that potentially offers improved performance over a wider range of paddler weights and conditions in the context of the 12'6" versus the 14' race board debate - but racing through shore break can sometimes nullify this rationale.

Why what fits on a plane is assisting in the evolutionary pathway

12'6" race boards or otherwise, are the upper limits of what (some) airlines will 'readily' accept, usually at a fee. While surfers have enjoyed relative freedom in travelling overseas with their stick, canoeists and kayakers haven't and resolve this through hire, loans, purchase on arrival or in some cases, inflatables. Any limit placed on design, external or otherwise, is fundamentally detrimental to the sport.

Regardless, it's reasonable to say that manufacturers have no control over the airlines, but then some creative thinking is required to over-come this problem - 2 part rigid boards or iSUP boards. The specialist downwind paddler requiring rigid 14' boards and over most probably suffer the most as a consequence of this limitation.

Rocker line

Rocker, relates to the degree of curvature running fore and aft along the longitudinal length of the board, measured from the underside upward to the extremities of the bow / nose and tail underside. A greater degree of curvature front to back, generally improves manoeuvrability at the expense of directional stability and vice-versa, but this can be offset partially by hard (sharp) rails or enhanced using soft rails. Flat water boards typically should have very little rocker to avoid creating a deeper 'depression' and pushing water and to maximise water line length. Open water boards, will lean more toward increased degrees of rocker. Rocker together with volume distribution, are key determinants of a board's 'sweet-spot'. Curved under-sides will tend to rock back and forth in open waters so as the 'footprint' shifts, the waterline length may consequently remain more constant.

Dave Parmenter's C4 V1 14' board of 2011/12 features cross-sectional rounded curvature and significant rocker fore and aft and represents a move away from an ironing board hull form as does his TGIF 12'6" board. Consequently this is not a flat water 'specific' board as it's design lines are suited to open water conditions - though its semi-displaced cross section improves flat water performance.

While these soft railed boards test the paddler's skills, the trade off in performance is there for those who persevere. The performance improvements elevate such a craft from being essentially 'dumb' to one which is far more 'intuitive' in conforming to the nuances of water and in reducing drag coefficients. In essence, the hull does some of the thinking for you at slower, displacement speeds in working with water not against it. When displacement windsurfing boards evolved onto the racing scene in the early 1980s, they proved so much quicker than the flat planing hull windsurfers of the time, a separate division was created - Div 2, on account of their superior speed in light to moderate winds.

The rocker curvature of the 14' C4 V1 shortens the boards waterline length to not much over 9'.

Ex pro-windsurfer, John Hibbard takin' it easy. The versatility of the sport is its primary saviour. There's just so many options available to you given the right day, in the right place, with the right kit.

Rudder mechanisms

Manufacturers (designers) have been slow to embrace the idea of rudder fitment (not helped by race rulings) when it seems plausible that even 12'6" boards, with optional fitment of a steering mechanism at the least, may expand the end-user's scope of use and offer more value in outlaying large amounts of money. While the use of the rudder may diminish the need for some skill sets, it certainly adds an extra degree of functionality and possibilities.

Paddle a rudder steered paddle board, get to grips with it in lumpy seas and a bit of a cross breeze and you'll never look back and yet they are about as rare as hens teeth. Why is this so. Cost? The hassle of fitment? Misunderstanding? A perverse need to keep things pure? Who knows, but if I can give you a very fitting comparison, to which you would not be aware of unless you were deeply connected to the sport of outrigger canoeing.

Deep out in the Pacific, in the French Polynesian Islands, the rudderless Va'a Hoe (solo outrigger canoe) has been used for centuries, mastery of which is a time honoured skill and right of passage. If you aren't raised from childhood to master these iconoclastic water craft of symmetry and beauty from lagoon to open water, you will struggle to come to grips with the art and skills required to gain control beyond all but the most perfect of still conditions.

In 1986, solo outrigger canoes were not present in the Hawaiian Islands, but in that year a solo va'a hoe was brought back from Tahiti and work began in earnest to add an enclosed deck and add a foot operated steering mechanism as used with surf skis. The purpose of this was to gain control in open water

Traditional rudderless va'a hoe of French Polynesia. Note the paddle without top grip. In every sense the bio-mechanical action and lineage associated with this sport replicates that of outrigger canoeing a fact unacknowledged for the most part by the stand up paddle boarding community. Worse still and by way of a total lack of respect and disregard for the cultural significance of this sport, is the way in which surfing organisations and emerging wanna-be governing bodies and even some training organisations continue to disregard this clear and obvious fact, thereby missing the relevance of the paddle by a few thousand years.

Contemporary rudderless (sit in side) Tahitian va'a hoe for open ocean racing. Not just rudderless, but no fin at all. *Photo: Steve West.*

conditions and in doing so created a safer, more controllable design which could be used in a far wider range of conditions without the need for super human strength or machine like precision paddle skills which incorporated a wide variation of steering strokes. The sport boomed as a result.

While this may have under-mined the need to develop exceptional paddling skills, the efforts of the designers resulted in a far more user friendly, manageable craft, which offered the end user vastly improved performance merits over its rudderless counterpart back in French Polynesia. What had been created by irony, was less of an evolution of the Tahitian va'a hoe but in essence a somewhat Anglo-Polynesian variation of the surf ski being as you sat on it, not in it and used a foot operated steering mechanism with an outrigger assembly fitment.

An early variant of the rudderless Tahitian va'a hoe, in Hawai`i, but with pedals and rudder fitment. Later the deck was covered and the paddler given a purpose made adjustable seat. *Rider: Walter Guild Photo: Jeff Hornbaker*

Anglo-Hawaiians went on to develop the sit on top, rudder steered (foot operated pedal controlled) OC1 which changed the face of big water downwind paddling and everything else in between. Adding such a system to high performance stand up paddle boards, not only makes sense, but will have you paddling more often in winds and conditions you never thought possible. *Rider: Rick Nu'u - Maui Photo: Steve West*

The point of sharing this with you is to help substantiate the benefits to be had for you the end-user in having a foot operated rudder system - at least to have it as an option, thereby elevating the range of safe, controllable conditions in which you can get use from your board. Why should you have to paddle on one side to counter the affect of side winds, when the rudder negates this problem together with controlling the board being bullied by nasty cross-chop or dealing with the the pull of a strong current or tidal flow. Indeed it could be argued not only is a rudder system advantageous from the point of view of performance and enjoyment, but purely from the viewpoint of safety.

These conditions transcend the notion of the sport being easy. A wider range of manageable conditions means more water time, more board use, more fun, more appeal of a sport currently being hindered by some unfathomable resistance to the addition of such a simple performance enhancing solution, in

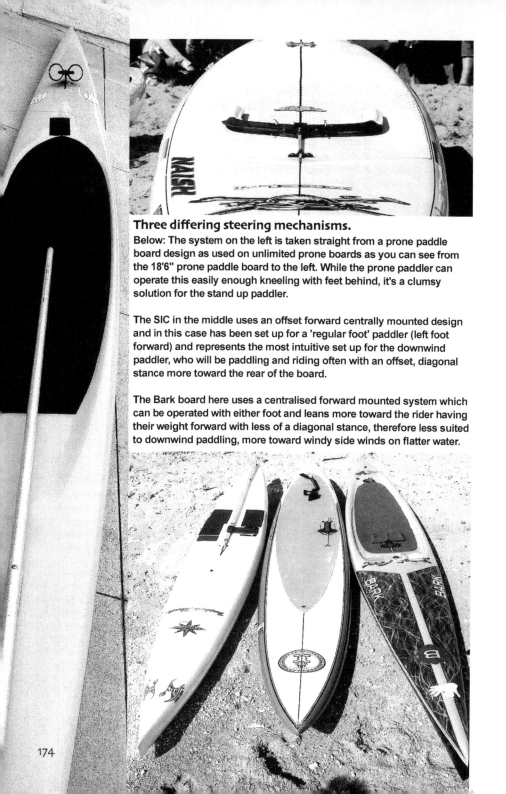

Three differing steering mechanisms.

Below: The system on the left is taken straight from a prone paddle board design as used on unlimited prone boards as you can see from the 18'6" prone paddle board to the left. While the prone paddler can operate this easily enough kneeling with feet behind, it's a clumsy solution for the stand up paddler.

The SIC in the middle uses an offset forward centrally mounted design and in this case has been set up for a 'regular foot' paddler (left foot forward) and represents the most intuitive set up for the downwind paddler, who will be paddling and riding often with an offset, diagonal stance more toward the rear of the board.

The Bark board here uses a centralised forward mounted system which can be operated with either foot and leans more toward the rider having their weight forward with less of a diagonal stance, therefore less suited to downwind paddling, more toward windy side winds on flatter water.

resolving a variety of limiting factors? There's no cultural precedent hindering this addition or ruling, but something's not right when it is constantly excluded. It's entirely probable, that this stems from the general mind-set and condition of designers failing to elevate their thinking beyond the concept of the craft being that of surfboard - when in fact, designers who use canoe or kayaking as their touchstone, are more receptive to inclusion of this device.

Foot operated steering systems are used on unlimited prone paddle board designs and it is the same / similar system that migrated its way into downwind stand up paddle boards - the system, elevates the boards somewhat primitive simplistic inanimate persona to that of a more sophisticated beast with animated moving parts offering genuine benefits to the end-user (see notes on use in downwind chapter).

Notes on stability

Whenever you jump between boards, you will experience three differing forms of stability; **Directional Stability** - how well it travels in a straight line, **Longitudinal Stability** - how sensitive it is to fore and aft movement from nose to tail as it moves under your weight and **Lateral Stability** - how sensitive is the side to side (rolling) movement. This is a very basic explanation, but all these factors are relative to the design parameters of the board itself and not just with regards to the basics (length and width) but also rail shape, bottom shape (cross section) rocker (fore and aft curvature) and micro-management issues such as, fin shape, number and position.

High performance OC1's have pointed bows and stern, rounded cross-sectional hulls (displacement) and more rocker aft than forward. These super quick canoes, are fast both in flat water, downwind and upwind. If you could stand on this and paddle effectively you would have yourself a quick craft. Averaging between 21' and 22' the water line length is ample for high speeds and the outrigger (ama) provides added stability which permits the designer to make a fast, inherently unstable hull. *Travis Grant*

Directional stability
(how well the board stays on course)

How well a board will travel in a straight line is reliant upon a combination of factors of rail shape, board thickness, length and width. Common to all boards is the driving force of the paddle along one side of the board, causing the board to veer off-line (yaw) turning away from the paddling side. This can be offset by a cross-wind opposing this force, hence why paddlers often end up paddling for extended periods of time on one side and where the use of a foot operated rudder system can negate this problem. 'Hard' rail shapes as opposed to 'soft' will improve directional stability, while long (12'6" +) and narrow beamed (<29") boards will hold a better line. Progressively shorter, wider boards will proportionally lack directional stability. When learning paddling skills, you

want a board with good directional stability, so as you can concentrate on paddling not zig-zagging.

Surf orientated paddle-surf boards are short and wide for manoeuvrability and deliberately lack directional stability. A common descriptive term 'track' refers to how well the board does or does not 'track' i.e hold a straight line. Negative outcomes of a board which tracks too well, is where it fails to respond to your efforts to alter it's course or where the rails dig in and causes the board to 'track' on its edge when you don't want it to, more of a problem with longer downwind boards at speed. Excessively hard rails may cause the board to 'trip-over' causing it to momentarily attempt to flip.

Longitudinal stability
(how your board pitches fore and aft)

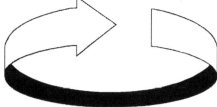

Refers to the boards fore and aft movement the variance of which is affected by varying points along the craft's length, which in turn determine the aspect ratio of the craft; the relationship between the length and width (beam). High aspect craft can be considered, long and thin and support weight at the nose and tail more effectively than a low aspect, short and wide design, though the 'fineness' of the bow and stern and rocker curvature (fore and aft curvature) also comes into play and in addition the degree of buoyancy (volume) at each end. All these factors determine how much pitch (movement at the bow and stern in an up and down motion) can be expected. Race boards and longer cruising boards are generally of a high aspect design; surf styled boards, low aspect.

Lateral stability (how stable your board is)

This concerns the board's tendency to roll or heel from side to side. Paddlers may term their board 'tippy' and much of this has to do with the bottom shape of the hull and how 'rounded' or 'flat' its cross-section is, amongst other considerations; rounded rails, board width. In more extreme designs, where bottom shapes are marginally rounded (displaced), of narrow width (<27") decks may be lowered, so as the paddler is level to or even below the water line in extreme cases, thereby lowering their centre of gravity in order to improve control / stability, being that stability is a factor of the relationship between the rider's centre of gravity and the board's centre of buoyancy (though the board also has its own CG).

Boards which dictate where you must stand, must be well matched to the paddler's body weight so as to switch on the 'sweet spot' of the board's inherent design. The paddler cannot move to counterpoise the shifting sweet spot and nuances of the board and therefore these boards are better suited to flat water. *Photo: Steve West.*

Boards which dictate your feet positioning

Boards which allow the rider to move fore and aft and side to side, permit micro-management of the nuances of the boards contact with the water, permitting greater control over these external factors. Boards which do not allow for such freedom of movement, greatly restrict the paddler from acting as a counterpoise to these movements and a constantly changing water line length and surface contact of the water. Such boards are better suited where conditions are near static (flat) and where the rider is suited to the board's design in terms of body weight in particular, as the gravity exerted has a direct affect on the board's trim and therefore 'sweet-spot' as designed into the board by the designer (hopefully). These factors in turn affect the board's run (glide) in relation to the board's design parameters.

Displacement hull shapes

Displaced hull shapes represent the extreme end of hull design. In the context of paddle craft the best examples include C1 (solo olympic canoes) and K1 (solo olympic kayak) paddle craft. These are unstable when stationary or at low speeds, on account of near semi-circular cross-sectional hull shapes of very narrow width, which leads to improved laminar flow of water. This ensures that the drag co-efficient is low and makes for a hull that glides through water (particularly flat water) with minimal resistance and as a consequence, requires less energy / power / force in order to generate speed against the resistance of water. Add to this, razor sharp bows and sterns producing minimal bow wave, clean release and 'closure' of the water behind and you create a fast (low drag) unstable craft. This design is essentially focused on being able to move through water with minimal drag with no attempt to lift and plane .

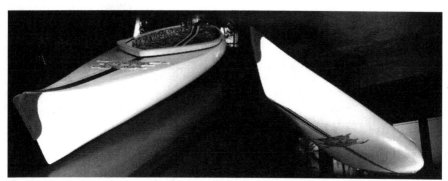

The late Jim Drake's, Starboard K15 represents one of the original fast flat water semi-displacement boards conceived and very much canoe-like inspired.

Jim Drake"s, semi-displacement stand inside Starboard K15.

A stand up paddle board design of this extreme nature (C1 / K1 shape) would demand high skill levels and may not be commercially viable at present. It may need to be very wide, which would begin to negate advantages gained on account of the added surface area and therefore drag. Essentially, a semi-circular hull cross section, acts much like a rocking chair; it naturally wants to rock from side to side, which makes for a 'tippy' board.

Overall, it requires less power to push a displaced hull design at its optimum hull speed over that of a flatter, planing hull design. The problem comes in making it feasible to stay on it, consequently stand up paddle race boards remain for the most part only very marginally displaced at best - most remain near flat which seems excessively cautious in the case of flat water race board design and contrary to all that we know of hydrodynamics.

Semi displaced hull shapes

A semi displacement hull brings us back to that holy grail of maxims, that of compromise. Predominantly these hulls are designed to move through water (push) with some ability to plane on the surface, made possible by flatter mid and aft sections, though some may feature single or double concave.

Terms used include fast displacement, semi-displacement, semi-planing. All of these are largely interchangeable. Semi displacement hulls typically have a

Photo: Dana Edmunds Courtesy of Ocean Promotions

Travis Grant's powers home to win the first SUP Survivor race in Hawai`i paddling a C4 TGIF 12'6" board which features a semi-displaced hull shape and upswept nose more associated with longer downwind styled boards, keeping the design essentially 'bowless'.

marginally rounded bottom shape (cross-sectional) with a tear drop shape running bow to stern. Such hulls, in broad terms, 'displace' or move water equal to the weight of the craft and naturally sit within the hole in the water created by its downward gravity, which is offset by the hulls buoyancy. Consequently such boards will only have minimal planing (high speed) characteristics. Once beyond 'displacement' speed these boards can become inherently unstable depending on the extent of roundedness.

Semi-displacement hulls are a compromise away from the extremes of a fully displaced hull and tend to have wider, flatter (square) rear / tail sections. One of the earliest examples of a semi-displaced hull is the Starboard K15 designed by the late Jim Drake, a unique design which has proven itself in many a long flat water race. In order to overcome stability issues, the paddler stands within its hull which has considerable width. It is in some sense a canoe without side walls - however race rulings have yet to address the issue of what constitutes a board per se and what does not - regardless, it is thought provoking.

180

Some (few) designers are now incorporating greater degrees of displacement in their hull designs as paddler skill levels improve demanding more challenging rides. This is being offset by increased board thickness, larger side walls and in extreme cases, lowered stand in-side hull recesses for the feet.

Semi-displaced hulls are designed to partially climb on top of the bow wave and separate the transom from the stern wave. It takes a lot of power to drive a hull in the semi-displacement speed range, when it incorporates a bow which is permanently 'engaged' - the biggest problem being, that once up to the board's upper threshold of speed, the required effort to push over the bow wave ultimately encroaches on the paddler's level of physicality.

Some designers have addressed this issue by simply disengaging bow contact with the water all together, in creating a swept-up nose, which relies also upon the paddler's weight to raise it free of the water line.

Jamie Mitchell's 14' board of 2010/11 was a recognition that greater board thickness was required throughout on race boards and with the addition of concaves and rounded rails the board raised the bar in terms of performance and the demands made of the rider. This was also used on his 12'6" design. A Pin tail ensures smooth release and closure of water as it leaves the board's under-surface. Added volume addressed the issue of stern-suction where the paddler's efforts results in bow lift and stern suction causing excess drag. Many boards during 2010 were released with low volume tail sections which led to poor performance on account of stern-suction in particular. This problem was addressed very quickly, with much greater volume being added throughout the board's entire length.

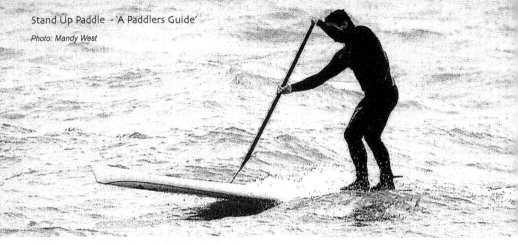

A good example of a board which looked to have a great deal going for it, the 12'6"
Starboard Pin, however the tail lacked volume which caused it to suffer from stern-suction.
Relatively short boards (12'6" and under) with very low volume rear sections, make it
mandatory to bias your weight forward of centre, to essentially disengage the stern, while
'engaging' the bow by lowering it. This however causes the bow to generate a greater bow
wave which is also a negative. The 'sweet-spot' on such boards are only within a very limited
range. Many boards have 'gained some weight' and got fatter as a consequence.

Photo: Steve West

Brian Szymanski's prone
paddle board inspired 'Surf
Race' design of 2010 saw
more volume added to the
boards length throughout
to reduce stern suction. The
nose is rounded and bulged
so as the water makes
contact with the hull first,
which therefore breaks
water up rather than
creating a definitive bow-
wave. Under the water, the
hull was semi-displaced
making it easy to catch
small runners and resulting
in less drag at low speeds
in flat water.

Boards designed for racing in a variety of water conditions / environments, including Battle of the Paddle (BoP) styled boards, tend to be designed with wave piercing bow lines with some degree of semi-circular cross sectional curvature within at least the first quarter of their length, flattening towards the mid and aft section into what can only be described as a flat planing surface. Such hull shapes are a compromise in cutting through waves and chop and on occasion 'surfing' back to the beach or perhaps catching runners when paddling downwind. On flat water, they remain relatively hard work, preferring broken surface-tension between the hull as you might encounter in choppy water.

Planing hulls

Planing hulls are designed to climb (rise) up out of the water at high speed and hydroplane on top of the water. Perplexing, is why so many boards fall into this category - the answer is stability, but the downside is a high degree of friction and drag at low speeds. At planing speeds, water is breaking cleanly from the rear and the hull is riding on its flat mid / aft sections. The greatest resistance at planing speed is frictional resistance. It takes greater amounts of power to climb out of the water, up and over a bow wave, than it does to maintain planing speed once reached, however, with up-swept nose rockers, a bow wave is effectively negated from the equation.

While hulls with a greater degree of cross-sectional curvature (displacement) in small choppy downwind conditions, will tend to latch onto runners with minimal (less) effort, they tend to fall off early if constant strokes aren't taken, whereas a board with less cross-sectional curvature of similar length and width, though it will require greater effort to get onto the runners, once latched on, will tend to ride this energy source for longer periods of time with diminished amounts of effort required to do so, on account of planing (lifting) free of the water thereby reducing drag. The higher energy expenditure here, is spent in getting to the point of planing, much like the power required from an engine to achieve planing speed. This is the domain of downwind board designers, who also go on to incorporate double concave hulls to further encourage lift at speed.

Original stand up paddle boards manifested from the basic longboard surfboard design, designed by surfboard designers whose world is essentially flat, save for a bit of rocker curvature on occasion (fore and aft) and a few

Water must flow freely from the tail / transom. Back eddies will serve to hold the board back in failing to release the water and this is easily evidenced by observing the water flow off. Slow speeds and square tail shapes do not make for the best release of water, hence why sleek rowing sculls have pointed bows and sterns and why some designs now, negate the extremity of the tail being in contact with the water. Wider tail areas are used on power boats with good reason; they are planing hulls which must cope with stern suction caused by the motor - fortunately the water 'hardens' at high speed. Stand up paddle boards are slow on account of the feeble amount of power a paddler can deliver - only when wave power takes over, do the rules change. The challenge for designers at the 12'6" end of the spectrum are diverse, not least of which is ensuring suitable volume in the tail section to prevent stern suction, yet allow for clean water release. Pin tails provide the cleanest release of water, but the least surface area and herein lies the problem, so as rounded square and square tails are common-place.

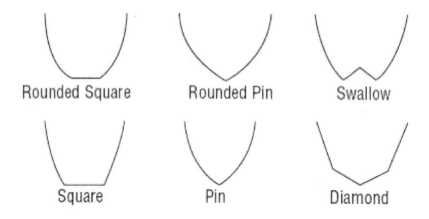

subtle curvatures here and there. Such hull shapes are in simple terms, a 'drag' when it comes to flat water paddling. Slow, but stable.

A flat hull shape is essentially a planing surface, which at low speeds on flat water, results in high levels of drag. High wind downwind paddling can result in the required speeds for such a hull to plane, offsetting the downward gravitational force (weight) of the rider and reducing drag.

Notes on stern design / stern suction

In regards to the evolution of race boards, some fundamental mistakes were made early on, more especially of race boards within the 12'6" range. All hull shapes generate lift at the bow and squat at the stern which causes some of the hulls weight to be supported dynamically. The faster the hull goes, the greater this affect. The ability of the design to negate this negative trait to bring about stability and a reduction in lost power through what amounts to

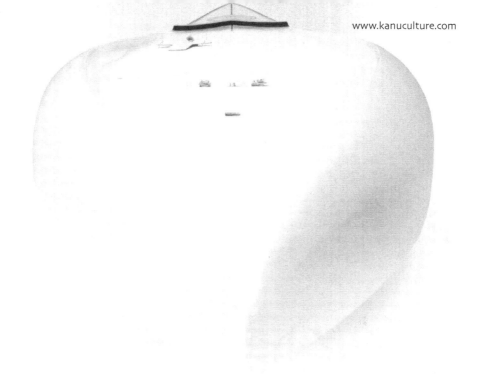

Pin tail designs offer the best water release regardless of slow or high speeds; however, the problem comes in designing adequate volume (buoyancy) into relatively short boards and 12'6" is still short when compared to say solo racing OC1 which is nearer 21ft. In purest terms, long, narrow streamlined is best always in paddling parlance. This is the rear end of a Starboard Point 14'8" Mark Raaphorst SIC design, a board ahead of its time on many levels; in terms of design and construction. 14'8" is not a lucky number for this board as it falls into no-mans land so far as race rules are concerned, but remains a board approaching a product of divine intervention, axed from the Starboard line up as fast as it came. It does however have a very flat hull shape, so as it 'sticks' to flat water and only breaks free at speed in the rough.

stern suction and therefore drag, will result in improved hull speeds. Many boards have been produced with tail volumes insufficient to offset this affect.

Ultimately, stand up paddle board (race) designs, are more restricted because of what is happening behind the centre-line as opposed to what's in front of it when talking in terms of improving hull speed through a reduction in drag. Therefore stern shape, form and function, is in fact more often than not, more critical than bow shape. By example, take a row boat, weight the bow so as the square transom breaks free of the water, then paddle it backwards so as the bow becomes the stern and it will perform better (faster) than vice-versa.

Hull trim is a factor of the physics and hydrodynamics of the fluid it sits in, which is not always entirely related to its contact against the water's surface. Lift at the bow, is generated by an increase in pressure against the skin (hull) relative to the nominal energy line (i.e. still waterline) and as a consequence, squat is caused by a decrease in pressure relative to the nominal energy line at the rear (tail). Additionally a board's relative buoyancy will be affected by whether the board is paddled in fresh water or salt, where fresh water results in the board sinking even further as a result of fresh water being less buoyant.

At speed, a displaced or semi-displaced hull shape is lower (relative to the still waterline) than when stationary, which results in some of the hull's weight being supported by the dynamic pressure differential, hence why they need plenty of volume to offset this factor.

Paddling harder eventually gets you to a point of diminishing return when you consider speed returned to effort applied. Being in tune with how this feels and at what point you have reached it, is a valuable learning experience. At this point you have very probably outgrown your board.

For any given board design, once to the point where the distance between the waves formed are about as long as the boards length, the tail wave will naturally be behind the tail and the bow wave forming somewhere about 1/4 of the way back from the bow. The tail will be stuck in a trough of its own

Square tailed Fanatic, Pin tailed Surftech 'Mitcho' board. *Photo: Mandy West*

making and the bow trying to push up over the bow wave. At this point and depending on the board's design, you will attain hull speed - where it then takes a disproportionate amount of effort to go much faster.

Tail shapes are critical to the release of water from the underside and rails of the board, a fact often considered more critical than bow shape - though efficient design of both is preferable. Most semi-displacement boards will have an immersed (in contact with the water) tail with adequate volume to provide lift above displacement (slow) speeds (preventing stern suction) but this creates turbulence and drag at slow speeds.

This turbulence occurs until the board reaches a speed where the water flows cleanly from the bottom surface (planing speed). True displacement hulls rarely have an immersed rear end. Lately, designers have been getting around this by adding rocker so as the tail is free of contact with the water at low speeds with the paddler stood further forward. At higher speeds the tail makes contact with the water, but is compressed and flows more freely.

When the underside passes through water, it must split the water, which naturally must join back together with its passing. This creates in effect a depression in which the board must sit. At planning speed, it lifts partially free from this hole. In parting the water, some is pushed aside and some is pushed down. As speed increases, it takes more effort to push it down, than to push it aside, as the water in effect, hardens, as pressure increases. High speed craft (power boats) which power their way onto the surface and skip over it like a stone, require relatively wide and flat rear sections.

However, in the case of low powered craft such as stand up paddle boards which remain low in the water, though may plane marginally (downwind boards) the tail is often upswept (rocker) and often sharp to close the water behind smoothly to avoid drag. For non-planing human powered craft, long and narrow requires less effort to achieve higher speeds, but they will generally handle less weight. Such designs minimise water disturbance, barely breaking surface tension of the water (i.e rowing sculls).

Bow or nose designed boards

Front end designs vary greatly. Some boards have definitive bows, others up-swept noses as a continuation of the board's rocker line. Boards featuring noses are not displacement boards on account of this singular feature - this is determined by the hull's progressive overall cross-section.

Wave formation is a major cause of bow lift and stern squat and as speeds increase, the waves formed by a bow, leads to an increasingly sharp 'V'eed' wave, resulting in greater drag and a deeper depression in which the board sits. One of the designer's objectives is to limit the size of the bow wave created.

Conventional Bow Shapes

Pointed bows create minimal resistance at displacement (slow) speeds. At faster speeds however, the wave making resistance increases exponentially because the board is trying to climb on top (over) the bow wave, meanwhile the stern is being sucked down by dynamic forces from the hole created in the water as the board moves forward, which can lead to lateral in-stability.

A conventional bow features a forward-sloping bow shape that starts at the extreme front of the vessel and drops down to meet the waterline. The beginning of the waterline is moved backward and its form is less sharp. The result is a bow that pushes waves, downward and forward. This absorption of energy slows the board. Waves created at the bow, equate as drag, which serve to deplete the energy of the paddler who must push against this uphill effect.

Sturgeon nose / Ram ended / Reverse sloping bows

A variance of the conventional forward sloping bow shape is the reverse sloping bow / nose shape. This has been associated with such craft as the sturgeon-nose or ram-ended canoes used in the interior of British Columbia and Washington by the Kutenai, Kalispel, Salish, and Sinixt people. Tahitian canoe makers have used this principle for many of their racing va`a (outrigger canoes) with great success.

A backward-sloping bow starts at the extreme front of the vessel. This allows for the sharpest possible continuos bow shape, which smoothly divides both waves and calm water. Increased volume above and up front allows the vessel to efficiently deal with larger waves. This design minimises spray (wave

Sturgeon nosed canoe of British Columbia tribes people.

generation) and promotes a soft entry into the waves. As the waves are parted efficiently, wave energy transfer is minimised. This means that speed losses are reduced.

Taken a step further, as the bow submerges, much like the nose of a dolphin riding the wake, the shape lends itself better to travelling under water than that of a conventional forward projecting bow which creates drag as it tries to resist submersion which leads to a slowing of the craft.

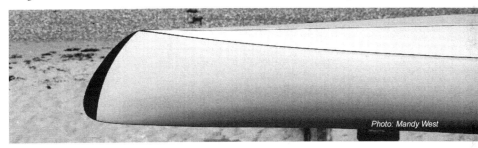

Photo: Mandy West

A Naish 12'6" race board incorporates a sturgeon bow. Below: A conventional bow shape tends to push the bow wave forward and wave energy is moved against the hull, making for greater speed losses (right).

12'6" remains a relatively short board in the context of stand up paddle boarding when you factor in boards of 18' at the upper end of the scale. The eternal hydrodynamical question becomes whether to 'engage' or 'disengage' the bow relative to the boards very short sweet-spot and the heavier you are, the less of a sweet-spot you'll have. The swiss designed 12'6" Nidecker features a sturgeon nose and low volume, so as it wave pierces rather than attempting to avoid nose diving.

Photo: Steve West

Jamie Mitchell engaging the bow.

Photo: Dana Edmunds Courtesy of Ocean Promo

Bow sections may cut the water cleanly and work well in chop (especially upwind) but they create their own bow wave in the flat, which once formed, create large amounts of drag to which end the paddler has to attempt to push over it for any significant gains in speed; near impossible. The raised rocker of the nearer of the two boards, without bow, breaks the water up in a random manner underneath and may not seem as efficient on first glance, but does in fact negate the need to push over a self-made bow wave in flat water conditions.

Concave Hulls

Commonly used on high speed craft, concave hulls are used by some downwind board designers. They are designed to be functional and efficient in extremes of conditions and speeds and will on occasion feature a 'V' tailed cross-section in helping to permit easier rail transition at speed on account of the water being compressed and if a concave is incorporated, water is further accelerated out the back.

Single and double concave designs, produce lift with laminar flow channeling water under the board. A concave creates additional lift when water runs into the aft section of the board's template, where the template turns into the tail and crosses the path of the water flowing towards the tail, lifting the tail under the rider's back foot. Air can be channeled between the hull and the water, breaking surface tension - reducing drag.

Photo: Steve West

When the paddler weights the rail and the underside of the board, they compress the water, channeling it through the concave when at high speeds. The rocker, template, rail and fin arrangement, provides the compressed water with a channel of escape out through the tail section of the board. This phenomena, accentuates the acceleration of the board through it's turns. These designs are prevalent on many downwind style boards providing added lift at speed, as the water is compressed and accelerated out behind the board.

An F16' SIC downwind board with double concave underside; an effective means of compressing and directing water while providing some amount of lift. Note the 'hard' rails.

Downwind board nose designs

Here the rules change for all manner of design parameters - rail shapes and designs all altered to suit. Such boards tend to feature 'noses' not 'bows' leaning more towards that of a windsurfing board style, designed to avoid nose diving by increasing the upward sweep of the rocker-line at the front, creating a board with a nose not a bow that is not in constant contact with the water.

Photo: Steve West

Two very differing designs. The 14' C4 V1, though not dedicated to down wind paddling, uses a combination of high volume, rocker and a definitive vertical bow to prevent nose diving. In contrast to the F16 next to it, the V1 is designed to punch through on-coming waves. The F16 is purely conceived to go down wind, where the designer aims to avoid nose diving not on account of volume, but simply through added rocker and the need for the rider to shift their weight to the tail to raise the nose - though the V1 paddler can also move their weight to avoid impact.

Nose diving at speed is a negative. Heavier paddle craft with greater inertia and horse power, such as an OC6, can nose dive with less negative outcomes. Indeed some Tahitian va'a are designed not to resist nose diving and are designed more along the lines of a torpedo or submarine form.

100% concentration is required when 'dropping in' in order to avoid nose dives in steep sections. Here, Connor Baxter works the rear of the board, weighting the rear foot to lift the nose whilst engaging the hard rails and ensuring the fin is fully engaged. The low volume nose slaps the trough here without fully diving.

Rail shapes

Rail shapes are really not that spooky or mysterious. They come in two basic variants 'hard' and 'soft', where hard means there is a definitive edge which separates the underside of the board from the board's edge (or rail) or soft where the underside of the board rolls around without a definitive edge. What needs to be understood is how these two types vary in affecting the board's handling and interaction with the water.

Hard Rails (hard edged)

Hard rails are added to provide additional directional stability in holding the board on a straight course, especially at speed. The hard sharp edges bite into the water and minimise lateral movement. Hard rails are more common on longer boards and you will find they are generally added into the rear and mid section, corresponding to where the board is likely to plane, while further forward the rails will tend to be soft. Rails remain soft from mid way up to the nose on these boards to avoid 'tripping' at speed when downwind paddling; the rail biting causing the board to react adversely. Rails toward the front are kept soft for this reason.

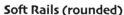

Soft Rails (rounded)

Soft 'rounded' rails of varying degrees and severity, offer the least assistance in regards to directional stability, which translates into making the board 'loose' for want of a better term. Soft forward rails will allow a longer board some lateral movement which in effect cushions some of the impact while preventing the board from being suddenly re-directed through the rail 'biting' in after re-entering. Softer rear rails, permit the board to turn with less resistance to sudden redirection and are common to stand up paddle surf boards.

Observation of these differing rail designs and how they alter or have been used in combination will provide you with a great deal of information with regards to the designer's intent for the board's handling. Hard rails for control at speed and directional stability; soft rails for looseness and manoeuvrability.

As a consideration, hard rails offer less resistance and drag than rounded and in effect permit the water to be shed with less suction or resistance, whereas soft rails, cause the water to bend (roll) around the edge of the board, leading to the water being somewhat more adhesive to the rails which increases drag.

Fins (single fin)

Fins as a basic principle, provide lateral (sideways) resistance in offsetting lateral pressure, which assists the board in maintaing forward momentum and for the rider to maintain control. They are in effect a counter-poise device. The downside of all fins, is that they generate drag as a by-product in providing lateral stability.

Much like the fundamental principles associated with blade size of a paddle, which must offer up just the right degree of resistance without too great a trade off of drag, fins must be matched to a number of basic considerations, which can extend into a micro-management of the board's handling characteristics.

The functionality of being able to change between differing fins (or creating differing fin configurations; single, double, tri or quad in the case of stand up paddle surfboards) is one of the micro-management, performance altering controls the paddler / rider has available to them. For the most part, off the shelf boards are supplied with only a basic fin, to keep costs down, with the intention that if you need to up-rate the fin from the factory supplied model, you can, but be prepared for the added expense which can be high. Cost will be a factor of material used, workmanship, weight and branding.

The design complexities of fins is akin to rocket science or at least the makers would have us believe so. They may be high aspect (deep and narrow) or low aspect (short and wide), possess various flex properties, variance of curvature and all in all it has been made into a complex science, some of the machinations of which are bemusing to say the least. Bemusing as it might be, getting it right is nevertheless important.

A fin for all occasions

Whether you're racing in flat water or water where there is lots of debris or sea weed, grass or kelp, or downwind paddling, these scenarios will affect the handling of your board. The ability to change fins, is in the same performance consideration as when changing between paddles and represents a micro-management factor you can evolve into your approach to paddling.

It's important to keep in mind that flat water race boards in particular are slow-speed craft and the temptation is to be sucked into fixing a go-fast fin offering more lateral resistance and consequently more drag than required. There are many considerations to take into account. Flat water K1 (racing kayaks) have very small rudders / skegs fitted for this exact reason. On the other hand, when downwind paddling, you will stray into high speed territory and the rules of engagement will change accordingly - hence we have low and high speed fins.

What is the pre-dominant shape of the board's rails; hard or soft? Hard rails will provide added lateral resistance, whereas soft rails will not. In this sense to what extent is the inherent design of the board aiding directional stability.

The relative width of the rear section of the board will be another factor to take into consideration and to what degree is the board high aspect (long and narrow) or low aspect (short and wide). High aspect boards with narrow tail widths will generally offer greater degrees of lateral stability, whereas the reverse is true of low aspect, wide tailed boards. For any given race day or paddling scenario, wind strength and direction will affect the board's line of travel as these external factors will serve to push the board off-line. In addition, side chop will want to push the board sideways. Upwind you will be more reliant on rail shape, though you don't want a fin so short, so as to 'pop' out.

Downwind you will need to consider wave steepness and the period (time) between wave crests and your relative speed. Long downwind boards in very steep sections can run the risk of the fin 'popping' free of the surface or loose traction on account of cavitation formed by air bubbles. At high speeds, low aspect fins will need to be replaced with longer fins of 9" and greater.

Your body mass is an additional factor, as the heavier you are, the greater the resulting lateral force will be acting on the board and therefore a longer fin depth (or one of greater surface area) should be considered and the same could be said of very strong paddlers, who may literally over-power their board.

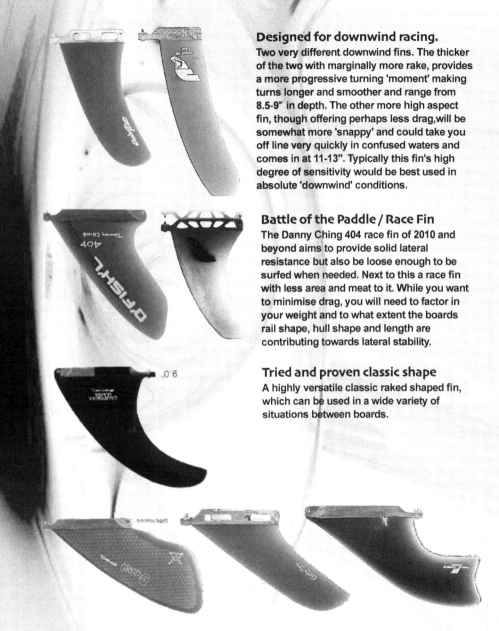

Designed for downwind racing.

Two very different downwind fins. The thicker of the two with marginally more rake, provides a more progressive turning 'moment' making turns longer and smoother and range from 8.5-9" in depth. The other more high aspect fin, though offering perhaps less drag,will be somewhat more 'snappy' and could take you off line very quickly in confused waters and comes in at 11-13". Typically this fin's high degree of sensitivity would be best used in absolute 'downwind' conditions.

Battle of the Paddle / Race Fin

The Danny Ching 404 race fin of 2010 and beyond aims to provide solid lateral resistance but also be loose enough to be surfed when needed. Next to this a race fin with less area and meat to it. While you want to minimise drag, you will need to factor in your weight and to what extent the boards rail shape, hull shape and length are contributing towards lateral stability.

Tried and proven classic shape

A highly versatile classic raked shaped fin, which can be used in a wide variety of situations between boards.

Weed fins

Throughout California in particular, sea grass, kelp and sea weed of all descriptions is omnipresent which has spurned an entire range of fins designed to keep you on course while the radical rake back permits the weed to roll off the leading edge. Always a good idea to keep one of these in your grab bag of extras.

The bottom line here, is that you are free to experiment and that fins do for the most part offer the paddler / rider the opportunity to 'tune' their board to a variety of circumstances. Be warned though, you can spend a veritable fortune on a singular fin which will promise you a list of benefits beyond your wildest dreams when in truth, there may be more to be gained from improving your paddling technique or fitness levels, before micro-managing at this level.

High speed downwind paddling

While you may be less concerned with lateral stability when downwind paddling, you'll want a fin which permits smooth, responsive rail transitions. If the wind is more on your quarter and you have to keep compensating, you may find a high aspect fin a handful, whereas something with a bit more meat in its width and angle of rake could help.

8

Synergy

Why it's good to know the paddle sport family tree,
the evolution of paddling techniques and where terms such as
'Hawaiian' and 'Tahitian' paddling styles originated.

The term 'waterman' has become over-used and abused with the advent of stand up paddle boarding; perplexing, given that a singular interest or skill in one water activity does not a waterman make

Nuka Hiva Marquesas Islands
Team Outrigger Australia.
Photo Steve West

Why it's good to know your history

Being that stand up paddle boarding has a very strong association with the sport of outrigger canoeing, whether you grasp this reality or not, it is a matter of fact and therefore some background regarding the evolution and traditional aspects of paddling technique and how they have evolved to this point, will I believe help provide a sound platform around which to understand your own paddling.

Ultimately, no reasonable discussion regarding paddling technique can be complete without some understanding of its evolution and acknowledgment of key events and interventions. For the most part, some self-proclaimed experts often take a far too narrow view of the issue; micro-managing the various phases of the stroke, seeking perfection while often missing the big picture of what makes some paddlers fast.

Many, if not most, world-class, rough water ocean paddlers have had little or no 'technique' training. Their skills are largely self taught and honed through a way of life dedicated to ocean paddling. This is often in stark contrast to the flat-water K1 (kayak) or C1 (canoe) paddler who emanates from a culture obsessed with technique, style and the science of paddling. This is not to suggest that the analysis of sound paddling technique and styles have not been considered – far from it, but there is also a great deal of intuition involved and natural ability.

1820 - Missionary intervention.
Purity and parity remain in Tahiti, but not Hawai`i.

Prior to the arrival of the missionaries in the Hawaiian Islands in 1820, (aboriginal) Hawaiians clearly had their own defined paddling style. For over fifty years however, there was an effective ban on paddling, resulting in the intricate nuances of the Hawaiian outrigger canoe paddling technique being partially lost.

The detailed intricacies of Hawaiian outrigger canoe (wa`a) paddling technique was reintroduced to Hawai`i, not through written text, but ideas passed down orally - a tribal dissemination of knowledge. It has been suggested that the so called 'Hawaiian Style' of paddling that was reintroduced, was not an accurate copy of the original, given that most of the elders had passed on, but it was near enough true to the original.

In contrast, on the islands of French Polynesia, no such ban was imposed, so it is considered that their technique remained true, unrestrained, free to evolve and in essence there was less adherence to tradition. In this context, two major variants of paddling techniques have been created out of these two canoeing cultures. This legacy remains to this day, with an ever continuing melding of interpretations and ideas from many different regions of the world. In effect, we now have a third major contemporary technique, which may be considered Anglo-Polynesian.

In the early 1880s, outrigger canoe racing was introduced to the July 14th Bastille Day events in Tahiti, however lagoon racing had been a way of life prior to this. Until 1976, this was the only official race in the region. From 1945 to 1965, there was a gradual increase in the development of organised racing with the creation of ten new clubs on the island of Tahiti. During the early '70s, the sport grew rapidly and the Ligue des Pirogues was established in 1973 to formerly administer the growth of the sport.

TEAM Maire Nui

The last five years of the '70s saw some of the most significant and contentious changes to outrigger canoe paddling technique and equipment. Hawaiian paddlers were confronted with the Tahitians joining the world stage for the first time at the Moloka`i Hoe (A race between the island of Moloka`i and O`ahu) of 1975. Over the course of the next four years, their participation and successes shook the foundations of a sport Hawaiians considered their own. For all that is good and noble regarding 'traditional' Hawaiian wa`a paddling techniques, it took other regions of the world, less constrained by tradition and more concerned with speed to break the mould.

At the start of the 1975 Moloka`i to O`ahu Canoe Race, three Tahitian teams took on the Hawaiians in their prestigious event. Fred Hemmings who at the time was steering the Outrigger Canoe Club team recalls, **'Three Tahitian teams blew off the line in a sprint with a stroke count of what must have been 65-70 strokes per minute. We were sprinting too, our stroke count went from the traditional 42 strokes a minute up to what was the incredible pace of about 48-50 strokes per minute. By Lauu Point, the three Tahitian teams had at least a 300 yard lead...we eventually ran them down in the Channel. The Tahitians spawned great revelations in canoe paddling. Hawaiian tradition was replaced with innovation and new techniques.'**

The Kaiwi Channel. The holy grail of ocean paddle sports testing grounds.

This was the first time Tahitian teams had entered the event and in doing so the legacy and legend of the Tahitian paddler was born. Maire Nui won the fibreglass division in 5:47:33 and their win was far from 'lucky', they had already been famous throughout French Polynesia since the club's founding in 1948. Not only did they win in their first attempt in the fibreglass division, but went on to win again in `76, `77 and `78 in the Koa division.

Another Tahitian crew, Te Oropaa, won the fibreglass division in 1976, in 7:54:40 ahead of Maire Nui. To add insult to cultural injury, this year's course was the longest ever run, 55.6 miles. Putting their success into greater perspective, at this time no formalised ocean distance racing existed in Tahiti, not until 1978; between Tahiti and Moorea and back.

How did these paddlers train, what paddles did they use, what was their paddling technique, how did they go so fast? Consequently, a great deal of analysis and melding of ideas between Hawaiian and Tahitian paddlers followed. These years were the most significant and affected the consciousness of every wa`a paddler throughout the Hawaiian Islands.

The Tahitians presented to the Hawaiians a paddling stroke which required less body motion, less reach out in front and less pull back past the hip. In addition, their stroke rates were way beyond that of any Hawaiian team and they used paddles that were uniquely teardrop in shape, with smaller blade area. If this wasn't enough, they introduced new, sleeker racing va`a, shaped by Tahitians living in Hawai`i, which in time would effectively be banned by Hawaiian rulings.

Fundamentally, these wins hit the Hawaiians right where their pride resided; ocean skills, athleticism and knowledge of what was 'their' sport. From paddle to canoe design, through to the act of paddling itself, the paddlers of French Polynesia together with their coaches, mentors and artisans, had elevated the sport of outrigger canoeing to a level of technical excellence and obsession from which all regions of the Pacific could only continue to marvel and learn from. While for many of us the sport is a part of our lifestyle, for the paddlers of this region it is more a way of life that carries with it much greater levels of meaning and raison d'etre.

'In no other country in the world is outrigger canoe paddling, or any other sport, as important as it is in the Tahitian Archipelago. We cannot yet ask why this is. Yet we should revel in the fact that it is so, and be inspired.'
Dr Hugh Fisher.

Photos Steve West

OC1 paddlers benefit greatly from stand up paddle boarding in core-strengthening and bringing into play hip flexors and the lower body, while the stand up paddle boarder can benefit from learning a more intimate lowered perspective of the water and the chance to work a little harder aerobically and improve general levels of fitness. Rider Chris Maynard. Many ocean paddlers also paddle surf skis or kayaks. The torque (rotational twist) as used in these sports has been added to good effect to the canoe / SUP stroke, however the notion of pushing forward with the top arm has diminished in recent years with more emphasis on a downward, lateral movement of the top arm. Rider Jasmine Kelly

C1 paddling in particular, as an Olympic sport, has come under a great deal of scrutiny because of the gravity with which Olympic sport is esteemed. By osmosis some of this intellectual study has passed onto outrigger canoeing because of the depth of research and in a sense by default this is now applicable to stand up paddle boarding. Whereas perhaps OC paddling needed to revert to C1 paddling for some technical insight, it remains exclusively a flat water pursuit, practiced kneeling and by nature asymmetrical, whereas OC paddling arguably emulates more similarities associated with the stand up paddle board stroke and is understood enough now to be the obvious chalice from which to sip inspiration. In the context of stand up paddle board sprint racing, C1 paddlers such as Jim Terrell, have adopted paddling on one side without switching, hyper-extended leg split with rear knee near to the deck.

Mainland USA influences

In 1978, while the Tahitians won the Koa (traditional wooden canoe) Division of the Moloka`i Hoe, the fibreglass division was won by Blazing Paddles, a Californian team who used what were considered to be very radical paddles at the time. The paddles were lightweight, short, had smaller blade areas and single bends with 'T' grips that were borrowed from Olympic class canoes. Attempts were made to ban this type of paddle. They were abandoned when it was discovered that the Bishop Museum in Honolulu had drawings and artefacts which included T-Grip paddles.

Billy Whitford a key member of this team, remains as one of the sport's off island legends. His lateral thinking contributed greatly to making the sport more ergonomic, through the introduction of river canoe paddles and new paddling techniques. He was also extraordinarily supportive in mentoring and coaching the most successful women's crew in the history of the sport, Offshore California.

The Californian's technique was considered an Olympic technique where the blade is placed close to the canoe hull and enters and exits vertically. The power was generated by vertical downward power, a technique which was adopted from marathon river canoe paddling. At this time, the blade areas were smaller than those being used in Hawai`i, had a square rather than tear drop shape and included lay back - a bend in the shaft. They did however, continue to pull the blade past the level of the hip, so the handle would be level with the stomach as recounted by Billy Whitford and their stroke rate was marginally less than 60/min. Over 60/min he believed at that time, was excessive, labelling it Slippy-Dippy paddling with elbows and wrist.

1980s Hawaiians begin radical change

At this point, Tahitian, mainland American and Hawaiian paddling techniques were all very different from one another, each one based on a different theory and belief. The Tahitians were going purely on instinct and evolving their technique naturally. Mainland Americans were considering what they had learned through Olympic canoeing and river canoe marathon paddling. While the Hawaiians continued to hold on to their traditional techniques and paddles.

Traditional Hawaiian notions of paddling technique were being challenged head on and not within Hawai`i, but from regions where tradition was not going to stand in the way of speed. By the early 1980s the Hawaiians, under siege since the mid 70s, had little option but to rethink everything they knew about the wa`a stroke and the paddles they used.

For the most part, the Tahitian style of paddling dominated the minds of paddlers, as teams moved towards higher stroke rates and even considered the use of double bend paddles as favoured by Tahitians. Clearly adopting any one particular style of paddling, makes it necessary to consider the entire package holistically; paddle, paddler, paddling technique and craft must all be suited to ensure the absolute best performance and the same can be said of stand up paddling.

It wasn't until 1981 that Hawaiian teams began serious experimentation with open river canoe paddle designs as introduced by the Californians. Gradually at first, then in a sudden dramatic shift, traditional designs were cast aside in favour of what amounted to a far superior design; a lighter, more efficient and ergonomically pleasing to use stick. The issue now became one of blending these paddles with paddling technique.

1990s - Aussies introduce aggressive hybrid stroke

The Australian's win in the Moloka`i Hoe races by Outrigger Australia 1991 and Panamuna OCC 1992, once again raised questions regarding technique, but also levels of physical fitness and professionalism. The sport had only been in Australia since 1978, relying upon a couple of imported Hawaiian 4 person surfing canoes and a Malia six person canoe imported in 1981.

Australian's initial interest was purely the attraction to an ocean sport and relished the idea of competing in Hawai`i and ultimately the winning of this prestigious event. There were no limits of traditional 'does and don'ts' and no cultural affinity with the canoe whatsoever for these brazen Aussies. In many ways, this allowed them to start with a blank slate as they took paddling technique to another level.

Both Outrigger Australia and Panamuna crews were comprised of elite surf ski paddlers (lifeguards and ironmen) who brought with them unique ocean skills and levels of fitness rarely seen at the event. It was yet another

While prone paddle boarders may use their hands for propulsion, the synergy with the stand up variant, resides in their intimate knowledge of the nuances of how their boards interact with the dynamics of the water on a craft which has many similarities. Eyeballing the water at surface level, a prone paddle boarder gets to see and feel the water in a unique way. Stand up race board design shares a close affinity with that of prone paddle boards, hence designers of these boards are ideally positioned to add input to current and future designs.

Photo Steve West
Currumbin Australia

cultural wake up call for the Hawaiians and indeed the Tahitians. Such was the physical prowess and ocean skills of these athletes, technique and style seemed almost a secondary factor in their ability to make a canoe move faster than most.

Though their sense of timing was less than impeccable, their technique was aggressive, explosive and ultimately unique to the sport. In addition, they used a fast stroke rate, upwards and at times over 70 strokes per minute, even faster than the Tahitian crews of the time. They used paddles similar to those favoured by the Californians and a variation of the Olympic Style paddling technique incorporating greater elements of body rotation (torque) as used in surf ski paddling and kayaking.

A magazine article following the 1992 Australian victory quoted, **'Then in 1991, the Outrigger Canoe Club of Australia won, broadening the competitive horizon by a few thousand miles. "Aussies are year-round professionals," says Kaakuahiwi. "To me, that's taken away from what the local people have been used to. For us, paddling is a lifetime thing, not something so painful that after a couple of years, you don't want to do it anymore. We have family programs. But the way the best crews train is so advanced now that if we (Native Hawaiians) want to win again, we'll have to start looking for thinner boys and thinner girls. And there goes our tradition. You don't see too many thin Hawaiians."'**

Putting the wins of the Australians into some perspective, most crew members, especially those from Panamuna, had barely spent any time whatsoever paddling an outrigger canoe. Some had but a few training sessions in such a craft, while others at best, three seasons of intermittent sessions, slotted between their respective primary sports, pitted against paddlers with up to 30 years plus experience, whose primary sport was outrigger canoeing. Their combined ocean skills, aggressive paddling skills, elite levels of athleticism and highly driven, competitive natures had much to do with their win.

Greater body rotation as used by surf ski and kayak paddlers was beginning to make inroads into outrigger paddling. Much of the emphasis centred on reach and power at the front of the stroke, with an early exit at the hip. This allowed for the generation of power from the larger muscle groups by rotating around the spine, with less emphasis on the downward drive as promoted in river paddling.

211

Tahitians adapt Australian technique

As a result of Outrigger Australia's impressive win in 1991, Gabby Lou - father of Lewis Laughlin, of Faa`a Canoe Club of Tahiti at the time, took notes and studied the Australian paddling style. He then blended this with the Tahitian style to create a winning technique which would help them win the Moloka`i Hoe in 1993 and 1994. Notably he increased the stroke rate upwards and over 70 strokes/minute and shortened the stroke length further, a style which became known as Chilly-Dipping on account of the short sharp movement. In 1993, for the first time in the history of the event, the time went below the 5hr mark with a crossing in 4:55:27 setting a new record. Within French Polynesia, Faa`a dominated during the late 1980s, through to the mid 1990s. Tahitian crews today are once again dominating the Kaiwi Channel.

The Tahitian stroke defined - 'Quick n' light'

It need be understood, that with regards to discussion of the Tahitian stroke, all that is known of what defines it, comes from what we know of their outrigger canoeing (va'a) stroke, in difference to the 'traditional' Hawaiian stroke. Significantly, it must also be noted, that the Tahitian preference for double-bend paddles, with some shaft flex and larger blade areas (in difference to those used for the Anglo-Polynesian technique) form an important part in carrying out the Tahitian stroke. Double bend paddles are yet to make inroads into stand up paddle boarding.

The technique is aerobically demanding and aims to keep the craft up and running being as there is very little time allowed for deceleration. The recovery distance is shortened and the entire emphasis is on working the front portion of the stroke, where some 75% of the propulsive power is believed to exist. A shorter shaft will permit a faster turn-over of the paddle and for the paddler to get behind and over the stroke, vital to making this stroke effective.

Quick (explosive, accelerated power phase), short stroke length (early exit at or even before the level of the hips), shallow entry (blade is not depth-charged beyond the level of the blades shoulder), elbows, wrists and shoulders are moved in a slightly exaggerated rotational manner and as part of the rotational movement, rather than the body. The top arm pushes marginally and lower arm pulls explosively, just as the shaft passes through vertical, the blade exited very soon after. When this technique is applied using a single bend paddle, there is no emphasis on pushing with the top arm when shaft is vertical - just rotation and some compression. The stroke rate is high and emphasis on the 'up-front' pull at all times.

Of note, Tahitian OC paddlers typically have excellent strength to weight ratios, in fact 'heavy' paddlers simply don't make their top OC teams as they believe there comes a point where your weight simply overtakes your strength endurance levels. High stroke rates aim to keep the craft moving at a high average speed with little or no deceleration time period.

The Hawaiian stroke defined - 'Slow n' heavy'
The 'traditional' Hawaiian stroke is in complete contrast to the Tahitian Stroke. Whereas the Tahitian stroke can be thought of as 'Quick n' Light' the Hawaiian stroke is 'Slow n' Heavy' by comparison. It's also fair to say, this stroke if emulated entirely, would be seen as fundamentally outdated, having been modified into what can be considered an Anglo-Polynesian variation.

The strokes taken per minute are significantly slower than of the Tahitian stroke, with emphasis on a long reach out front to initiate pull and a long push past the level of the hips. This is essentially a pull / push stroke. There is greater exaggerated body movement, with a falling forward from the hips motion, the blade driven deeply at entry, beyond the level of the neck so part of the shaft is significantly submerged, the blade then actively pushed past vertical and beyond the level of the hips.

In the context of stand up paddling technique the paddler would more than likely be compressing downwards and lowering the knees, which results in a somewhat rotational stroke, whereby the blade follows a crescent shaped path under the water, rather than a more consistent lateral one. This technique leant itself to a long shafted paddle and certainly suited larger, heavy paddlers of old, who relied upon this less aerobically demanding stroke, with a slower rating and more reliant upon strength than strength endurance. The very much longer recovery time due to the added distance required for the paddle to be lifted and carried back to the point of entry, provides a longer period of deceleration in which the craft can slow. Historically and culturally speaking, the stroke suited the heavy indigenous Hawaiian paddlers, canoes and paddles of the time.

The Anglo-Polynesian stroke - 'Torque n' compression'

This essentially melds the Tahitian and Hawaiian techniques and adds in elements used in surf ski, kayaking and C1 paddling, discarding what is seen as surplus to requirements and adds in some critical elements such as greater emphasis on torque (twist) around the spine, so as the larger muscles are engaged making the stroke more sustainable.

This is the stroke that is used today in Hawai`i, California, Australia as the old Hawaiian way of paddling has long since been diluted with the advent of shorter paddles, smaller blades, higher stroke rates. A long reach out front is seen as critical, the body is twisted away from the paddling side during what can be considered the wind-up, the blade is entered by lowering the shoulder. Once the blade enters, the paddler begins to un-wind, twisting into and towards the paddling side.

The emphasis remains on the front section of the stroke (Tahitian) with an early exit. In the context of using the double bend paddle, the blade is angled forwards and at an upward slant by bringing the top arm back so as the elbow is bent, near level with and behind the top shoulder. This is a critical factor. If the top arm enters straight out in front, reach will be lessened and the paddler cannot get over the stroke in order to compress the blade downwards and across the body resulting in a significant loss of lift on entry.

The blade is driven downwards and laterally through the upper hand, the lower arm initially pulls, then the arms are locked as the body rotates keeping the shaft as vertical as possible for as long as it takes for the lower elbow to naturally fall away and bend. A single-bend paddle is used and the shaft length is cut as short as is feasible so as the paddler can get over the stroke and so as a relatively high stroke rate can be maintained. Importance is still placed on exiting the paddle early at near hip level.

Overall this is quite an aggressive, explosive stroke. Smaller blade surface areas, flatter blade templates demand compression of water against the blade face, from the moment the catch begins.

Evolution of the stand up paddling stroke

Evolution of the standing paddling forward stroke may well be considered to be only just reaching some levelling out, but one thing is certain, being a new sport, it would be naive to think that the act of paddling is something new to the likes of those who hail from a lifetime of active

Photos: Steve West / Fiji International Rudderless Va'a Hoe (V1)

215

Mana

participation in paddle sports, more notably outrigger canoeing and of course river canoeing. Some level of disrespect is certainly given unwittingly by those who are unaware or ignorant to the many hard core paddlers who are now stand up paddle boarding and what it is they bring to the sport.

Add to this river paddlers, whether Canadian Open Canoeist or Kayakers across the USA and perhaps Dragon Boaters and all others in between, no doubt they will bring their own variations. The overwhelming influence in so far as ocean stand up paddle boarding is concerned, this has initially manifested from outrigger canoe paddlers of the Pacific and currently include such luminaries as Dave Kalama, Aaron Napolean, Jamie Mitchell, Travis Grant, Danny Ching, Thibert Luissea, Todd Bradley, Kai Bartlett and many more besides.

From 1995 to the present day, there has been a gradual refinement of paddles and of paddling techniques. Paddle makers have worked with paddlers, as shapers would work with surfers and many participants are rising to the

Photo: Steve West / London Boat Show
Rider: Annabel Anderson

217

challenge by improving their fitness levels and improving their skill through cross-training.

With a significant number of outrigger canoe paddlers from Hawai'i, California and Australia in particular entering the sport, they bring with them all that they have learnt and known of the variations of paddling styles and techniques, of paddle design and training. The Tahitians loyalty and love of their national sport of outrigger canoeing (va'a) may well see them sit back for a while before we see the sport becoming mainstream there, however their love of paddling will make it inevitable and significant.

Many arm-chair theories regarding the optimum application of biomechanics (technique) of the forward standing paddle board stroke exist. What we can say with certainty is that if we had to identify a direct lineage to that of another paddle sport, then we could safely say the outrigger canoeing forward stroke, as the closest descendant, being that outrigger canoe paddlers of Hawai'i, then California and Australia quickly took up the sport in true pioneering spirit, applying what they already know of outrigger canoe paddling theory and technique.

Elite Australian ocean paddler Kirsty Holmes at full stretch, exemplifies the Hawaiian outrigger canoe stroke which has been embraced as but one of the major identifiable standing paddle board techniques.

Photo: Steve West / Raiatea
French Polynesia / Vahine Race Hawaiki Nui Va'a
Paddler. Kirsty Holmes

Any theory surrounding paddling technique must take into consideration the craft, the paddle and the paddler. Your biggest challenge will be in rejecting other people's reality and replacing it with your own, that is to say, you will over the course of your paddling lifetime, hear many differing variations of 'how to' however, you should not alter your technique for the sake of it, in the absence of reasoning behind it.

Different strokes for different folks - Technique and style

'I believe in moving the board past the paddle with the larger, stronger muscles. Don't pull the paddle through the water, you won't go as far per stroke. Most important is planting the blade before pulling on it. Exit at your feet. My race pace and hard training pace is about a 10-minute mile (6-6.5 miles an hour) depending on the wind and currents. My stroke rate ranges from 44 to 50 strokes per minute.' *Jim Terrell.*

'Depending on conditions, I like to paddle with a quick stroke pace, where the stroke ends at your feet.' *Chuck Patterson*

'I like the Tahitian stroke because it is lighter and places less strain on your muscles and joints…it's easier on the lower back, because you keep your back more upright. It's more about rate and technique than brute strength, so it also doesn't create as much lactic acid. You can accelerate quicker too, when you're trying to catch a swell. I don't use it 100% of the time, though. Going back and forth between the Tahitian and Hawaiian (longer, deeper stroke) helps to minimize fatigue.' *Dave Kalama*

In a rapidly changing sport, paddlers are increasingly concerned with perfecting a personal paddling style. While we may define a particular paddling technique as 'best' for a given paddle craft, we must remember that there is no one style that is best for all paddlers. Technique is essentially a defined how-to. Style is inherent to (and often limited by) the bio-mechanical and physiological make-up of the paddler. What suits the individual best, is what tends to work best.

If we can think of ourselves as machines providing power to drive the board through the water, each paddler is essentially a different engine type attempting to achieve a similar goal. Bio-mechanically, we all operate in a more or less similar fashion, but 'more or less' means a lot in regard to the different ways we apply and move our bodies to create the

Photo: Steve West / London Boat Show
Rider: Bobby Cooper / Mandy West

most efficient pulling of the board up to the blade.

So far as what affect the differing Hawaiian and Tahitian strokes have had as a cultural island divide in approaches to paddling styles with regards the stand up paddling stroke, we can see it is significant, if not confusing. Understanding of these origins, as defined by these rival paddling island nations, where outrigger canoeing is a national sport, will always remain significant.

Static and dynamic paddling techniques

Comparisons with Olympic canoeing can provide us with some understanding of the variety of paddling techniques used. Two primary techniques relate largely to the degree to which the paddler bends from the knee and hip during the stroke, while the movement of the upper torso remains essentially the same in both.

These are referred to as, 'static lower body frame' and 'dynamic lower body frame' techniques.

Spend any time watching a variety of paddlers and you will notice how some remain relatively upright during their stroke cycle. They rotate only in a twisting fashion from the hip and waist with a dropping of the upper shoulder to plant the blade (Tahitian). Others rotate marginally and lower their entire torso almost squarely from the shoulders, moving low to the board, seemingly pushing the blade in more energetically, while maintaining a hunched over position at the exit phase of the stroke (Hawaiian). This in some regard defines 'traditional' paddling techniques.

When short bursts of speed are needed its a natural response to 'choke' the lower hand down the shaft in order to deliver more direct power to the blade engaging the smaller muscles of the arms, pushing harder downwards and across the body line. By definition, this is a form of 'dynamic' paddling.

The paddler applies greater body weight 'over' the stroke and the lower arm aligns at a more efficient level to deliver greater direct force to the shaft.

Having shortened the distance of the lower hand relative to the blade face, but having widened the gap to the top hand, the lever arm has essentially shortened. As you lower your body, your top hand and elbow may be above your head if your paddle is overly long.

Photos: Steve West

What seems obvious is that many paddlers, rely on a mix of both techniques, both static and dynamic - perhaps more static for distance paddling / adventuring / cruising and more dynamic when short bursts of speed are required for race starts / chasing runners / wave catching / sprint racing. Some paddlers however adopt either technique regardless in all circumstances. Ideally, you need to learn a variety of paddling stroke types in order to blend with the circumstances / conditions.

Dynamic paddling

Dynamic technique incorporates leg movement as well as that of the torso and because of this, it is also referred to as 'inertia transfer technique'. Dynamic technique relies on a substantially greater amount of the body weight during the entry and pull of the paddle. There is a reliance not only on upper torso rotation but on a thrusting motion from the hip and knee, where body weight adds inertia (forward energy).

There is active movement of the upper body in the stroke. The body is leant into the stroke at the reach phase, with a bending and twisting around the hips. This is generally practised by smaller paddlers, women and junior aged paddlers.

The body should bend forward from the hips in combination with torso rotation and a slight degree of alternate bending and straightening of the leading leg; the offside leg remaining stable. This allows for greater reach and utilisation of body weight. By marginal straightening of the legs during the power phase of the stroke, we emulate dynamic or inertia paddling technique to some degree. This being said, the dynamic technique is by nature technically harder to perfect. It is therefore preferable to learn the static technique first.

High, top arm action at the set up phase just prior to entry, ensures the elbow is raised above the level of the head. The upper torso dips low in order to achieve maximum application of body weight during the power phase of the stroke.

One of the obvious problems that comes to mind with the dynamic or inertia technique, is that such large movements creates a potential for longitudinal and lateral instability of the board. This could cause it to sink and rise both lengthways and sideways in time with the forward and backward motion of the paddler. This is undesirable as it increases then

Photo: Mandy West / Hayling Island England

decreases the wetted surface area of the hull and causes the board to be subjected to varying degrees of resistance and theoretically reduces its glide.

It is critical that the paddler rotates from the hips, while lowering the leading shoulder to ensure smoothness in this motion. This technique is predominantly used by shorter, lightweight paddlers. Single-bend paddles are better suited to this style of paddling.

All too often, stand up paddle boarders 'throw' too much of their energy downwards, not enough forwards, coupled with 'pushing' the paddle way past the level of the hip and feet. All of this amounts to greater degrees of counter-productive movement, when longer, smoother, more lateral pull will bring about more speed, with less effort and drama.

Static paddling

Predominantly, this is a more upright paddling position, suited to taller individuals who have plenty of leverage and upper body strength, though it is also used for lower speeds and cruising.

Static technique requires that the lower frame, below the hip, remains relatively stationary while the upper torso leans forward and rotates. This is the only movement.

Static **Dynamic**

Paddling in a more 'dynamic' way, requires excellence of timing, lots of trunk rotation and leading with the shoulder. Smoothness is essential to counter greater body motion. 'Bobbing' squarely downward from the hips is counter-productive as it simply drives the board downward.

The arrows attempt to reflect the energy flow.

Static technique relies predominantly on the power and leverage of upper body to pull the board through the water. Generally speaking, tall paddlers, both male and female, tend to adopt a more upright, or static paddling technique.

Technique - The quest for perfection

Technique and its analysis is an intellectual process that demands complex thought processes. In order to become a technically advanced paddler, you need to apply yourself to consider just what makes efficient paddling. Facts without thought can be dangerous and often misleading. If someone has told you to paddle in a certain way, with no explanation or reason given, then you have no knowledge as to why you are doing it. This often makes you less inclined to continue. On the other hand, if you are informed about why a certain action will have an effect on board speed or paddling efficiency, your understanding will motivate you to use that technique, especially if you see and feel improvement.

Technique versus style

Technique is a defined, 'how to' while style relates to any variance of this technique, brought about largely by physiological differences between individuals tending to create differences in bio-mechanical movements and hence uniquely differing styles to suit.

Variation of stroke types

If you are confused regarding the efficacy of using either fast, slow, long, short, deep, or shallow strokes in any manner of variation, the simple answer to this is that a truly accomplished paddler, possessing great paddle skills, will use all of these variants when required to blend with the liquidity of an ever changing dynamic as is the nature of wind and water.

Talking in terms of one stroke type, or one stroke rate which works best for you, is to presuppose a static environment. You will need to learn them all and know when to use them (this is not to suggest that one particular variant does not suit you best, it simply will not work in all circumstances).

A touch of physics

All paddle sports are based upon the use of a lever (a paddle) to apply leverage (power) in order to move and control a water craft. Some basic understanding of the principles will perhaps ensure you are armed with some thought behind the facts and thereby apply yourself to what can amount to a lifelong quest to perfect such principles.

Torque

Also called 'moment' or 'moment of force' is the tendency of a force to rotate an object about an axis, fulcrum or pivot. Just as force is a 'push' or a 'pull', a torque can be thought of as 'twist'.

Fulcrum

The problem with many leverage theories as applied to canoeing or stand up paddle boarding, is that all wrongly assume a fixed fulcrum point in the equation, when in fact no such thing exists in the context of these sports. Rowing yes. The fulcrum point, is the point at which energy is transferred to a fixed point (lower hand) about which the lever (paddle) moves. While the lower hand may act as a fulcrum point, it is a NON-FIXED FULCRUM POINT, considerably less effective than a fixed-fulcrum point.

In terms of physics, when we speak of the paddle being referred to as a first class lever, this is an over simplification often made by academics who don't paddle. Consequently, there has been a rethink of how the paddle (lever) is best used in order to move the board (load) which can also be thought of as a lever in itself.

Lever

A rigid rod or bar (paddle) to which force is applied to overcome resistance.

Leverage

Using leverage to wield power. Knowing where the optimum fulcrum point along the shaft is located, allows us to position our lower hand around this area (throat) in order to gain the greatest gains in leverage and delivery of power to the blade.

Centre of Gravity (CG)

Also called the Centre of Mass, is the point in any solid where a single applied force could support it; the point where the mass of the object is equally balanced.

TOP ARM PUSHING FORWARDS

This assumes the lower hand is a fixed fulcrum point and the paddle is used as a first class lever. Pushing forward with the top arm, will move the blade prematurely past vertical and encourage use of smaller muscle groups and only minor core muscle groups at best. This represents a more 'circular' blade path, the top hand going on to 'push' way beyond the lower.

The blade should be 'anchored' on account of clean catch and compression of water on the blade face. What you feel on the blade is 'resistance' in the context of levers, which resists your efforts to budge and in doing so, the net result is that you pull the board up to it. You could use a combination of techniques, but the lower is the preferred for sustainable power and activation of core muscle groups.

TOP ARM PUSHING DOWNWARDS and TRANSVERSELY

This technique aims to keep the blade 'vertical' for a delayed period when it is most efficient and acting positively with your efforts to move forwards. Rotation (torque) delivers a sustained, powerful lateral pull. The initial compression downwards, followed by a transverse movement in allowing the shoulders to follow the hips, adds to the rotational force, but importantly generates 'lift' at the outset of the stroke. This also allows the hips to be 'engaged' during the power phase. This creates a more 'lateral' blade path.

237

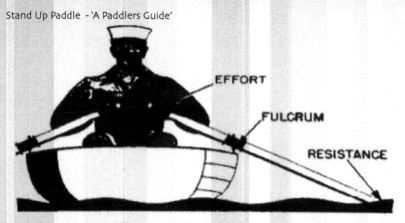

Figure 1-3.-Oars are levers.

The row boat has a fixed fulcrum point acting through the rowlocks (oarlock) which permits the oar to be used as a first class lever. No such mechanical advantage for stand up paddlers or canoeists who must cope with a non-fixed fulcrum point of a relatively puny lower hand, gripped around the throat of the shaft, which is far from fixed.

The Board

The board itself is by definition a first class lever, its fulcrum located at its centre of gravity (i.e its point of balance, somewhere around the mid section). When force is applied, the board rotates (moves) around its centre of gravity to accommodate the applied force plus any weight carried.

Photo: Steve West / Hayling Island England

Here the paddler is using a dynamic technique, the back can said to be 'planked' whereby it assumes a near horizontal plane. Hands are stacked, hand-over-hand and the paddle at this point is neither a first or a third class lever as such, until the top hand moves over the lower at which point it becomes a third class lever. The limiting factor in this instance is being able to follow through with enough rotational torque from this position. Emphasis here can be too centred on downward trajectory, rather than lateral pull.

Changed perspectives

The recent evolution of canoe paddling techniques, has led to a redefining of the classification of the lever type by which the paddle can be defined. In simple terms, the original premise was that, '**The paddle is a combination of first and third class levers, being a first class lever momentarily, up to the point where the bottom hand acts (poorly) as the fulcrum for forces produced by the upper hand when pushing forward (when in-front of the upper hand) and a third class lever when the upper hand acts as the fulcrum for forces produced by the lower hand through pull (when level with and moves behind the upper hand).**

First class lever

Pushing (punching) forward from the top arm, using the lower hand as a simple, non-fixed fulcrum point, defines the paddle as a (poor) first class lever. This however, in combination with pulling with the lower, prematurely shortens the efficiency of the power phase, as the blade goes into an early stalling pattern, so it has little or no time spent in a vertical plane, when the forces of compression acting against the blade are greatest.

Third class lever

This is said to exist as the top hand moves forward and passes beyond the lower, the mechanics shift to being that of a very poor third class lever, again on account of the top hand progressively becoming the non-fixed fulcrum and the lower, the provider of increased power through rotation.

A new approach

Studies within canoe sports, reasoned that bio-mechanically you cannot consider either the top or lower hand at any point, being suitable as a fulcrum point capable of providing quality leverage points for the paddle to be used as an effective first or third class lever. What was needed was a rethink. During the latter part of the 80s, the technique of pushing forwards with the top arm in particular came under scrutiny.

Rather than using the paddle as a mere lever, it was considered that surely it was more efficient to maintain the blade upright for as long as possible, by rotating the torso around the spine engaging the larger muscles of the torso, resulting in increased pressure and sustained drive to the blade. In effect the torso, winds-up (recovery / set up phase) and unwinds (entry / catch / power phase) delivering the bulk of the power, which transfers to the body's gearbox, the hips, legs and feet which bring about forward movement via this linkage.

'In a sense the paddle was now being considered less of a lever and more of a tool around which torque was created through the rotation of the body, as if the blade were cemented vertically into the ground below and the shaft, a vertical pole which you reached and rotated (pulled) yourself up level with. In essence think of your board sliding on rails and ahead of you a series of vertical poles to be reached out to and grabbed.'

This became the most defining recent change of mindset which has evolved as being the best way to use the paddle, not so much as a lever to be pushed forwards with the top arm, thereby engaging the blade, the lower hand acting as the fulcrum point (first class lever) but more so as a fixed object, upon which force is applied through torque (rotation) around the spine, using the larger muscles of the core, to deliver greater sustained power and therefore force.

Push

Non-fixed Fulcrum

Load

So far as utilising the paddle as a first class lever it is fundamentally flawed, as the fulcrum point is non-fixed and the musculature for pushing with the top arm is essentially weak when compared to the more powerful rotational core muscle groups. It's essential to understand the folly in over-simplifying the use of the paddle.

What happens when pushing from the top hand

Pushing forwards with the top arm, causes the blade to pass through vertical prematurely, lessening the efficiency of the blade's surface area necessary for efficient 'anchoring' through water pressure against the blade face. Additionally, the resultant offset angle of the blade as it passes through vertical, serves to pull the craft downwards, not entirely forwards.

Much is said of using core muscles, however minimal propulsive power can be generated via pushing using the minor trapezium muscles when compared to rotational torque and power generated from the larger core muscle groups associated with unwinding from around the spine. In addition, it encourages pulling of the lower arm, which triggers use of other minor muscles such as the biceps, not nearly as powerful or able to maintain continued power to the blade over time (strength endurance).

While the paddle will momentarily act as a very poor first class lever at the catch and initial pull, the object has become to keep the blade in a delayed, vertical plane, so the paddle is in effect, acting neither as a first or third class lever, the hands stacked, hand over hand, while using torque (twist) as the principal means of power delivery.

In some sense the laws of physics and principles of leverage are made complicated on account of the dealing with not one lever, but two, the viscosity of water and the lack of a fixed fulcrum. Naturally as the top hand passes over the lower, for a brief moment you enter the realm of a third class lever, but the top hand never remains 'fixed' as it naturally wants to travel as part of the process.

What to do with top arm

The top arm works most effectively in a 'downward' and 'transverse' direction across the body over towards the paddling side (not forwards) following the line of the shoulders, which follow the line and rotation of the hips, being driven by the larger muscles of the torso. In addition, it follows the direction of travel of the upper shoulder and works in a rotational fashion at the exit and recovery phase - clockwise when paddling on the left, counter-clockwise when on the right.

This is often translated or seen as pushing forwards, when in fact this is incorrect. In a sense the top arm is acting to bring about lift as the angled (off-set) blade is being driven downwards. The angle of the wrist and positioning of the top arm is critical throughout the stroke as it largely governs the relative position of the blade at its extremity, while the lower hand functions more in controlling placement and delivery of power to the blade face.

What to do with the lower arm

Correct total paddle length, relative not simply to your height, but to a combination of factors; height, arm length, board thickness while essential, will be compromised if the lower hand is not positioned at an optimal distance from the blade. Experiment for yourself in moving your lower hand up and down the shaft, to feel the variance in control and pressure delivered back along the shaft to your body. Take note of how this alters your stance in particular at the point of blade entry and which muscles are engaged.

As the lower hand moves further down the shaft, reducing the lever arm length (measured from lower hand to the centre of effort of the blade) this will encourage leaning further forward and downwards. Up to a point you will feel you are able to deliver more power to the blade and have more control over its movement.

Arms too wide apart, will lead to reduced rotation and reach and an increased use of the smaller muscle groups. Fatigue of these smaller muscles will set in early. Added downward pressure to the board through the feet due to this stance will affect board run and sustainable, smooth paddling is hindered. This is not a sustainable or efficient technique for extended periods, but may work for short burst of acceleration.

Torso 'wound-up' ready to 'un-wind'. Note position of top hand high and already poised to travel down and across the body-line to the paddling side, lower arm is not hyper-extended. This is still part of the recovery phase (swing through) and the leading hip is still travelling forwards and body rotating.

Paddler Travis Grant Photo Dana Edmunds

Due to the extreme length of the stand up paddle when compared to canoe paddles, when combined with paddling in a standing position, the positioning of the lower hand in particular has a critical bearing on your ability to manage the load acting on the blade face. Additionally, because the lever arm (shaft length) is much longer than that of a canoe paddle, where the paddler is seated, the power required to efficiently offset an increase in leverage is much greater, so that rotation around the spine, bringing into play the larger muscles using torque is far more effective than attempting to lever oneself forward as such.

Spacing of the arms

While optimising your leverage is your objective, there is a 'sweet-spot' for the lower hand around the throat, acting as the non-fixed fulcrum point, when ahead of the upper hand. Either side of this optimum point, will often result in negative trade-offs. As you narrower the gap between your hands, the less power and control you will have over the blade.

Photo: Steve West, Hayling Island England
Paddler: Mark Slater

Narrowing the gap between top and lower hand, by moving the lower hand upward to be shoulder width apart, will length the lever arm (distance between the centre of effort of the blade and the lower hand) moving the non-fixed fulcrum point away from the blade so as you gradually loose control over delivery of power / force to the blade itself.

The lower arm at the entry phase of the stroke should not be hyper-extended, there must be some bend remaining in the elbow and this again represents a rethink, which equated that straight arm chin-ups are substantially harder and more inclined to lead to injury and tendon strain as against having the arms marginally flexed at the elbow. At the catch phase, when the blade is buried and water is first compressed against the blade face, the lower arm will pull momentarily, backward and downward from the elbow (forearm, bicep and tricep) to initiate lift and drive. As the board moves up to blade and the shaft approaches vertical, both top and lower arms momentarily lock and rotation around the spine through the torso increasingly takes over in generating pull.

Hand-over-hand (vertical shaft) sometimes called 'stacking the hands'

As the shaft reaches vertical, we need to align our top and lower hands, 'hand-over-hand' maintaining rotation around the spine, controlling the power to the blade by temporarily locking the arms during this rotational power phase, until such time as the lower arm naturally wants to bend and therefore relax. This is generally when the blade is level with the hips.

This is only achievable if; the top arm is angled across the body line from the rear shoulder, the pull has been transversely executed, torso rotation and stance are correct. Failure to have your top hand over towards the paddling side at the point when the shaft is vertical, generally results in the pull not being parallel to the rail, the blade sweeping progressively away from the board resulting in direction of travel being pushed away from the paddling side.

When shaft nears vertical, continue rotation and cease downwards pressure of the top arm, keeping shaft vertical until lower elbow, naturally wants to bend and relax (near hip level) at which point the blade is exited outwards and upwards, away from the side of the board. Ensuring the blades angle of travel is close to the rail of the board, will contribute in breaking surface tension (in flat water) between hull and water as the blade edge travels partially under the hull.

When you move yourself past the blade

Past this point, pull becomes push and the blade in affect, stalls as it progressively angles upwards. Continued push past this point, will keep the blade 'loaded' and prevent water spilling off the blade face, pulling the board downwards negating varying degrees of the propulsive power delivered to the board during the forward power phase of the stroke.

A quick snappy exit away from the side of the board, whilst feathering the blade is the recommended technique.

Note: Continued pulling past the level of the hips (not pushing) can have a positive affect on the directional stability of the board if required. The first part of the stroke will tend to push the nose of the board away from the side you are paddling, however once the blade passes the level of the hips and continues a parallel line of travel, the resulting forces tend to work to pull the nose of the board back towards the paddling side. This can be useful and so long as the blade is maintained relatively straight during this period, board run can be maintained without pulling it downwards.

Postural issues

One of the most difficult technical aspects of delivering power to the blade is avoiding paddling in a 'hunched' over style as this effectively negates a great amount of residual drive and power available through the inherent weight of the upper torso. Paddling with hunched over back and shoulders contributes to driving the hull downwards during the power phase of the stroke and to some degree even during the recovery phase (swing through to entry).

Arching the small of your back just prior to the recovery phase of the stroke, potentially creates a cantilever effect (your weight will tend to transfer marginally to the heels). Arching forwards progressively over the stroke, transferring power to the balls of the feet, will mean that you have essentially driven your upper body into the stroke, thereby adding weight and added power to the blade face resulting in greater forward pull and drive to the board.

This can provide relief to the lower back muscles when padding for extended periods of time and assumes a similar attack as the pole vaulter would when driving the pole into the ground.

The pole vaulter cantilevers (arches) their back, then through compression through the arms down through the body, the back is straightened then moves forwards to achieve the most efficient range of motion in driving the pole downwards.

9

Stance

Being that standing is the significant point of difference over other forms of sit down or kneeling performed canoe sports, it's fitting to consider this from the outset.

Foot placement is critical on many differing levels relating to board control, balance, engagement of the hips, reach and overall efficiency and effectiveness.

Determining to what extent your hips and feet are engaged or disengaged during the paddling process is central to delivering force generated back down to the board.

Balance, stance, centre of gravity

The action of paddling while standing ensures that we should spend some time considering the importance of the variance of stances we can adopt and address the issue as a matter of importance, as standing whilst delivering power to the blade is central to the sport.

Consider how many other board sports warrant or dictate the feet must be aligned, side by side and facing the direction of travel? Surfing and windsurfing demand the rider is essentially 'offset' in varying degrees in relation to the direction of travel for reasons of control and stability in countering the forces at play. Windsurfing is probably our best example being that the forces are essentially transverse, yet the resultant direction of travel, forwards.

In doing so, this sets up the rider in what is termed 'footedness' in the same way as 'handedness' dictates whether someone favours the left or the right hand, though for the windsurfer, the feet alter each time they gybe or tack but even so, many windsurfers will still favour a regular or 'goofy' stance for jumping or wave riding.

It's a natural response to want to adopt a counterpoise position in resisting being pulled forwards (as experienced when paddling) and part of this response should naturally be to offset the feet, if only marginally, so as to create a fore foot and a rear foot. Importantly the forces generated by the blade which are initially felt as lift and then a pulling forward progressively and transversely to one side of the paddler, requires that the best stance should be somewhat marginally offset, either toward or away from the paddling side and not square on as often advocated.

Neutral Stances

Neutral stances represent the least stable position to assume. The narrow base of support formed allows only for small shifts in torso movement past the level of the feet before the body's centre of gravity falls outside of the centre of pressure exerted by the feet.

Natural Stances

Natural stances can absorb lateral (side-way) forces (choppy waters) but are not ideal in dealing with the resulting forces of lift, forward or transverse pull. This stance represents normal stationary standing.

'Regular' Offset Stances

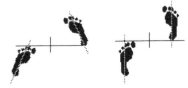

'Goofy' Offset Stances

Side Stance Left

Side Stance Right

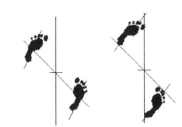

'Regular' Diagonal Stances

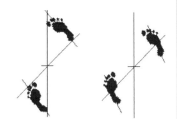

'Goofy' Diagonal Stances

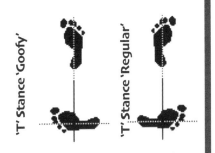

'T' Stance 'Goofy'   **'T' Stance 'Regular'**

Diagonal stances form the basis of much improved balance encouraged through a widening of the base of support area, coupled with a lowering of the centre of gravity through varying degrees of crouching. These stances form the basis of what we relate to with surfing in particular, but form the basis for sound, solid stand up paddling positions. Paddlers should learn a 'switch-foot' technique in shifting between regular or goofy stances to optimise sound bio-mechanical positions for paddling and dealing with variations of conditions.

Stability is everything

Pushing forwards with the top arm, hips square-on and limited engagement, shoulders working independent of the hips / waist area, standing in either a neutral or natural stance, serve to shut-down the core, negating rotational forces of torque and compression, which in turn lead to a lack of stability. Stand up paddlers who are inherently 'unstable' on account of poor connectedness to the board, are quick to label many boards 'tippy' when it is they who are tippy, not the board.

Equal distribution of pressure on both feet using either regular or 'goofy' stance.

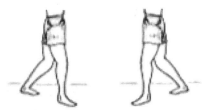

Greater pressure on the forefoot weights the nose to encourage 'dropping-in', turning, controlling angle of nose.

Shifting pressure to the rear foot, commonly used when avoiding nose diving or when paddling over on-coming wave / shore break.

Paddler Travis Grant

Outrigger canoeing (OC6) relies upon a leading leg as does C1 paddling and therefore the paddler can be considered to be paddling offset. Fencing requires a leading and a trailing leg, the advantages of which are improved balance, stability, control and power in thrusting forwards or retreating backwards. Boxing and martial arts are all centred upon balance, posture and an ability to deliver power through the arms through body rotation.

In consideration of stand up paddling, we must factor in the paddle as a vital component in assisting balance (not hindering it) and how this affects a shift in our centre of gravity as we swing through the stroke and how torque created through rotational forces, can be best delivered.

The study of stance and balance is known as anatomical kinesiology. Bio-mechanically, balance is determined as the ability to maintain a vertical line from centre of gravity (near navel height) through to the base of support (the feet) with minimal postural sway.

Balance requires coordination of input from multiple sensory systems including the **vestibular senses** - organs regulating equilibrium, the **somato-sensory senses** associated with **proprioception** or the sense of awareness of the relative position of neighbouring parts of the body and strength of effort being employed in movement and finally, **kinaesthesia senses**, associated with the sense of body motion through the joints (limbs) and our visual systems.

Sway

Can be considered as the horizontal movement of the centre of gravity, present even when stood upright and stood still, inevitable due to micro-functions within the body as might be associated with breathing through to gross motor movements associated with shifting body weight from side to side or shifting weight from the forefoot to the rear foot in controlling external sources as one experiences when stand up paddling.

Proprioception

This has been described as being for example, what allows someone to learn to walk in complete darkness without losing balance. During the learning of any new skill, sport, or art, it is usually necessary to become familiar with some proprioceptive tasks specific to that activity.

Without the appropriate integration of proprioceptive input, a paddler would not be able to swing a paddle without visually watching its motion in relation

Above: Regular - Below: Natural (Neutral)

Below: 'Goofy' *(named after the Walt Disney character)*

251

to the feet and hands, nor the ballet dancer be able to perform without having to watch their feet and calculate how to stand without falling over.

These proprioceptive senses can be sharpened through the practice of a variety of exercises. Standing on a wobble board or balance board (indo-board) is often used to retrain or increase proprioception abilities, particularly as physical therapy for ankle or knee injuries, which has automatically led to stand up paddling being identified as a useful activity for rehabilitation for those who may have experienced some degree of impairment of this function.

Several studies have shown that by closing the eyes when performing certain proprioceptive exercises, it encourages a more intense learning, being that the eyes give invaluable feedback in establishing the moment-to-moment information for balance.

Looking down when paddling - don't

When learning, it's common to want to look down at the feet in order to take in the information as part of proprioception learning - programming of the body's understanding of the board's nuances in relation to the water around it.

Studies however, have shown that keeping the eyes focused on a more stationary constant, often the horizon in the case of stand up paddling, will provide better balance outcomes.

The way I like to think of it, is that by looking at your feet in rough water, your conscious and subconscious minds are at odds with each other. On the one hand your subconscious mind understands you will need to respond to altered states of equilibrium (balance) yet your conscious mind is struggling to understand just what to do about it. Looking away and keeping your eyes up and letting these proprioceptive responses figure it out negates interference of the conscious mind freaking you out.

Kinaesthesia

This is well known to Olympic paddlers nurtured through constant technical training and monitoring and is central to muscle memory and hand-eye coordination. Training can improve this sense. The ability to swing a paddle, with bio-mechanical precision time after time, requires a finely tuned sense of the position of the joints. This sense needs to become automatic through training to enable a person to concentrate on other aspects of performance, such as maintaining motivation, reading external factors such as the water, tidal flow and the relative position of other competitors.

The senses must detect changes of body position with respect to the base of support, regardless of whether the body moves or the base moves or changes size. Stand up paddling ensures that all three of these senses are bombarded - the rougher the water, the tippier the board, the greater and more attuned (and well practised) these senses must be.

Centre of gravity

The centre of gravity is the theoretical point where our body weight is concentrated or the theoretical point about which the body weight is evenly distributed. Assuming a uniform body density and a symmetrical shape, the centre of gravity is in the geometric centre.

The body's centre of gravity shifts with each body movement. When the distribution of a person's body weight changes, the centre of gravity will shift toward the greater weight concentration. External loads will alter the position of the centre of gravity. When an external load is added, the concern is the combined centre of gravity of the load and the person.

Photo Steve West Paddler Ryan James

Line of Gravity

Base of Support

The only reason the paddler does not fall forwards and off the side of the board when planting the blade with downward force, is that the resultant combined forces pushing back upwards, generate pressure back to the paddler, assisting in keeping the feet firmly on the board, even though 'lift' is the initial force felt. Pushing downwards not only generates initial lift to the board but greater board and paddler stability. Here the paddler's upper body is beyond the level of his base of support. Downward pressure combined with powerful rotation on the blade provides stability. The base of support is restricted here due to the stand inside deck.

When the person lifts or carries a load, the combined centre of balance must be kept over the base to be in balance.

The greater the external load or the greater the distance the load is held from the person's body, the farther the combined centre of gravity will be from the person's centre of gravity. In the case of the stand up paddler reaching outward and way beyond their usual base of support, while applying downward force to the blade, a load is said to exist at the blade face, which must be resisted or it will pull you over. Creating a counterpoise of pressure, ensures the paddler remains stable during the power phase of the stroke. The less power you apply, the less stable you will be.

Line of gravity

This is an imaginary vertical line that passes through the body's centre of gravity and represents the direction gravity acts on a body.

Centre of pressure

This relates to the forces acting downwards into the feet in a very rudimentary sense. The CP must be in equilibrium with the persons' CG in order for balance to be maintained comfortably.

Balance

There are two types of balance: Static balance, when a person remains over a relatively fixed base (static 'upright' paddling) and dynamic balance, when a person is in motion (dynamic 'leaning into' paddling).

Stability

Stability is a quality relating to the degree to which a body resists being upset or moved. The major factors that affect a person's stability are: The area of the base of support. The relationship of the line of gravity to the edge of the base of support. The height of the person's relative centre of gravity. The mass of the person.

Area of the base of support

Several structural characteristics of the human body relate to the base of support. Static balance is achieved by ensuring that the position of the centre of mass lies inside the base of support. The size of a person's feet is one factor in determining the area of the base. In a more complex manner, the size of the pelvis is a limiting factor. Whenever a stance is larger than the dimensions of the hips, the legs form an oblique angle to the surface and this position could be detrimental to stability if there is inadequate friction to keep the feet from sliding outwards.

It is uncomfortable and often unnecessary to stand with feet apart edge to edge in a neutral stance, as this only serves to push each rail downwards more

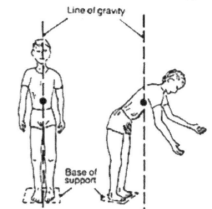

Base of support

Line of gravity

Base of support

Centre of gravity outside base of support - fall over

dramatically. It is better to move the feet away from the edges and rely upon the boards secondary point of buoyancy to return the hull back down level. Working more towards the centre line will generally allow for better board performance.

Relation of line of gravity to the edge of the base

Increasing the horizontal distance between the line of gravity and the edge of the base, will enhance stability. If a higher degree of stability in all directions is desired, the paddler should assume a stance with the line of gravity falling in the middle of the base.

Mass

Mass relates to the quantity of matter in a body. Stability is related to mass in that the greater the mass, the better the degree of stability. For a body to be moved, there must be sufficient force to overcome inertia and friction, both of which increase proportionally with an increase in mass. So to some degree, it could be said a heavier paddler's net mass, means on the basis of this singular factor, they may be more stable than a lighter paddler.

Height of the centre of gravity (CG) or centre of mass (CM)

The centre of gravity (CG) or mass (CM) is the balance point of an object if it were balanced on a pivot. However it may well not be its geometrical centre (GC). When the body is balanced around its centre of mass, it is said to be in a state of equilibrium. The centre of mass can be referred to as a pivot point around which the body can revolve, using the rotational equivalents of force, known as torques, which rotate the body clockwise or counter-clockwise using the various muscle groups.

A person's centre of mass is slightly below their belly button, which is nearly the geometric centre of a person. Males and females have different centres of mass - females centres of mass are lower than those of males because of the relatively larger mass in the hips and higher in males, because of the relatively larger mass in the chest and shoulders. It can vary with age and body build. On average, the centre of gravity of an adult standing erect lies within the pelvis / sacrum region.

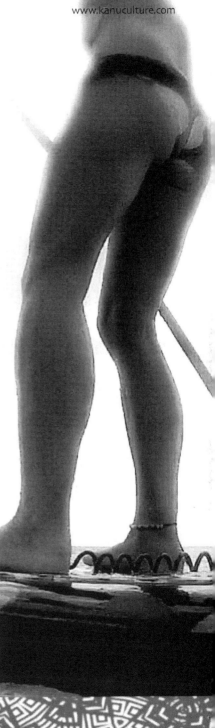

Lowering the body's centre of gravity increases stability, as it enlarges the distance the centre of gravity must be raised before it falls outside of the base of support.

Translational and rotational motion

The first condition of equilibrium is that upward and downward forces balance. There are two general types of motion caused by forces acting on an object. The first, translational motion, is the kind of straight motion which is an example of the system falling downwards under its own weight if it were not balanced by upward forces. The second kind of motion that could result from these same forces is called, rotational motion.

The rotational effectiveness of a force is equal to the amount of force (power delivered through the torso around the hips / waist) multiplied by the distance from the line of action of the force (reach) to the axis of rotation you are considering.

Universally it seems, stand up paddling is often taught in a manner in complete contrast to all of these notions, where the feet are side by side, in effect in neutral and as a consequence, in what could be called a disengaged stance, which is essentially unstable permitting the rider little or no margin for countering the many rotational forces at play, let alone the forces generated from the paddle itself.

The way in which this inherently unstable position is compensated for, is by the paddler over-exaggerating the entry phase of the stroke with enormous force as if wishing to dig a hole. While gentle cruising it could be said may warrant a relaxed, disengaged, side by side stance, the reality is, that even at slow speeds in calm water, it's only natural to want to favour a leading leg and so any amount of slight off-set should be encouraged.

Amazingly some race boards in particular, are designed to actively encourage the idea of a disengaged, neutral stance by limiting deck space or carving out a recess in which you must stand. Though at first glance, top level competitors may appear to be standing in a natural stance on flat decked boards, they generally have a preference and one foot will be marginally ahead of the other as a natural instinct.

Establishing footedness in the stand up paddler is important. If you don't take your paddling into the surf or do much down winding you may not even be aware if you are a 'regular' or a 'goofy' foot paddler? Unlocking this bit of information is essential to your overall 'set up' and advancement as a paddler.

Footedness and pedidexterity

There are several ways to determine footedness. Once you have this identified, this will give you a clue as to how you can begin to apply this to your paddling. There are some big advantages to be had in nurturing fancy footwork in leading to greater board control, management of rougher water and getting greater enjoyment from your paddling.

Regardless of your footedness, nurturing pedidexterity so as paddling with either foot forward is ideal, as it opens up a wider range of control over the nuances of the board and direction of force from the blade to the feet.

When first learning a new board sport, riders / paddlers very quickly adopt a preferred stance. Regardless, significant amounts of practice can yield high levels of pedidexterity between stances. Many stand up paddlers can switch between feet (switch stance) and more especially those who come from a windsurfing or kitesurfing background.

1. Stand feet together, have someone push you firmly from behind and see which foot you place forward to prevent your falling over.

2. Stand feet together and imagine you are going to push a scooter along using your foot, which would you use. The one you use is your leading leg.

3. From a prone position, spring up to surfing stance and see where you end up in terms of your feet.

4. Stand feet together, out-stretch your arms and have someone pull you toward them and see which foot leads out to prevent you falling.

5. Close your eyes, jump up in the air and turn and land and see which way you naturally turn and land.

There are anomalies in these tests and some folk can become confused as to which stance they prefer. In the context of stand up paddle surfing, you will at least determine which leg your leash attaches. The rear.

Anatomical kinesiology notes

The CG of your body refers to its balance point or that point in which your body balances without any tendency to rotate. For the latter reason, the CG is that point where all of the weight of your body is concentrated. The CG in an adult is normally within the pelvis region / upper third of the sacrum during the normal standing position.

The human body is capable of assuming a variety of positions, therefore the CG tends to shift as we move. As you change positions of the body segments, the CG may even be located outside the body.

Body build, age and gender affects the location of the centre of gravity. The CG in women averages 55% of their standing height, 56.18 percent for a man. A women's CG tends to be lower because more weight is concentrated in the pelvis area and thighs compared to a man.

Stable equilibrium results when CG is lowered. Crouching in the case of stand up paddling will lower the centre of gravity and increase stability.

Unstable equilibrium exist when only a slight push or pull will destroy it.

Factors affecting your CG, include the size of the base of support, the relationship of the line of gravity to the base of support and the height of your CG.

Lowering your CG by crouching, assuming a marginally diagonal stance, widening of foot placement and use of the paddle as a brace when downwind paddling or in the surf should be an instinctual response to altered forces attacking your equilibrium.

The wider your base of support, the easier it is to maintain balance. But this is not to suggest you stand with your legs wider than the width of your hips and certainly not with your feet out to the outer edges of the board as every reaction has an equal and opposite which could lead to pushing the rail up and down from side to side as the forces shift.

If you raise your arms, your CG is shifted upward and it becomes more difficult to maintain balance over your base of support. Lowering your CG, allows for greater angular displacement of your CG within the bounds of your base of support. There will be less tendency to be off-balance, hence why paddling with a diagonal stance improves stability.

The human body has less tendency to be off balance when the line of gravity falls at the centre of the base of support. If you are not certain from which direction an external force is going to act on your body, it is best to make yourself stable by having your line of gravity fall over your centre of base of support. However, the paddle can and should act as a brace and provider of stability, if used correctly, providing instant counter-balancing forces to offset loss of balance.

The greater the mass, the greater the stability. Why? Force=mass x acceleration. Stability of an object is increased, as its mass is increased, therefore taking a greater external force to set the object off balance.

The greater the friction between the supporting surface and the parts of the body in contact with it, the more stable the body will be, which requires your deck to be super non-slip.

The lower your CG, the greater your stability. Paddlers should assume lowered positions for greatest stability and for power delivery to the blade. Downwind paddling and stand up paddle surfing (river or ocean) in particular, require this lowered stance.

You will obtain greater stability if the base of support is widened in the direction of the line of force, which requires that you address these forces stood off-set diagonally ie leading forefoot and rear foot stance.

To maximise stability, the line of your gravity should intersect the base of your support in such a way that it provides for the greatest range of movement within your base of support.

The paddler who knows he will be pulled from the front and side should shift his line of gravity forward (lean forward) so that he can 'give' in a backward direction without losing balance. On occasion you will need to lean backward (move the line of gravity back) in order to absorb the forces encountered when dropping into a wave.

The greater your body mass, the greater your stability. Heavy, solid individuals are more likely to maintain balance than lighter individuals.

An individual maintains better balance in locomotion when focusing on stationary objects, versus disturbing stimuli. Look up, not down!

10

Technique

With some understanding of the sports DNA,
how can we apply this to the sport of stand up paddle
boarding to develop a range of techniques mixed with
personal styles used at appropriate times?

While it is said there is no one particular way you
should paddle, the fact remains, there are certainly
ways in which you shouldn't.

Before we begin

It's important to lay some foundations before getting too far into this section. I acknowledge two differing doctrines in situ which have manifested as a result of differing cultural standpoints, geographically offset by thousands of miles and influenced by respected paddlers within the paddling ohana (family) around the world.

These doctrines include that of the C1 paddler and the OC paddler. I will address the C1 doctrine from the outset. My experience of C1 paddling extends to training with a C1 Hungarian paddler who was ranked 7th in Europe which is credible and worthy of mention. Coming from the C1 paddling culture and myself from the doctrine of OC the differences seem profound on some levels, similar on others.

Significantly, C1 paddles are straight shafted, blade areas are substantially larger, sprinting is limited to flat water, the paddler kneels on one knee and paddles on one side only. Watch videos of C1 racing and what comes to mind is how closely the 'style' resembles the 'Old School' Hawaiian OC stroke - long out front, lopping, hyperextended arms and on occassion, significant push out the back, the top arm very high, driving downward and while there is emphasis on body rotation, not to the same degree as that of OC. (Jim Terrell has addressed this issue and has modified a technique to suit of which I share a similar view).

The C1 craft, paddle and techniques used seem to resemble many old school traditions largely limited on account of the nature of the paddle used and the craft itself. In comparison, the stand up paddle originates from the

modern day OC paddle, both in terms of blade shape and the single bend. Lessons learned of the advancement of the OC stroke in line with required advancements in paddle designs covered in 'synergies and secrets' all apply here as the preferred and more bio-mechanically efficient pathway, but with regards to stand up flat water sprinting, elements of the C1 stroke very probably take on more relevance.

On undulating water, fluidity of body and mind, in-tune with board, paddle and the nuances of the water, take on greater significance. OC paddlers of the world, are stacked deep and wide in terms of those excelling on the Pacific-wide racing scene with many more yet to come. In Europe and elsewhere, stand up paddle boarders are investing in solo outrigger canoes for cross-training purposes.

The overall picture
It's a confusing world where you have such variance of styles all based on a narrow principal of technique and then an even narrower principal of basic theory. As we move away from the theory, however scientific, the nuances and idiosyncratic difference between people soon manifest in wide and varied altered perspectives of how to paddle.

The fastest paddlers, not always the best technicians
Many consistent winning paddlers, cross the line first on account of many varied factors which could include; fitness, superior equipment, course knowledge, a will to win / sheer determination, high pain thresholds, youthfulness, experience, preparedness, natural ability, lack of quality competition numbers - but not all are winning because of superior technique, though naturally they would need to possess at least an above average technical skill level to excel.

At the time of writing, we're seeing very young and talented paddlers dominating particular race forms - on account of natural talent and having been born into water sports as a way of life; windsurfing, surfing and now stand up paddle boarding. They represent the sport's evolving generation. Naturally high levels of aerobic capacity, as associated with youthfulness, coupled with long lean fast twitch muscles, long levers (arms), lightweight body frames, equating to high strength to weight ratios, are clearly proving advantageous over many older, heavier less aerobically fit paddlers who may well in truth be technically superior.

But the fact remains, some of the fastest paddlers have somewhat unique styles far from text book, but the important issue here, is what is going on under the surface of the water.

This being said, many elite paddlers, regardless of how many line honours won, could still benefit by time spent in consideration of their technique and this is why Olympic level paddlers devote a great deal of time to perfecting excellence of technique and therefore efficiency.

Simply put, two paddlers of equal amounts of all other factors, will generally result in the better technician winning out. If you're looking for a role model, a mentor for your own paddling technique, it would be easy to always focus on the number one winner, which may lead to a somewhat blinkered view of things, which would be a mistake as it's important to consider variance of techniques and styles across a range of differing paddlers not at the very top, but maybe just off of it.

We've become obsessed with giving a consistent winner all the attention and kudos without considering some important questions. Who is the fastest paddler within a certain height or weight group and how does this relate to your own physiology? By this I am pointing out, that some paddlers excel given that they may not have all the attributes they may need to win, but one thing they may have, is excellence of technique.

Typically as the sport matures there will be a changing of the guard in terms of who dominates the racing scene. In flat water events, the bigger, heavier, powerful men who initially dominated, are being replaced by lighter weight, pocket-rocket type paddlers, where brute strength and some intimidation has taken a back-seat. This was true of outrigger canoeing as OC6 crews gradually became smaller, where strength to weight ratios, strength endurance and technique has won out over time and no truer is this than in the way Tahitian paddlers have evolved in this manner. As an extreme example, indigenous Hawaiians of very large build, have long since been unable to keep pace with their skinny Anglo-Polynesian / Pacific rim counter parts.

A great deal of myth and thoughts without facts are being served up as being the correct way to stand up paddle. Without providing facts without explanation is simply lip-service and hot air and some of this is coming from paddlers who excel in the absence of good technique.

How it often looks

The general impression formed when you watch many stand up paddlers (and many winners) is that they appear to be trying to dig a hole or drive a stake into the ground just ahead of them, but thereafter it seems there is a disconnection between the bio-mechanical action and what it is they are actually setting out to achieve; simply move across and over the surface of the water as quick and as smoothly as possible as if sliding on rails. Those who learn visually, watch others and then are simply emulating this with little thought of interpreting whether it's right or wrong.

If there's one thing stand up paddlers aren't for the most part and that's smooth. When many paddlers want more speed, they seem to resort to digging an even deeper hole, by pushing downwards with ever greater force, in the belief they are making significant gains.

The net result is that their boards 'bob' up and down in response to the paddler's movements, literally driving the hull ever deeper down into the water, thereby increasing the wetted surface area of the board in contact with the water at entry and subsequently killing off board run (glide).

It seems the more movement and wayward flailing you bring into your paddling technique, the faster you must be going on account of your limbs and the water flying about and the board's manic movements in smashing the water all around it. What is the thinking here and level of thought being advocated and what problems are associated in paddling this way?

Well they are multi-faceted, but it all comes down to the fact that one of the key qualities associated with any paddling technique or style, is that of smoothness. Smooth paddling, smooth board run. Rough paddling, rough board run. Not so hard really. It's bad enough that your board has to paddle within the depression (hole) it creates, but for you to make that hole deeper through poor technique is unproductive.

Many stand up paddlers have yet to grasp the importance of rotation, reach, smoothness, alteration of stroke rate and depth and application of sound paddling technique (let alone understanding of how a paddle actually works) which has manifested an altogether novel, inefficient, unsound, idiosyncratic style, unique to the sport, which falls way short of what could be called definitive, reflecting what seems a step backwards along the evolutionary tree not forwards so far as the art of paddling goes.

The triangular window, created between upper and lower hands, the shaft in-between and body line, forms a powerful bio-mechanically strong and sound form. The stroke form can also be thought of as triangular, where your top hand is in effect the apex. As the blade enters the water, it needs to be driven downwards only so far as needed, just beyond the neck of the blade, thereafter parallel, lateral pull upon the blade face through rotation maintains this form. In this instance, Travis Grant maintains loose hips in allowing the board to follow the contours of an undulating sea. The overall impression is one of fluidity. **THESE WELL KNOWN PHASES MAKE UP THE BASIC FORWARD STROKE.**

Phases

Downward

Upward

Backward

Set Up

Recovery

Entry

Exit

Catch

Power Phase

258

On flat water, here Jamie Mitchell is hyper-extended, creating a huge amount of reach. Lower arm is hyper-extended but at the point of entry, brought about by a lowering of the leading shoulder, the elbow bends in anticipation of the pull. Much like performing chin-ups with straight arms, the power generated is limited when compared to when some flex is added in, assisting the joints in being cushioned. Paddling with 'stiff' arms may work for you in flat waters, but in rough open water, stiff-arm paddling, will simply tense you up. Adopting a stiff / rigid upper and lower body, arm swing and pull, will cause the board to stiffen up and become erratic in its movements. You need to flow with it, not against it.

Reach

KANU
CULTURE
publications since 1994

Many paddlers start out with a solid triangular form, until the stroke takes on a circular path. Body falls forward, top hand pushes forward, lower hand pulls backward, blade rotates through vertical without delay. Lateral pull is limited, board is driven downward and a laboured push of the blade past the hips, then pulls rear of the board downward.

Phases of the standing forward stroke

The forward stroke, has traditionally been broken down into simple phases or components so that it may be better understood by the paddler and importantly so as instructors can teach and demonstrate each of these phases in some logical linear method.

What is critical in understanding your own learning curve of each of these phases, is that they are symbiotic. The success of each phase is largely dependant on the quality of the phase before it. Mastering each component is essential for mastery of the forward stroke.

Set Up Phase The point just prior to entry of the blade. Maximum twist, rotation and reach have been obtained. **Entry Phase** Placement of the blade into the water, buried cleanly with minimal 'splash'. **Catch Phase** The precise moment the paddle is fully buried and 'primed'. **Power Phase** Paddler applies load to the paddle through a combination of compression, pulling and rotation (torque). **Exit Phase** Removal of the paddle at the end of the stroke from the water into the air. **Recovery Phase** The swing through to set up.

Stand in-side boards can limit foot placement and demand smooth paddling technique. Ryan James here demonstrating long reach, lowering of the shoulder in searching for the water and at the exit point, demonstrates a clean, snappy release and a return to near standing straight position in preparation for the 'wind-up' to the set up phase.

Photos Dana Edmunds Courtesy of Ocean Promotions Paddler Jamie Mitchell

GLIDE PHASE

The glide phase is in fact a part of the sum total of the forward stroke. Knowing the glide quality of your board in glass like water conditions, will help determine optimum stroke rates, relative to your power output - measured as a percentage of effort (100% being flat out - 75% being near race pace etc).

Short 'water line length' boards will tend to require higher stroke rates per minute, as they will decelerate quicker than those having longer water lines, leading to longer glide times. Longer boards therefore, can allow you to slow your per minute stroke rate, so as to benefit from longer glide times.

Some 14' boards, only have 9' water line lengths, on account of the degree of 'rocker' added in, which will compromise glide times on flat water.

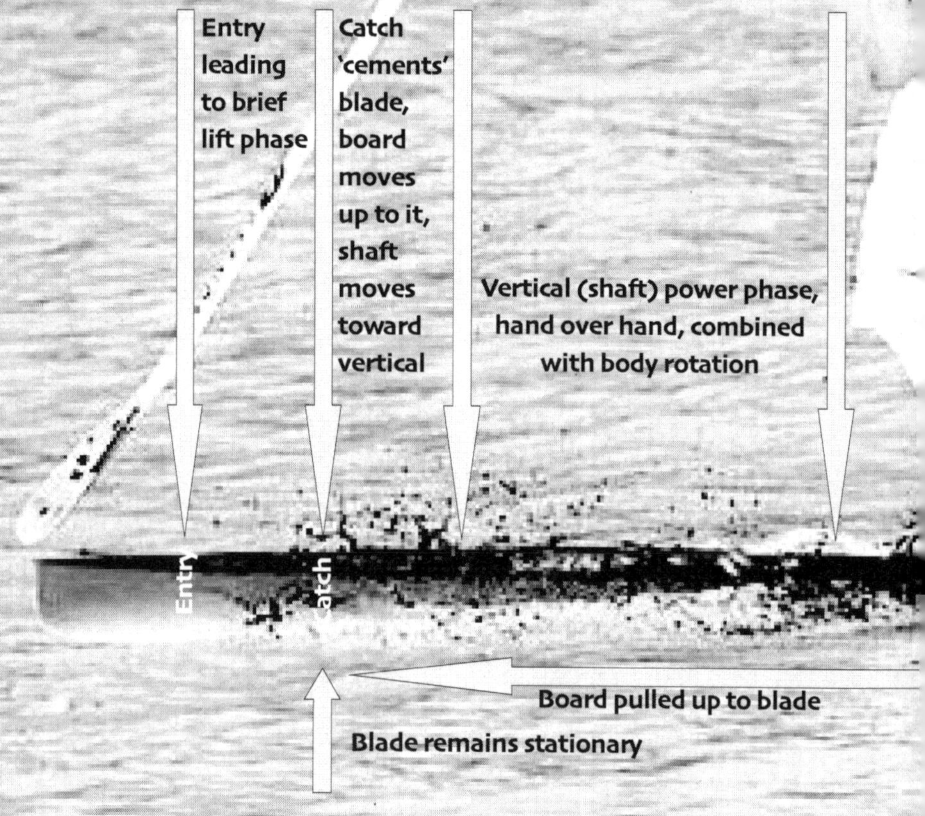

Entry leading to brief lift phase

Catch 'cements' blade, board moves up to it, shaft moves toward vertical

Vertical (shaft) power phase, hand over hand, combined with body rotation

Entry

Catch

Board pulled up to blade

Blade remains stationary

264

Jamie Mitchell

The primary power phase can be considered to commence after the catch is made and pull begins up until the point where the board has travelled up to the blade, approaching knee level, thereafter power diminishes as the paddler enters into the exit phase, to the point where the blade transfers into the air. The glide phase can be considered to be the distance measured from the exit point of origin, just behind the feet x distance travelled prior to re-entry of the blade. Glide distance tends to increase as waterline length increases. Shorter boards have less 'glide time' hence the need for quicker recoveries and stroke rates (or greater power) to avoid any significant loss of glide / speed.

Exit

Glide Phase

Total distance travelled per stroke is measured from entry to exit + glide distance, ending at blade entry.

KANU CULTURE
publications since 1994

265

A dynamic image of Travis Grant demonstrating drive downwards of the top arm, lower arm locked but not hyperextended, powerful torso rotation, shoulders following the line of hips, legs taking up the tension transferring the power down to the board, vertical shaft being maintained during rotation, top arm elbow level with the shoulder during maximum power and clearly his paddle cut down to size for ease of handling and to ensure the body can get over the stroke.

All too often onlookers will conclude that quality paddlers are pushing forwards with the top arm.

Here you can see the lower shaft is near vertical the lower hand over the level of the blade, but the upper hand has moved ahead of the lower, not on account of push, but on account of flex of the shaft due to the rotational forces being delivered.

Photo: Dana Edmunds
courtesy of Ocean Promotions

The forward stroke in brief

The power phase consists of generating compression of water against the blade face, through tension and torque predominantly engaging the larger muscles of the torso, transferred to the board through the hip flexors down through the legs to the feet. The arms act as levers in combination with the paddle acting as the lever arm, engaged through rotation around the hips ensuring the shoulders follow in alignment, with the top and lower hands, 'hand-over-hand' the blade running parallel to the board's rail. The top arm is pressured downwards (not forwards) with the lower arm locked.

Consider that an estimated 75% of the propulsive power of the stroke occurs approximately within the first 7"- 12" of pull, reinforcing the importance of the set up, entry and catch phases of the stroke.

The first part of your stroke should initiate lift as a result of the angular entry of the blade and downwards force applied, not forwards. The arms must not be hyperextended (old school). A marginally bent lower elbow brings about greater blade control and power delivery while permitting the muscles to contract more efficiently and prevent ligament injury. Avoidance of push forwards through the top arm (old school) through the trapeziums is critical, as this negates the vertical positioning of the blade prematurely and engagement of the smaller, minor muscle groups.

Note: Water is compressed against the blade face with sufficient force, so as not to spill away from its edges. It anchors itself. Poor blade shape, poor entry, can generate air bubbles along the power-face of the blade in particular, encouraging blade slippage, which may sometimes result in 'fluttering' (blade oscillation) during the pull phase as the blade moves within the air pockets. Small, flat blade areas require explosive controlled catch and pull in order to compress water against the blade. Think in terms of turning a liquid into a solid as a result of compression.

The set up

The set up, is the moment just prior to entry. If the paddler is not set up correctly before entering the blade, many things can and will go wrong. In many respects the set up defines in bio-mechanical terms, a great deal about the way in which the paddler applies themselves; in other words the technique which they are relying upon.

Fusion

Simply layering two images taken from movie clips, we can clearly see the OC1 and SUP strokes mirror imaging each other very nicely. Travis Grant simply thinks of stand up paddling as 'outrigger canoeing stood-up' as does the likes of Lanikai legendary steerer Jlm Foti and many more who hail from an OC background. For the outrigger canoe paddler, being able to practice your primary sport stood-up, serves to use the body in a more dynamic manner, but ultimately the benefits work both ways.

KANU
CULTURE
publications since 1988

For the OC paddler to engage the hip flexors and use the legs as demanded by the stand up paddling stroke, is in physiological terms a relief and added bonus as decades of sitting down on the job, can have its down sides in terms of isolating the legs partially from the paddling process even if they remain critical to OC technique.

The set up phase needs to be dynamic; think of the body being a coiled spring ready to be released. You're aiming for a long reach, clean blade entry and if you haven't any rotation going on, then it's presumed you're going to be pulling with your arms only.

Freeze-framing a paddler at this point, will show you immediately such factors as; have they rotated around the hips / spine or are they square on. Are the legs bent, straight or is one leg bent, one straight. Is the top arm elbow high and behind the level of the head or out in front and is the lower arm hyperextended or bent. Are the feet in a neutral or natural position (side by side) or an off-set and engaged position. All of these factors and more are micro-management issues which can tell the trained eye, how the paddler will deliver power to the blade.

As you move from the set up to the entry, the position of your body and legs remain more or less unaltered. Contact of the blade with the water is achieved predominantly by lowering the leading arm and shoulder. Sometimes, particularly when flat water paddling, you can incorporate an almost undefinable pause prior to entry.

Extend the paddle as far forward as comfortably possible by twisting around the spine from the hips and reaching out with lower shoulder, upper shoulder moves backwards to angle the blade. This will increase blade angle (and therefore lift on entry) and reach (entry point of the blade). The blade tip touches the water and enters as a result of the lower arm and shoulder moving downwards. Lower arm is slightly bent - not straight, chin and gaze remains upward.

It is also essential that the top arm is bent at the elbow so the grip of the paddle is closer to your body, ensuring blade angle is increased. Top elbow is raised but level with head and partially flexed, leading shoulder remains as low as possible.

Ensure a clean entry with minimal splash. Just prior to the catch, the latissimus muscle is stretched and the rubber-band affect of this stretch together with some pulling with the lower arm, is the first force that initially propels the board.

The body must be balanced, the blade over the board edge and parallel, head relaxed and along the centre line of the board. Your head is very heavy and any adverse movement will affect board stability.

In the sport of outrigger canoeing during the 1990's, it was advocated that the lower arm should be hyper-extended, however recent studies support a marginally bent elbow provides greater stability for the paddler and greater control of the blade. In addition, ensure your forearm is not angled downwards, as this will ensure an upward trajectory of the blade, rather than a lateral one. Look to keeping your forearm level with the board.

It's common practice to enter the blade as close to the rail as possible. Feathering of the blade during the recovery phase of the stroke by an inward rotation of the wrist and rolling relaxation of the lower shoulder, permits the blade to be sliced in sideways at the point of entry. It then becomes parallel with the hull as the paddle moves through to the catch.

The advantage of the blade being entered progressively from one corner, rather than flush with the surface of the water is that it produces a cleaner entry with less chance of aeration occurring along the length of the blade. Additionally, the width of the board often makes it difficult for all but a few to achieve having both hands over the side of the board on entry. This is generally achieved progressively throughout the stroke, but needs to occur as soon after the pull commences.

Common set up errors (but not limited to)

If we assume the set-up phase of the stroke is the first cycle of the forward paddling stroke, it's safe to say that if it goes wrong here, the flow on will directly affect the quality of the next phase; the entry. The following is a list of common errors associated with this phase.

Arms and hands

Lower arm too straight. Top arm elbow too straight or high (can occur if paddle length is too long). Hands gripping paddle too hard. Incorrect lower hand position on the shaft - too high, too low. Paddle not angled sufficiently to the water and parallel to the board. Forearm angled upwards, not horizontal.

Posture / body

Leaning too far forward. Hunched shoulders. Lack of rotation. Excessive lean out from side of the board. Excessive bending or hunching through the middle and or upper back. Shoulders not rotating. Standing too upright. Hips not engaged, knees too straight.

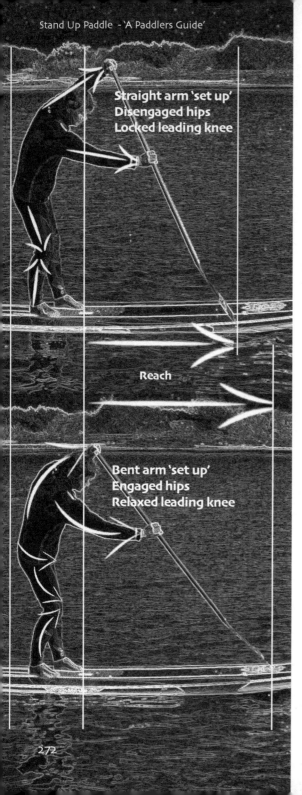

Straight arm 'set up'
Disengaged hips
Locked leading knee

Reach

Bent arm 'set up'
Engaged hips
Relaxed leading knee

Paddler has an offset 'regular' foot stance in both examples. The first example negates effective use of the hips, the second encourages active engagement.

The stroke and the follow through, must engage the hips and permit the knees to follow. Here the top arm is well above the level of the head, the lower arm is near straight (hyper-extended), there is little body rotation and marginal flex in the leading leg. Blade placement requires the paddler's entire torso to fall downwards, pushing the hull downwards increasing drag.

In this image, the top arm is nearer the level of the head, the lower arm has a marginal degree of bend and there is greater body rotation. Blade placement can be initiated by lowering the leading shoulder, keeping the body rotated lessening the affect of the upper torso weight baring down on the board. Potential reach is increased and greater power can be delivered to the blade as the body unwinds during the power phase of the stroke.

Note: The leading hip is following a natural in-swing and the inside leg is bending downwards, inwards and transversely accommodating the line of travel of the hips as part of the rotational process.

Arrows attempt to reflect pathway of trave
shaft, body and flow of energy. Paddler is
marginally offset with a regular (left forefoot,

The set up

Here the paddler is 'winding-up' turning the body away from the
paddling side. Shoulders and hips should be kept in alignment,
working in sync not independent of one another. This will
encourage core muscles to be activated. Inside (leading) leg
bends downwards, inwards and transversely in order to
accommodate the in-swing of the hip, which is following the line
of the shoulders as part of the rotational (wind-up) process.

Entry through to the Catch

Entry of the blade should be clean (especially in flat water) and pull avoided until catch is achieved, often considered the most critical part of the stroke. The paddler aims for clean entry and to gain 'lift' from the blade face trajectory. Top hand control is critical for placement of blade and its trajectory. It must move over to be on the paddling side.

Torque

Power phase

The body begins to 'un-wind' delivering power much like a coiled-spring through torque to the blade face. Paddling with offset stance, in this case left foot marginally forward, the drive to the leg shifts from the inside leg (right) to the outside leg (left) as the paddle passes through vertical. Here the shaft is vertical and blade face at its most efficient. The paddler is essentially rotating around the grip and throat of the shaft, which momentarily keeps the blade face in a delayed vertical plane.

Fluidity not rigidity.

Relax. Breathe.

Exit and recovery phases

Relax and remember to breath! This particular exit and recovery technique, uses a lateral exit away from the side of the board, a rolling of the lower wrist inwards in order to 'feather' the blade, the lower elbow kicks out and away from the body and the shoulders relaxed. This initiates the smoothest means of adding twist to the hips and in keeping hips and shoulders following a similar path.

Search and reach for water. It won't come to you. Lead with the shoulder.

Dynamic entry
A more 'dynamic' ('inertia transfer') approach to the entry and the power / pull phase that follows. Greater body lean into and over the stroke. Ensure continued rotation and lowering of the leading shoulder to bring about contact with the water. Avoid dropping squarely downward from the shoulders and hips.

The top hand

The top hand is often overlooked but represents an important controlling factor of the fine motor skills required for excellence of paddle skills. It works in an anti-clockwise direction when paddling on the right, clockwise on the left, within only a relatively small range just above and below the level of the head.

Micro-management

Fingers

Pressure should be on the lower three fingers ensuring correct wrist alignment. Thumb / index fingers provide axis point around the throat. Grip is relaxed not squeezed.

Lower arm

Note the angle of wrist, elbow and forearm relative to the board and direction of travel. At this point it is locked and the latissimus dorsi and core muscles are performing most of the 'core' work.

Where's your top hand?

If at the end of your stroke (at the point of exit) your top hand is much beyond your mid-torso, it's a sure sign your stroke is more 'circular' than 'lateral'. The top hand need only move within a relatively small range from just above the head to just below.

Where's your lower hand?

If at the end of your stroke (at the point of exit) your lower hand is below mid thigh level, it's a sure sign your stroke is more 'circular' than 'lateral'. It should be operating between the mid torso and mid thigh level.

Head / neck / face
Head hanging down, gaze focused down. Tension of the neck, facial muscles / clenched teeth.

Legs / feet / hips
Feet not braced on the board. Too much pressure on the balls of the feet. Feet too wide apart or close together. Feet too near the rails. Hips not engaged during the rotation or working out of sync with the shoulders.

Blade entry
The blade is entered through lowering of the leading shoulder, the top arm cocked marginally backward at the elbow, thereby angling the blade face upward and extending your reach, encouraging lift from the moment of entry through to the catch.

Straight top and lower arms, will diminish reach. Contact with the water using this method, is brought about by 'falling' forwards from the hips (square on) which in turn drives the hull downwards, bringing about greater drag and resistance negating board run.

If the paddler fails to rotate around the spine and enters the blade by falling forward from the hips with shoulders square on to the board, the result is downward drive, through upper body weight, which negatively affects the boards glide. This is often referred to as 'bobbing'. Universally and for reasons hard to define, the stand up paddling stroke has manifested largely into this form. 'Chilli-Dipping' is a name which comes to mind, once used by Hawaiians to describe how some Tahitian (outrigger) paddlers appeared in difference to their, at the time, long-lopping stroke.

Most importantly the entry must be clean in avoiding imploding water around the blade face which in turn creates a pocket of air which will be taken down the blade and result in blade slippage. Pulling on the blade prematurely before it is fully submersed, is a common error. You need to drive the blade deep and clean in order to achieve good catch.

Common entry phase errors
The entry phase of the stroke is very controlled yet dynamic. The paddle is neither smashed into the water nor delicately placed, you need deliberate purpose, commitment and precision. Poor entry will doom the rest of the

stroke. The key element here is to ensure the blade does not take air down with it. Ensure that no effort is made to pull before the blade is fully buried in the water.

Arms
Upper arm pushing forward before contact with water, so the blade is moving backward at entry. Paddle not parallel to the edge of the board.

Posture / body
Failure to drop the shoulder and lower arm to push the blade deep. Excessive lean over the side of the board. Early rotation causing the paddle to move backwards prior to entry.

Blade design issues
A poor paddle design can hinder poor entry. Heavily scooped paddles can cause 'plopping' which is the sound of air generally imploding on the back face of the paddle. Thick edges or poorly angled blade faces can all lead to inefficiencies.

The catch
This is the shortest phase of the stroke and the most perplexing, sometimes confused with the entry. A poor quality catch, often relates directly to entry errors. As it suggests, catch is the exact moment when the blade is fully submerged and catches or grips the water.

This requires that water is 'pressured' against the blade face. The term 'lock and load' provides a good visual narrative. The blade has been placed, 'locked' into position, then 'loaded' under pressure. The quality of the catch is largely determined by the quality of the entry and the manner in which power is applied to the blade and the design merits of the blade itself. Many experts suggest the catch phase is the most important part of the stroke. No matter how hard you rotate, pull and drive, if the blade has poor catch (grip on the water) it will simply slip backward and fail to pull the board up to the blade.

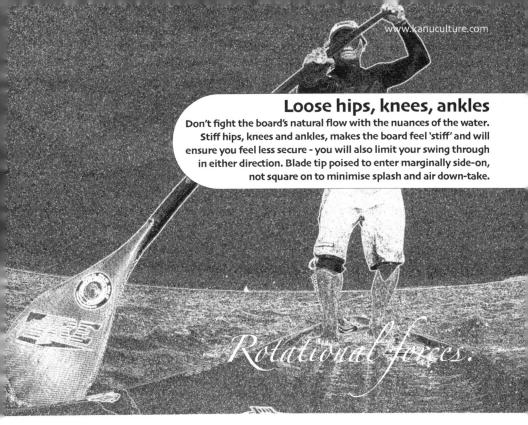

Loose hips, knees, ankles

Don't fight the board's natural flow with the nuances of the water. Stiff hips, knees and ankles, makes the board feel 'stiff' and will ensure you feel less secure - you will also limit your swing through in either direction. Blade tip poised to enter marginally side-on, not square on to minimise splash and air down-take.

Rotational forces.

The blade can be anchored or braced against the water once fully submerged. It is still being directed in a downward motion by the top and lower arms, shoulders, upper body and through the body's rotation.

Catch is achieved by a synchronised pull with your lower arm and rotation of the torso from the hips, so as you unwind from the reach position. The paddler's centre of gravity is marginally lowered as the blade remains close to and near parallel with the rails. A solid catch is essential for the next phase of the stroke to ensure the maximum use of the power-face, which should be 'primed' to take the load that will be transferred to it during the power phase.

Common catch errors

The catch is the first true 'feel' phase of the stroke. A poor catch as opposed to a good one, feels very different – a concept newcomers often struggle with. The difference equates to paddling with a butterfly net as against using a solid mass against which to pull on account of a lack of anchoring.

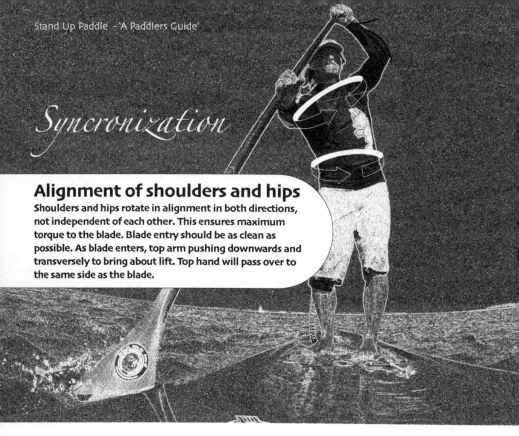

Syncronization

Alignment of shoulders and hips

Shoulders and hips rotate in alignment in both directions, not independent of each other. This ensures maximum torque to the blade. Blade entry should be as clean as possible. As blade enters, top arm pushing downwards and transversely to bring about lift. Top hand will pass over to the same side as the blade.

Experienced paddlers know the value of good catch and can quickly recognise how effective they have been in achieving it. An efficient blade shape is a key element The potential for a good catch is only as good as the quality of the entry. The blade must be nearly free of air along both faces.

Newcomers with no previous paddling experience, can benefit from a larger blade face which offers more resistance and drag, so they can feel this loading of the blade. Smaller blade faces, require greater precision of placement, speed and power in order to achieve adequate pressure.

Arms

Lower arm bends (pulls) too early in anticipation of the pull. Upper hand pushed prematurely over the lower hand. Lack of power / strength / speed.

Posture / body

Applying power to the paddle by early rotation, thereby rushing to the power phase. Excessive lean over the side of the board. Failure to commit fully to the stroke. Lack of power / strength / speed in the rotation.

Anticipation.

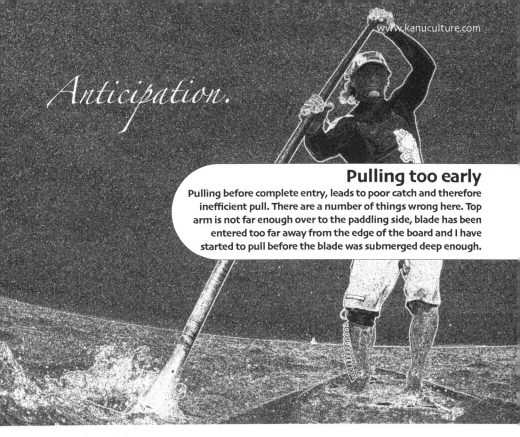

Pulling too early

Pulling before complete entry, leads to poor catch and therefore inefficient pull. There are a number of things wrong here. Top arm is not far enough over to the paddling side, blade has been entered too far away from the edge of the board and I have started to pull before the blade was submerged deep enough.

Legs / feet / hips

Not braced to take the load, too straight, too bent or feet out of position.

These common errors affect the blade's performance in terms of its potential to anchor solidly against the water. Rushing to the power phase of the stroke before establishing a good catch will negate the effectiveness of the power phase to come. Entering the blade into the water quickly and cleanly, applying downward motion of the lower arm and downward drive by the top arm so the blade is fully immersed, followed by torso rotation, will ensure the best results.

Poor catch when starting from a stand-still is common, as paddlers rush to the power phase prior to loading the paddle correctly. This is usually characterised by large amounts of splash at the entry and exit of the blade.

The power phase

The notion of 'surprising' the water should be emphasised, so the torque of the body and pull of the lower arm can be executed in an explosive yet smooth manner. This quick and sudden compression of the power-face against the water provides little escape time for the water to flow off and around it - especially critical with smaller blade faces.

"Herein lies a revelation. The blade remains stationary in the water on account of water being pressured against the blade face, which enables you to pull the board up to the blade. If the blade is moving backwards through the water, you've failed to compress the water, metaphorically speaking, from being a liquid into a solid, for the brief amount of time needed to pull the board up to blade. Never think of pulling the blade through the water. This is not what is meant to be happening!"

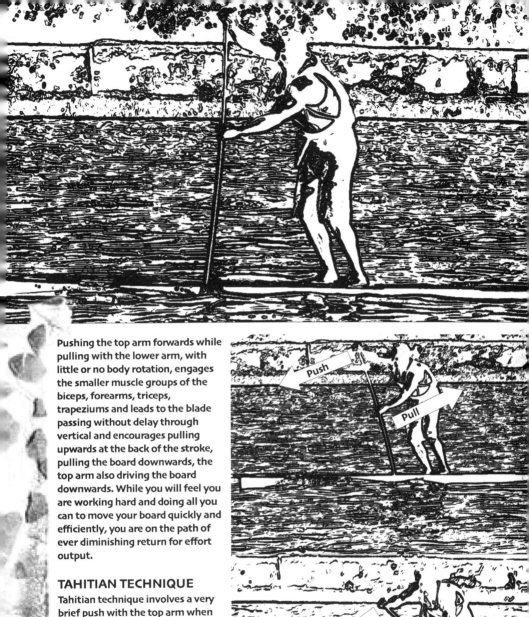

Pushing the top arm forwards while pulling with the lower arm, with little or no body rotation, engages the smaller muscle groups of the biceps, forearms, triceps, trapeziums and leads to the blade passing without delay through vertical and encourages pulling upwards at the back of the stroke, pulling the board downwards, the top arm also driving the board downwards. While you will feel you are working hard and doing all you can to move your board quickly and efficiently, you are on the path of ever diminishing return for effort output.

TAHITIAN TECHNIQUE

Tahitian technique involves a very brief push with the top arm when the blade has just passed vertical. But be clear. It is a short, explosive push only; never laboured or extended and the top arm remains high and does not pass downwards. In addition this popular technique originates entirely from outrigger canoeing, using double-bend paddles.

At the moment of entry and take up of the catch, lift will result. The top arm comes across to the paddling side very shortly after and the shaft of the paddle remains as near straight as possible for a delayed period, so as the blade is vertical and at its most effective. Lateral pull comes about as a result of your rotation and maintaining the hand-over-hand relationship during this brief, but powerful moment.

As the top hand passes below your head, it's already time to think about exiting the blade.

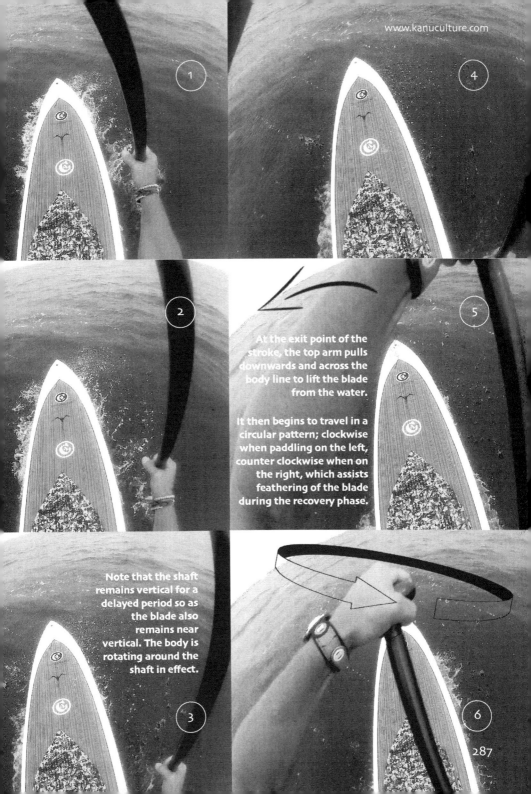

(1)

(2)

(3)

Note that the shaft remains vertical for a delayed period so as the blade also remains near vertical. The body is rotating around the shaft in effect.

(4)

(5)

At the exit point of the stroke, the top arm pulls downwards and across the body line to lift the blade from the water.

It then begins to travel in a circular pattern; clockwise when paddling on the left, counter clockwise when on the right, which assists feathering of the blade during the recovery phase.

(6)

Photos Mandy West

Parallel Pull

The width of the board can be problematic in achieving a direct hand-over-hand vertical and parallel pull through and indeed this is not necessarily the best bio-mechanical position from which to generate maximum torque and power for everyone. Some marginal benefit may be gained if the paddle is slightly offset, as it permits greater power to be generated from the body's rotation which is transferred to the blade. This is where surfski and kayak paddlers excel in using this technique because it is a natural extension of the kayak stroke. However, ensure your stroke does not 'sweep' away from the side of the board as this will diminish the forward propulsion.

Getting 'over' the stroke

Creative visualisation or at least having a sense of what you are trying to 'feel' during the power-phase of the stroke is a valuable tool in self analysis.

You want to have the idea of pole-vaulting yourself over the top of your paddle. The grip needs to be in front of you, not above you. You need to feel you are working over the stroke, not behind it. The shaft and your top arm will tell you a lot about whether you are achieving this, especially when the shaft is vertical.

An overly long paddle, will fail to give you this feeling, as your top hand will be too high above your head and is the common cause of shoulder injury and or discomfort.

Pull is initiated by the lower arm, originating from the elbow and leading shoulder, wrist and forearm, following a natural path of travel. Avoid over-reliance of the lower arm as the primary power source.

Direct the pull in a downward and lateral trajectory. Your upper arm keeps pressing forcefully, until the shaft reaches vertical, avoid pushing forward for maximum effectiveness. Keep your upper hand angled back toward you for as long as possible to keep the blade angled forward to improve power transmission and increased lift for a longer period of time.

Once your upper and lower hands are nearly (stacked) 'hand-over-hand', the body rotates around the spine, utilising the larger muscles of the upper body. Direct pulling from the lower arm ceases and simply transfers torque from your body to the blade. The sensation is one of 'squeezing' or 'compression' and rotation of the body using the the latissimus dorsi and core muscle groups.

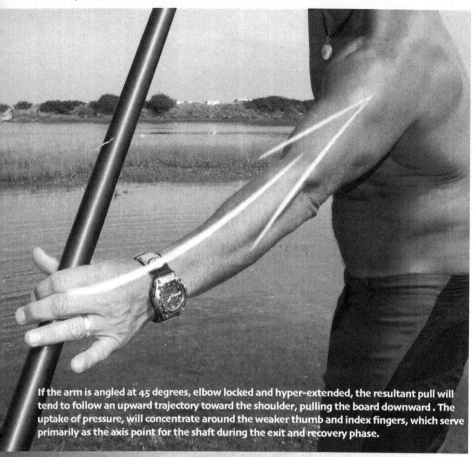

If the arm is angled at 45 degrees, elbow locked and hyper-extended, the resultant pull will tend to follow an upward trajectory toward the shoulder, pulling the board downward . The uptake of pressure, will concentrate around the weaker thumb and index fingers, which serve primarily as the axis point for the shaft during the exit and recovery phase.

Bio-mechanically speaking, this assumes you aim to 'push' forward with your top arm to generate 'pull' from the lower, non-fixed fulcrum point. This is counter-intuitive, given that all that we know and understand about canoe paddling and it's associated family tree, centres on the bio-mechanical mantra of pulling through torsional and rotatational application, not the weaker mechanism of pushing.

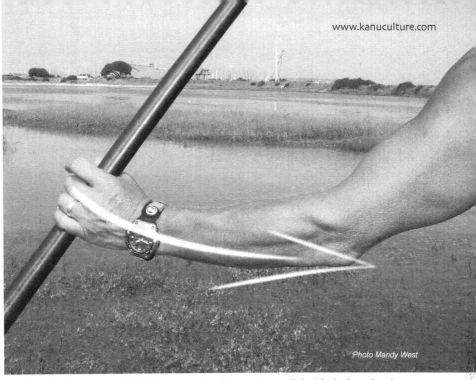

Photo Mandy West

Bending the lower elbow like this, ensures the forearm is parallel with the board and following the direction of pull and travel. The wrist and elbow are on similar angles of plane at the entry, to limit strain. Pressure should be on the middle and ring finger, not the weaker index and thumb - you wouldn't do arm-curls or chin-ups with these fingers. This encourages greater twist, torsional application, reach from the leading shoulder, engagement of the hips, bending inward and downward from the leading knee and ensures the pull corresponds to your efforts. Fingers should be relaxed, the pull should keep fingers secure provided the shaft is of suitable shape and dimension.

291

Aim to keep your upper and lower hand, hand-over-hand for as long as possible while rotating around your spine to ensure maximum vertical blade time and use of torque. Any premature push or movement forwards with the top arm, is often referred to as 'breaking the top arm' ie it simply gives-in to the load and takes the path of least resistance, resulting in the blade going into a negative incline and delivering diminished power.

Avoid moving your body excessively forward as this will encourage 'push'. As the torso unwinds, your leading shoulder moves back, while your offside shoulder moves forward, until the shoulders are square.

Once the shaft moves past vertical, as a result of the board being pulled up to the blade, your lower arm will naturally need to bend at the elbow and the top hand just below the level of your head. This signals the end of the stroke.

Summary
The initial catch is followed by a continued period of 'lift' as the angled blade is pulled down and back. Once hand-over-hand, the body then begins a powerful rotation until the shoulders are square-on. Once the board has been pulled up to and past the blade's stationary position, near level with your feet, the lower arm will naturally bend, your wrist and shoulders will relax, the top hand grip should be just level or below the sternum. The blade is then sliced outward from the water.

Lift / blade angle and the lower arm
When initial pull is applied to an angled blade, lift is the result with greater amounts of forward drive being generated as the blade moves through to almost vertical.

This lift effect has become increasingly recognised as critical. There is now increased emphasis on the pull being considered in terms of moving downward and backward while attempting to keep the blade face angled for longer and keeping this lift happening for longer.

As the blade moves to vertical, emphasis is then placed on rotation around the spine to generate torque. Consequently, we can talk in terms of a 'lift phase' which then transfers to the pull phase.

Common pull phase errors

Top Arm

Pushing the top hand forward so it passes over the lower hand prematurely, prevents the blade being vertical during the most powerful phase of the stroke. This indicates poor rotation and is often used as a way of avoiding pressure experienced during the subsequent rotation and pull.

Little power is gained by pushing forward with the top arm. While your top arm must push down at the early part of the power phase, acting on the angled blade to provide lift and drive forward, paddlers will sometimes continue to generate downward thrust past the point where the shaft is vertical, failing to rotate and pull back. This creates a circular blade path, rather than a lateral one.

Lower Arm

Lower arm pulling too early, rushing the stroke. Pushing blade too deep. Jerking the pulling action of the lower arm. Timing and execution of the transition between catch and the power phase is critical. Do not bury the blade much beyond the neck of the paddle.

Posture / bend

Back too straight. Excessive hunching. Insufficient body weight applied over the paddle. Rotation of upper torso not coinciding with gradual lift of the body as it moves to being square on, affecting energy transference along the shaft through to the paddler's body, the hips and feet. Power applied only after the blade has travelled past vertical. Blade driven deeper as it passes knee and hip, as body leans over board edge. Head not aligned and relaxed.

Legs / hips

Poor leg drive and lack of engagement of the hips or flexing of the knees.

Paddle design issues

Multiple issues can arise on account of poor paddle design including too much flex between neck of blade and shaft, too much shaft flex or not enough. Blade morphs negatively under load allowing water to spill away from edges. Inappropriate blade area relative to paddler's body mass / strength.

Exit phase

Ensure leg drive and transference of energy through your hips and feet to the board is in a forward direction, with stability around your trunk and spine. Soon after the shaft passes through vertical, your lower elbow will want to bend, this defines the end of the power phase of the stroke. Tension is released from the body and the exit phase of the stroke can begin. In flat water conditions, a clean whirlpool, 'footprint', near free of air bubbles should be all that remains after the exit. This indicates that a clean entry and good catch was achieved at the beginning of the stroke cycle and that the exit was executed at the correct time.

Upper arm is near straight and hand is level with or just below head or level with the sternum. The upper torso should now be almost upright, shoulders square, relax the lower and upper wrists and shoulders.

Your lower elbow will naturally find its own limits and bending as the blade moves towards being level with your hips.

The blade is now angled marginally backward. Draw the top arm across the body-line slicing the paddle out of the water and away from the board as it reaches the hip, the lower wrist rolls inward and the elbow outward. The blade is either lifted directly upwards and 'carried' up and forward, or 'swung' outward using a 'feathering' technique.

Common exit phase errors

Continued pulling at the point where the blade is level with the hips, will result in 'push' and 'pull-down', the reverse of the forces at play at the beginning of the stroke.

These are counter-productive. It is universally agreed that the paddle should exit the water soon after it has reached the feet or hips. This ensures that you avoid pushing and loading of the paddle, which serves only to pull the board downwards, adding drag on the blade, retarding board run.

Posture / body
Paddler fails to rotate body. Paddler over-rotates so their torso now faces outward on paddling side.

Arms
Stiff wrists, elbow and shoulders. Paddler pushes and lifts paddle past the hips, scooping the water, pulling board downwards.

Blade design Issues

The main concern here is in having a blade with too much scoop (concave) which holds water like a bucket at the end of the stroke, increasing drag, consuming paddler energy and slowing stroke rates. The blade design must promote water release at this point of the stroke.

Recovery phase

Relaxing, letting go of tension and remembering to breath are all vital elements of the recovery phase. This is a time to focus and concentrate in a relaxed state during the move through to the set up phase.

As with all canoeing typing strokes, the paddle stroke involves a gliding and a propelling phase and hence the recovery phase is essentially a part of this gliding phase. Too long of a gliding phase will permit the board to decelerate to a point where high energy output is required to regain

Remember to relax. You've done the hard work, now relax breath in and ensure the exit and swing through (recovery) phase is as relaxed as possible even if paddling at a high stroke rate. Use the wrists to roll the blade in order to 'feather'. The top arm has not moved much beyond the level of the shoulder. Relax from the hips and shoulders. Exiting the paddle in this manner, sets in motion the twisting of the body away from the paddling side. The alternative to this involves a vertical lift up and over square recovery, which is less conducive to encouraging rotation.

Relax and breathe

speed. **You need to develop a kinaesthetic feeling for your movements and learn to balance the two phases to maintain a smooth average speed.**

The smooth action of your recovery is essential to avoid unnecessary downward pressure on the board. Your pull has set the board in motion, it is important you don't interfere with this. Fluidity needs to be your goal.

At the mid point of the recovery, usually twice as long as the stroke itself, the upper arm reaches its highest point and your body begins to move from vertical into a controlled rotation around the spine, so your leading shoulder begins to move forward and down.

Your body remains relaxed and your lower and upper wrists begin to prepare the blade for entry once the set up has been reached.

Flicking. Don't.

Flicking - When using the sliced exit, avoid over working the top arm wrist action. As the blade leaves the water, relax, to allow tension to leave your body and to ensure a more fluid recovery. Exit of the blade, should feel effortless with minimal drag at this point. Too much could mean you're pulling too far past the hip. If the blade has any amount of concave, you will need to take the blade out super early or in a more upward trajectory to release the water.

Variance of exit and recovery techniques

The blade can be exited and swung through the recovery phase in two generally accepted way, both are overtly different and constitute a major variation in technique having a direct affect on entry, catch and power phases of the stroke.

1. Lifting and 'carrying' the blade squarely forward

The blade is lifted directly upwards at the exit, a consequence of the paddler having rotated to near upright (chest near vertical, shoulders square) and removing the blade upwards (not outwards) through the action of the lower and upper arms and a 'shrugging' of the shoulders.

Once free of the water, the blade is 'carried' back through the recovery to the set up and entry. The paddle travels in an 'up and over' pattern - up, forwards and downwards. This is common to dragon boat paddlers.

Limitations of this technique: Tends to encourage a 'bobbing' motion of the body upwards and downwards and fails to encourage rotation of the body at the exit or through the recovery. Tends to raise the paddler's centre of gravity and fails to encourage feathering of the blade and can set in place a circular paddling motion, rather than a lateral one. Blade can travel too high above water so as a quick bracing stroke out wide becomes difficult to execute. Encourages paddlers to fall short of full reach potential, entering the blade too early in attempting to maintain a high stroke rate.

Blade designs affecting exit and recovery: Curiously, blade angles have been modified to suit this technique by some designers. Blade angles relative to the shaft have been lessened to as little as only 3 degrees in some instances, away from about 10 degrees, negating some lift at the beginning of the stroke, permitting the blade to move through a vertical plane quicker, requiring the blade to be exited early and upwards. These blades tend to be high aspect in shape. It has been suggested this lessening of blade angle, permits higher stroke rates (but lessening of reach) which in some sense seems regressive in moving back towards straight shafted paddles, argued by some as preferable in the context of sprint racing.

2. Feathering and 'swinging' the blade

Your lower shoulder begins to relax as the blade begins its exit. Your elbow, as it continues its bend, is relaxed and angled out from the side of the body, while the wrist is relaxed as the blade begins to exit the water outward from the side of the board.

Your lower wrist rolls inward so the blade face opens out into the feathered position for the commencement of what can be called, the air transfer phase. The top hand works in a clockwise direction when on the left, counter clockwise when on the right.

Once free of the water, the paddle commences a low arced trajectory across the water in a 'C' shape away from, then back to the side of the board in a 'feathered' position to reduce the effect of wind resistance.

As a consequence of this low arched recovery, some paddlers will tend to 'slice' the blade in sideways on entry as opposed to a more 'vertical' downward entry. This can create a smoother, cleaner entry as air is less likely to be trapped on the back face of the blade, bubbles on the front face. Practice grazing the inside paddle edge over the water in a 'C' shape as you swing through the recovery. When the blade reaches the point of entry, snap the paddle to be parallel to the board, while slicing it sideways and downwards to form the entry part of the stroke.

Here the blade is skimming across the water, following a low trajectory, allowing the paddler to swing through smoothly during the wind up while making a wide bracing stroke out wide if needed, by pushing downward on the back of the blade. *Photo Mandy West*

"It don't mean a thing, if it ain't got that swing."

MOECKER

12'6

Common recovery phase errors
Arms
Lower elbow and / or wrist not relaxed - should turn inward. Top hand wrist not relaxed and failing to control paddle when feathering. Exit is jerky. Leading arm too low.

Posture / body
Upper body excessive movement. Commonly, blade is carried too high over the water back to the set up during the recovery, slowing stroke rates and raising centre of gravity.

Notes on double-bend paddles associated with the Tahitian stroke
The difference between single and double bend paddling technique is far from subtle. The additional bend in the upper shaft provides a crank which, when the shaft is almost vertical, provides you with a degree of mechanical advantage. While there are a few double bend paddles available as stand up paddles, the majority remain single bend with a few quad bends now emerging. Greater explanation is given in the chapter on paddles.

Set up and entry of the blade
The degree of body rotation is less than when a single bend paddle is used. Chest is canted forward, lower shoulder dropped toward board, upper shoulder moves further back than with single-bend because of the additional upper bend placing the grip further back toward you. Avoid over-rotation. Lower arm tends to be straighter to account for reduced rotation in achieving good reach, chin and gaze remains up, lower arm moves down to bring about entry, top elbow is often angled marginally down, shoulder remains as low as possible, top arm is two thirds flexed because of additional crank in upper shaft. Catch is as for single bend.

The pull (power) phase
At the mid-point of the stroke, with blade nearly vertical in the water, the effectiveness of the double bend paddle comes into its own. Your lower arm is now bent to an almost 45 degree angle and the top arm remains with elbow cocked, in a marginally downward angle. The paddler now goes through a transition, where they actively 'pull' with the lower arm and at the same time 'push' forward with the top arm, in one short powerful burst. In doing this, the 'crank' within the upper shaft is used to good (mechanical) effect.

The bend that exists in the double bend shaft, three quarters of the way up or so, is often referred to as a 'crank' and with good reason, in real terms that's exactly what it can be for the paddler. Provided that it is a well designed double bend, this crank or fulcrum point can act as an additional lever in providing drive and power to the blade. This short push forward with your upper arm and trapezium muscles can generate a powerful force, combined with a powerful pull of the lower arm using your smaller forearm, tricep and bicep muscles. It is not uncommon for this stroke to travel beyond your feet as a consequence of push from the top arm. At the end of the stroke, your top arm is straight (see image below).

Exit phase

Lift the blade from the water when it reaches your feet, continued pulling will become push and lift, pulling the board downwards. Because your lower arm pulls and the top arm pushes to use the upper crank in the shaft, it is better if the blade is lifted upwards first, when level with the feet, rather than sliced outward away from the board. Commencement of feathering can occur once free of the water, chin and gaze remain up and forward.

Common errors

Same as for single-bend technique, but also failing to synchronise push with top arm and pull with lower arm when the shaft is almost vertical and continuing to pull and push for too long past vertical, pulling the board down at the back of the stroke.

Tahitian preference for double bend paddles (amongst male paddlers) is well known, to which they have mastered a unique style and relationship with. Here the blade even features a significant 'scooped' blade face - the Tahitian stroke however exits very early even when compared to the anglo-polynesian stroke using single bend paddles. Tahitians are known for avoiding convention - they are quite simply the fastest ocean canoe paddlers on earth. At this point, Tahitian stand up paddlers are seemingly using single bend paddles, which will mean they will be modifying their technique to suit, though the quick 'n light method and all 'up-front' power band remains.

Photo Steve West Team Shell Va'a Tahiti Hamilton Island Ausfralia

KANU CULTURE

Choking down

Connor Baxter and Kai Lenny going head to head. Connor has reverted to choking down for a short burst of speed via increased stroke rate.

Connor Baxter has probably brought more attention to the 'choked' down paddling method than any other paddler on account of his obvious mastery of it and his standing within the SUP community. The technique permits an increase in stroke rate and relief of pressure from the upper shoulder in particular. Old school Hawaiian paddling techniques relied upon this method on account of a lack of T-grips.

The technique may seem to fly in the face of logic, however, choking down in this way, shortens the paddle and if the lower arm is also choked down toward the blade, the lever arm length is also shortened and greater control and power can be delivered. This permits an increase in stroke rate, though decreases reach and leverage. Pressure on the shoulder (rotator cuff) is reduced and it can resolve some discomfort and give time for you to recover. Your CG will be need to be lowered, some compression and torque may be lost - but can be offset by an increase in stroke rate. From this position, it's difficult to pull past the hips.

Mastery of the technique, combined with very high stroke rates and a lightweight body frame and long levers (arms), clearly pays off for short bursts, hence why it is used by some at the start of races in order to break free of the pack, when short bursts of speed are required (even downwind) and when paddling upwind when shoulders begin to fatigue.

Smaller muscle groups can be activated which can amount to an 'active rest period' of a type, but overall the technique is more aerobically demanding

301

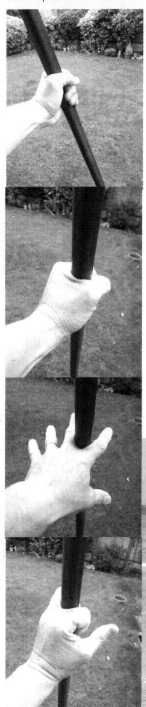

than conventional stand up paddling technique. It must be stated that the technique does not suit all-comers, particular heavier, slow twitch muscled paddlers.

Historically it's interesting to consider, that before T-grips were fitted as standard to outrigger canoe paddles post 1978, this was how outrigger canoe paddlers would paddle, with paddles which had no grip whatsoever.

It's all in the grip

Grasping the upper shaft with the upper hand in a conventional manner (regular closed fist grip) as in the top two images, encourages pushing forwards with the top arm from the shoulder and offsets the wrist in a way which is uncomfortable and may lead to strain. Splaying the index and middle finger and placing the shaft up into the web of the fingers, alters the angle of attack, off-setting the wrist so as the shaft presses into the palm from top to bottom making it secure. Importantly, it refocuses the drive from the top arm with a greater amount of downward trajectory, by encouraging the elbow to angle downward. Narrower, tapered shafts make this grip a little easier and an oval shaft provides a better fit between the fingers, with greater resistance to twisting off axis.

Photo Dana Edmunds Courtesy of Ocean Promotions / SUP Survivor Race Waikiki

11

Paddle steering

Steering and controlling the board using your paddle are
central skills which must be developed. Differing boards will
respond in differing ways, while the influence of winds,
tidal flow and wave action all play a significant
role as factors affecting your direction of travel
and the strokes you will employ to counter those forces.

KANU
CULTURE

Ocean and paddle Skills

It cannot be overstated that it is profoundly important to not only understand (thought) what it is you are trying to achieve through your paddling technique (fact), but that you learn this as early as possible, before you begin adhering to strict on water training sessions.

On water training sessions, utilising poor paddling technique with little or no comprehension of the dynamics of what it is you are actually seeking to achieve, even to the extent of a lack of knowledge of how a paddle functions or how your craft interacts with the elements, is not a winning approach. In short it will chisel your body adversely and the unlearning process can often be painful. The need to be efficient and technically sound is paramount in any endurance sport.

Add to this a lack of ocean knowledge; how to chase 'runners', backwash and an understanding of how wave particles work, the affects of interaction, how and when to use long strokes, short strokes, when to go deep or shallow or rate high or slow, how to wake-ride (if allowed) and milk the most out of the energy contained within the ocean or any body of water, will keep you working much harder than your opponent and / or limit your enjoyment.

There is no substitute for on water time, spent on a variety of craft in the true waterman spirit.

Board skills

Like any skill, board skills cover a variety of abilities both natural and learned. Fundamentally, excellence of board handling skill encompasses the ability to control the board's direction and movement over water in a variety of circumstances, in such a way as to allow the board to perform to an optimum level within its design constraints.

Ultimately while you may become familiar with the nuances of one board design, allowing you to switch between similar designs, board designs at either end of the spectrum, surf or race boards, are by their nature, more demanding of the rider, being more specific to the purpose. While designers create beginner boards to be first and foremost stable at slow speeds, more radical designs generally only become stable at relatively high speeds, assisted by wind and waves or wave power alone.

Consequently while you may feel quite skilled over time in managing your first board on flat sheltered waters, advancement to say an ocean racing board, could very well have you learning all over again. But this is the perverse nature of ocean sports and the challenge true waterman and women constantly seek out. Highly refined designs for extremes of conditions, more often than not, demand high skill levels of the rider, the net rewards of which, is to enjoy the sport at its zenith, because at this level, your level of participation takes on a whole new meaning as does your relationship with the elements.

The single best way to learn good board skills is to play, to experiment, to accept that falling off time and time again in the process of coming to terms with the nuances of your board and your own limitations, is the best way to acquire excellence of board handling skills and at the same time paddle skills.

Board handling includes issues such as steering using either weight placement alone, paddle placement (steering strokes) or a combination of both. Balance, while fundamental to the process of learning good board skills is not ultimately a defining quality to be confused with good board handling skills. Just because you have 'good balance' and rarely fall off, does not mean you have good board handling skills. It just means you have good balance. It's your ability to control the board with blade and feet, to be its master.

When the sport alludes to having a synergy with windsurfing, there is merit to the extent that the rider stands, uses their body weight to control board direction but importantly, relies upon some element of pressure transferred to the feet through a counter-poising force; the boom in the case of windsurfing and the paddle in the case of stand-up paddle boarding.

A windsurfer's relationship to the boom and how they control energy to the mast foot and feet are critical in obtaining maximum speed and control. Consequently when a windsurfer takes to stand up paddle boarding, they instinctually understand the relationship they must form between paddle and board, while a paddler (any paddler) of merit, would also understand this relationship. It is the key, the missing link many have yet to tap into. For the stand up paddler, the relationship with the paddle and how they direct energy from the blade to the feet is the fundamental essence of the sport.

Variance

When it comes to maintaining a straight course, variance of board width, length, fin arrangement / size / type, rail shape vary enormously. Boards designed specifically for the surf are designed to be 'loose' with a high degree of manoeuvrability, while most race boards of any length, are generally designed to be 'stiffer' so as to track and hold a straighter line, so as paddle power translates into forward motion, not sideways.

There is a wide variance in the way board designs respond to differing types of steering methods over others. Steering your board is actually quite complex even if the basics may seem easy.

There are many different ways to bring about a change of direction using a variety of steering strokes learned from canoeing, combined with weight placement learnt through surfing and to some extent longboard freestyle windsurfing. The greater the board's 'foot-print' (wetted surface area) the greater the amount of effort required to bring about a change of direction, but of greater relevance will be the board's length. The longer the board, the greater the lateral resistance. A shorter board of say 10' will turn more willingly and with less effort than a board of 12'6", regardless of average widths and this applies exponentially.

Going straight - an uphill battle

Regardless of how perfect your forward stroke may be, there are many things working against you which by their nature move the board away from the side you are paddling; if paddling on the left, the board will want to move right and vice-versa; assuming no cross-winds or currents.

Sound paddling technique, will certainly help minimise adverse directional issues and an understanding of what's going on may help you deal with the frustration it can cause. An understanding will have you on the way to mastery.

Blade entry

Ensure you enter the blade well forward and parallel to the equivalent straighter mid section of the board, not so as it is following the curvature of the board, as this will increase the turning affect, as your stroke will follow its curve and will act to 'sweep' the front away from your paddling side. Ensure your top hand is over the side on which you are paddling otherwise your stroke will certainly sweep progressively away from the side of the board, again increasing the turning affect.

Blade Entry

Cutting the blade in slightly side-ways on entry, so as the inner leading edge cuts inwards, is a common technique used to reduce air being drawn down with the blade, rather than 'splatting' the blade downwards and parallel to the edge of board. The top arm travels downwards and transversely across the upper body so as to be over the corresponding side of blade entry, which quickly aligns the blade parallel to the boards rail. When hands are aligned 'hand over hand' (stacked) you know the paddle is vertical and parallel. At the moment of catch (blade fully immersed) it should be parallel to the boards rails and by tucking under the board, surface tension can be be partially broken along and under the rails of the board.

The top hand is critical in controlling the angle of the shaft and therefore blade angle. Being that it is at the extremity of the shaft, small adjustments magnify the relative position of the blade. Moving this hand forwards, backwards or laterally through adjustment of the elbow, top shoulder, wrist or angling or rotation from the waist / hips, with lower hand relaxed, will alter the blades angle of attack throughout the stroke cycle. Note the top arm at entry is about to move across the line of the head to be on the same side as the blade. The blade is entered cutting in sideways, not 'splatting' in tip first, the blade reverts to being parallel as a result of the top arm moving over towards the paddling side.

Entering (cutting) the blade edge-on, rather than tip first, can reduce air take-down with the blade at entry and permits for a very clean entry. This is far more achievable as a result of employing a relaxed low sweeping recovery action rather than a high, square on recovery as used commonly by C1 and Dragon Boat paddlers.

Power phase

Ensure direct and linear blade alignment so as when the board moves up to the blade, it is close to the rails of the board. If you have driven your paddle to an optimum depth and the blade's template shape is well thought out, the shoulders should partially tuck-under the hull, the benefit being, that some of the vortex of water, will pass under the hull and assist in breaking surface tension. As you move through the stroke, when the shaft reaches vertical, your top and lower hands should be hand-over-hand (stacked). This will ensure your pull is parallel. If the hands aren't stacked, or near stacked, the stroke tend not to follow a lateral parallel path, sweeping away ever progressively from the side of the board.

Turning forces at play - in simple terms

From the moment you 'lock and load' the blade in the water (Fig1) the resultant forces act to turn the front of the board away from the side you are paddling, noticeably when starting from stationary. As the board moves up to the blade so as to be more toward the centre of the board, this angular force diminishes due to the greater surface area and increased board thickness resisting this turning force. At this point the board will tend to be following the path of the pull (Fig2). If the blade is maintained relatively vertical past the hip, the force will turn the front of the board marginally back towards the paddling side (Fig3).

PADDLING ON THE RIGHT (Example)
The stance shown is as 'natural' - feet side by side and the stroke and resultant forces would apply to either side of the board. In a natural stance, pressure remains predominantly on the inside (paddling-side) foot, throughout the stroke.

When paddling at a diagonal, the body is better angled to deal with the resultant forces created by the body's rotation. In this image, the left fore foot serves to redirect the nose back towards the paddling side as the energy from the legs intersects and transfers progressively from the rear foot to the fore foot as the blade reaches near vertical and the board moves up to meet the blade at the level of the hip.

Countering cross-winds

Cross winds can be partially offset by paddling using a diagonal stance so that the rotational forces around the hips down into the feet serve to counter the wind pushing you away from the paddling side, more especially towards the latter part of the stroke regardless of which side you're paddling. In simple terms, you are aiming to keep your chest turned into the wind as much as possible, which means you may need to switch feet from regular to goofy or vice versa. As soon as you turn your back to the wind, you can be sure you are setting yourself up to be blown off-course, downwind.

The advantages of paddling offset (diagonally) relative to the direction of travel are numerous, but in addition to improved rotation you will be able to direct energy when required to the board through the feet in such a manner, that you will be able to control and re-direct many of the external forces acting on the boards direction of travel.

Use the rails

Rounded rails and side-walls, will permit you to roll the rail downward on the windward side, to increase waterline and lateral resistance which can assist.

When adopting a diagonal stance, if you don't switch stances between changing paddling sides, on your forehand (leading leg) side, your reach out front will be greater and you will tend to exit the blade early due to the angle of your hips and shoulders. On your backhand (rear foot) side, your reach is shortened, but you can pull back up to and past the level of the hip so that both sides have equal amount of length. When the blade passes the hips, keep as vertical as possible (top hand over lower).

One of the primary benefits in being able to direct the flow of energy through the feet in a way which can assist the board's direction of travel, is that it allows you to keep delivering power to the blade in a uniform manner, parallel to the rail without the need to resort to alteration of the angle of the blade's forces; having to execute power steering strokes which can be exhausting and often result in drag and loss of speed.

Pulling up to and beyond the hips

As the board moves up to the blade and the blade moves past vertical so as to be level with your hip, it's generally accepted you should think about blade exit. If you extend the stroke past the hip, progressively twisting around your spine, ensuring the blade remains close to the rail, the blade will be momentarily angled inwards towards the rail and even under it, the resulting forces moving the tail away from your paddling side. Because the pull has now moved inward toward the rear of the board, the forces are reversed, so long as you pull inwards. The negative element to adding in this active sweeping stroke as a continuation of the forward stroke is that it slows your stroke rate, places greater demands on your skill levels and adds increased drag (resistance) at the end of your stroke. However the trade off for gained directional stability may be worth it.

Over steering

When paddling, it's tempting to over-steer so that each time the board wanders even marginally off course, you find yourself adding in steering strokes, cancelling out the boards naturally tendency to turn away from the side you're paddling on. Beyond this there's the affect of wind, wave and tidal flow hampering the direction of travel.

Developing a sense of anticipation, thinking ahead as to how the board's direction will be affected by your paddling and all other factors is a crucial skill to develop, one which ultimately becomes instinctual.

In calm conditions, in the absence of any steering stroke, passive or active, you should aim to learn to change sides frequently in order to maintain a straight course. Many small, frequent corrections are more effective and desirable than having to execute longer, drawn out corrections, leading to greater drag, compounding all negative consequences and slowing the boards forward momentum. **With time, you can practice paddling on one side only, without the need to change paddling sides, incorporating passive and active steering strokes.**

To become proficient at paddling alternate sides so as to maintain course, takes time in nurturing the ability to instinctively know just how much is enough. Anticipating the nuances of the board, even before they occur, is truly a skill learned only by spending a great deal of time on the water in a variety of conditions and often specifically between different board designs.

Accomplished paddlers will tend to be very dynamic in working either side of the board with speed and accuracy, while incorporating forward strokes and pitch strokes. They are by nature 'workaholics' constantly alternating between differing strokes to control and contribute to the boards run and direction of travel.

Body alignment - brace yourself

Whenever you make a steering stroke of any type using the paddle, the resultant forces (drag) will often compromise your balance, therefore you must assume a strong bracing posture, often best achieved by lowering your centre of gravity, bending at the knees and assuming a strong positive connection with the board through the feet. Being pulled off the board by the forces acting on the blade when steering, are not uncommon. Anticipation of what's coming just prior to blade placement, will help you deal with these forces. The longer the board, the greater the lateral resistance; the larger the blade area, the greater the resistance against the blade face.

Rail steering

Surfers are dependant on applying pressure to alternate rails of their board through weight transference through the feet, in order to bring about a change of direction on the wave. Leaning and applying pressure to either the left or right rail, depresses the board's edge, creating a leading edge which bites into the water, creating drag and producing subsequent forces which turn the board towards the direction of pressure applied. The degree of responsiveness is somewhat dependant on the board's relative speed, rail shape, buoyancy, fin shape and riders weight.

Rounded rails permit smoother turns, sharp rails will tend to cause the board to track off in one direction, while greater degrees of buoyancy (thickness and tail width combined) will require greater amounts of pressure to bring about a change in direction. When paddling at relatively slow speeds, the water is generally 'soft' so as the rail can be depressed with ease. The faster the board is travelling ie when surfing or chasing runners, the 'harder' the water will be and therefore greater amounts of pressure will be required.

Regardless of when on a wave or on flat water, stand up paddle boards respond to alternate weight placement upon the rails so long as the board has forward momentum. Whenever initiating a turn left or right through the application of a steering stroke, applying pressure to the inside rail relative to the direction of turn, will assist in bringing about the change of direction.

When applying a sweeping stroke on the right, to turn left, weight applied to the left rail will create added drag along this side of the board and assist in turning the board left and vice-versa. Rail pressure can also be used to help counter the boards tendency to turn away from the side you're paddling. If paddling on the right, the board will tend to want to turn to the left and by applying pressure to the right rail, this can help counter this tendency and vice-versa.

The speed of response and tightness of the turn is also dependant upon board shape, size, board speed, amount of weight applied, foot placement

In the context of stand up paddle surfing, the paddle is still fundamentally secondary to the importance of pressure applied to the rails as the primary means of turning the board. The paddle in this instance is being used as a means of steadying the rider, so as greater pressure can be applied to the rail without loss of balance. The performance gains derived from the use of a paddle, especially in smaller surf conditions as used by the stand up paddle surfer, is what ultimately provides at least some advantages over conventional surfing in being able to execute extreme moves through the use of the paddle to bring about aggressive turns, greater body lean and subsequent bracing as provided by the paddle itself. *Rider John Hibbard*

314

relative to the sides, rear or nose of the board and how the paddle is used in combination with each of these factors.

In the 1970s, 'Freestyle Windsurfers' using longboards, sailing on flat water, got to grips with the use of applying weight to alternate rails in order to bring about turning, aided by moving the sail sideways. Moving their weight towards the rear of the board, the board turned quicker and in a much shorter distance or arch, in combination with using the sail to 'scoop' the wind, the board literally spins on its tail. The paddle can be used in this same way. Taken a step further, 'Freestylers' would cut their fins down to size so as to improve the boards capacity to 'spin' on its tail.

Step back pivot turn

Moving your weight to the tail of the board will tend to lift the nose of the board out of the water, thereby shortening the water line length, reducing the wetted surface area and therefore drag. As a consequence the board can literally spin on its tail very quickly and efficiently aided by a sweeping stroke. The shorter the board, the tighter and faster the turn will be.

Long board freestyle windsurfers learned to depress the inside rail and sweep the sail across the front of the board when gybing in the same manner as the stand up paddler can depress the inside rail and sweep the paddle away from the board. These 2 images are the corresponding equivalents of turning a board right using a paddle or windsurfer on the tail.

Little rail pressure is required as the force generated by the paddle, having to cope with less drag from the board will suffice in bringing about a turn.

Passive (paddle) steering

Passive steering relies upon static bracing and angling of the blade against the flow of water to initiate a change of direction. In the case of most passive strokes, the paddler ceases to contribute to the forward propulsion of the board and in effect becomes a 'dead weight'. Additionally the stalled blade and the 'turning moment' of the board inevitably produces drag and a loss of speed, even if momentarily. This 'passive stroke', consumes the board's momentum.

Most passive strokes require that the board have forward momentum, working much in the same way as a rudder on a boat. Changing sides frequently in adverse conditions using quick, short, sharp passive steering strokes in combination with the forward paddling stroke, can maintain momentum, unless you need to make a large course change, in which case you can hold the passive stroke for longer and for as long as you have momentum. In the case of fast flowing water, the passive stroke will also be effective as used in stand up river boarding.

Passive steering strokes, can be classified as 'bracing strokes' in so much as the paddler braces the paddle against the flow of water and directs tension from the body to the blade while using the feet to control the resulting forces away from or towards the blade. Lowering your centre of gravity by bending the knees and ensuring firm and sure placement of the feet is essential to bring about stability through the body.

Kahi (Hawaiian kah-hee = to cut)

This is a powerful and effective passive stroke and essentially involves the paddler reaching forwards and outwards from the side of the board, planting the blade in a static braced position, steering the board towards the side where the paddle is positioned.

This particular stroke can be made anywhere from level with the feet to as far forward as you can reach. The further forward you reach and place the blade and the further out from the side of board you can place it, the greater the turning effect.

Rotate your body, lean marginally towards the rail and slice your paddle downwards and forwards in on its edge so as the grip is angled back towards you. The blade should act as a 'brace' by being steadily pulled inwards towards the board, just enough to prevent the blade from moving as this is a steering stroke, which pulls the board towards the blade.

You can choke your lower hand down the shaft to gain better control of the blade and this will allow you to bend your knees. Your lower arm needs to be bent nearly 90 degrees to keep the blade vertical while your upper arm is bent and high, so you can apply pressure.

Kahi (Hawaiian kah-hee = to cut)

An all time useful passive stroke which controls the front of the board when planted around half way forward of your full reach. Try paddling on one side for extended periods of time on either side while keeping a straight course. An excellent stroke to use when countering side winds or tidal flow or in bringing about stability - in this case a wind blowing from across the paddling side, in pulling the nose back on track. You may know it as a bow-rudder stroke.

While the kahi is a passive stroke, it is best finished with a a sweep toward the nose / bow of the board achieved by keeping the blade face near 'open' allowing water to flow off its edges. It's moments like this that you value a good blade shape and one that is a 'clean' and with ample amount of flat area.

A kahi being planted just behind the body-line, then swung forward into the stroke - used for stalling the board then pulling the front back over toward the paddling side.

Reverse Kahi (infront of the body-line)

Paddle is transferred to opposite side, legs are bent to lower CG in anticipation of lateral pull. Blade is planted at near 45 degree angle and initially held in place. Forward momentum of the board will create adequate pressure

Reverse Kahi (behind the body-line)

Executing a reverse kahi from behind the body line, stops the board and turns it on mid axis. You need to brace yourself even at low speeds and avoid have the paddle ripped out of your hands or being pulled off the board. A fun way to turn and great for skill development.

321

Turn the power-face so as it opens outwards, towards the on-flow of water, by about 20 degrees relative to the board. In this way, water will flow against the blade face and leading edge causing drag.

The position is held braced and locked. The more you open the blade face to the on-flow of water, the greater the turning effect. By opening out the blade face, the board is steered toward the blade. The blade will want to pull away from you, so be prepared for this force.

Before the board looses momentum, you can sweep the paddle inward. To end the kahi, pull and release the blade as normal and resume paddling. In this manner you can paddle and make constant adjustments, to pull the board towards the paddling side, without changing paddling sides (use as a drill).

Upright Reverse Kahi - This low speed kahi begins forward of the body line in a reasonably upright position. The blade is pulled inwards and back toward the line of the feet. A more radical method, would be to execute the kahi behind the body line, ensuring a strong brace or be pulled off the board! Depress the rail.

The side brace can take varying forms. On the left, at speed, a kahi is being performed out wide to bring compression to the feet and to redirect the board to the right. Alternatively, you can brace yourself using the back of the blade face with shaft at a low angle, where no alteration of travel is required.

Reverse kahi (see images)

The reverse-kahi, is based on all the same principles, the difference being, the paddler swings the paddle across the board, without changing hand positions and plants the blade forwards on the opposite side.

Side brace

This is an effective stroke used to stabilise the board in rough water or to counteract strong crosswinds or choppy waters. This stroke is often used in conjunction with a pitch stroke as a means of resuming paddling or finishing off the correction.

Rotate your body and lean out over the water, by about one half your potential and place the blade in the water in a near vertical position. The paddle should act as a 'brace'. Your lower hand can be choked lower down the shaft to allow you to bend at the knees and gain greater control over the blade.

Keeping the blade vertical and parallel relative to the board, apply a strong even pull directly towards you, while marginally opening the blade face to the oncoming flow of water, ie turning it out from you. The blade will want to pull away from you, hence the need to apply pull towards the board. The more you open up the blade face to the on flow of water, the greater the turning effect, however the harder it will be to maintain control of the blade.

Your lower arm should be bent into a nearly 90 degree angle to enable you to hold the stroke strongly. Your upper arm should be slightly bent, with elbow upwards or level with your head, to apply downward pressure.

This very powerful and effective stroke needs to be used when the board is only marginally off line as it is only effective in bringing about a relatively subtle and slow response from the board. A particularly useful stroke in combination with the forward stroke. You will only ever hold this briefly.

Brake stroke

A brake stroke is an essential stroke for stopping the board. It is a stroke, which all paddlers need to know. The blade is placed away from the side of the board with blade face open so it acts like a brake. Depending on the boards rate of travel, the paddler will need to apply quite a lot of force in a forward pushing manner with their lower arm in order to hold the stroke. If time permits, reverse the blade face to prevent breakage, if possible. Lower your centre of gravity by bending your knees.

Brake stroke.

Active (paddle) steering

Employing an active paddle steering stroke, involves the paddler continuing to paddle using a compromised forward stroke, which has a degree of pitch to it. This is also known as 'power steering' as it requires strength for successful execution. Unlike a passive stroke, the paddler is attempting to paddle and steer at the same time, so as to minimise loss of momentum.

The forward stroke, while contributing to the forward movement of the board, always results in producing some degree of unintentional active steering away from the side on which the stroke is being made ie if paddling on the right, the board will tend to move towards the left and vice-versa.

The initial catch and power phase of the stroke ahead of the body-line of the paddler and the board's centre of gravity, produces the greatest gains in forward thrust. As the blade moves behind the paddler's body line and past the board's centre of gravity, the blade's propulsive power acts to turn the board away from the stroke.

This constant wandering of the board from right to left and left to right is known as 'yaw' which can either be of benefit or hindrance.

The Pitch Stroke

The pitch stroke is frequently and erroneously called a J-Stroke as used in open canoe river paddling, compensating for the canoes tendency to drift away from the side the paddler is paddling on. The J-Stroke is a forward stroke with a 'hook' added to the end of it, outward from the side of the board and held in position or pushed outwards. It works in an open canoe when seated at the very rear of the craft, but when stood on a board at its centre of gravity, the middle, a J-Stroke is largely ineffective and will feel much like you are being pulled off the board.

A pitch stroke is a dynamic and powerful forward stroke with a directional factor incorporated into its length. This forward stroke begins out wide from the side of the board forward of the paddler and is pulled inwards up to about level with the feet and results in pulling the nose of the board towards the paddle. The angle of pitch away from the side of the board can be up to 45-degrees depending how great a turn you need to initiate. This stroke can be used when the board is moving or stationary.

Anticipating when to execute the pitch stroke is essential. Timed correctly, it requires some effort as it is by definition a powerful correctional stroke. Timed badly, it can become nearly impossible to make a difference, a static steering stroke becoming your best alternative. In light winds and seas, this stroke is relatively easy to execute. But as winds increase, especially side-on, it becomes progressively harder to perform successfully, to the point of being ineffectual, draining the body of energy.

Sweep Stroke - 'C' Stroke

A sweep stroke as it implies, originates either wide of the side of the board or forward and close to the side of the board and is drawn in a wide arch around and in towards the board, either finishing at the paddler's feet or behind. The sweep stroke is used when the board is moving or when stationary. A useful stroke in countering cross-winds.

It is a more subtle form of pitch stroke delivering a little less power and often used when turning the board radically on its tail contributing to the turning movement and less substantially to forward movement.

The Sweep Stroke (C-stroke) - works best from the extremities of the board aided by weight added to the rail. Here the stroke is being used when paddling downwind at speed, so as to pull the board to the right.

The Draw Stroke

This powerful turning stroke pulls the board towards the side the blade is on and only truly effective when the board is moving at slow speeds or stationary. When executed from the rear of the board it will cause the board to turn on the tail away from the direction of pull, while from the middle of the board, it will tend to simply pull the board towards the direction of pull of the blade rather than initiate any turning-movement.

When stationary, it is a very useful stroke and acts as a brace providing stability to the board and paddler when executed from the mid section of the board. In Canadian canoeing, the 'Bowman' uses this stroke to keep the canoe head to wind or current. At speed, when headed in a straight line, this stroke is less effective because the forward movement of the board works directly against the paddler's efforts. When the board has already begun to turn and loose some forward momentum, the draw stroke becomes easier to execute.

To execute a draw stroke, to initiate a turn, ensure you move towards the rear of your board, rotate your body on your paddling side, leaning out as far as possible over the water and place your blade in the water in a nearly vertical position. The blade should act as a brace. Your lower arm should be nearly straight while your upper arm is slightly bent with elbow upwards so your force is downwards and inwards. Keep the paddle shaft vertical and blade parallel to the board edge.

Pull the blade directly towards you with your arms progressively bending as they near the board. This is intended to be a powerful stroke. Use your entire upper body and some body weight behind the stroke. Finish the stroke by driving the blade under the board, to push the 'dirty' water under the hull and break the surface tension between the board and the water. Don't go too far under, as the blade may get locked up under the board. Slide the blade out of the water by lifting directly upwards with your lower arm and moving your top arm forward.

In a stationary situation, to repeat the stroke, you need not remove the blade from the water. All you need to do is twist the blade 90 degrees putting the blade perpendicular to the board edge, slicing it back out through the water to the starting position. Be mindful not to over bury the blade. The board may spin quite quickly as a result of the paddle's propulsion so be prepared.

Back-Paddle / Back-Water

The back-paddle or back-water stroke, is the reverse of the forward stroke, though bio-mechanically it cannot be performed in the same manner and is used to move the board backwards. While back paddling you can use shortly executed draw strokes in order to control the direction of travel. Reverse the blade when executing this stroke with any force, to prevent stressing the neck area and to gain greater control.

You can reverse your upper hand grip if you feel you can gain more purchase and control over the blade. Position the blade at approximately a 65 degree angle to the waterline and behind the line of your body, being mindful not to extend too far behind or the paddle will generate too much downward force rather than the required horizontal force.

Push the blade forward using your lower hand, while rotating your body through the stroke, so you can use your body weight. Pull the grip towards you. Keep the stroke relatively short and push hardest when the blade is vertical, keeping the blade parallel to the board. When the blade is only slightly past vertical, remove it from the water by dropping your upper hand down across your body, lifting your lower hand and moving back into the entry position behind you.

Adding a directional component, reach behind and place the paddle as far out from the side of the board as possible, keep the paddle at an angle so the grip is near your ear. Pull the paddle towards you with your lower arm, push away with your top arm and remove the paddle when near your hip and repeat. This is essentially a form of reverse draw stroke.

Push Over Stroke

The push over stroke is used when the board is stationary; turning the board away from the side the paddle is on. Though it's a weak stroke, it's useful for precision manoeuvring.

Place the paddle vertically level with your feet, blade face open and push the paddle away from the side of the board with your lower hand. Your upper hand remains more or less stationary. Return the blade by closing it and slicing back through water to the vertical position. Open face and repeat.

Practice, practice, practice. Set drills for yourself to get to know your board and above all, have fun doing it. Skills learnt through play can be used at critical moments when needed.

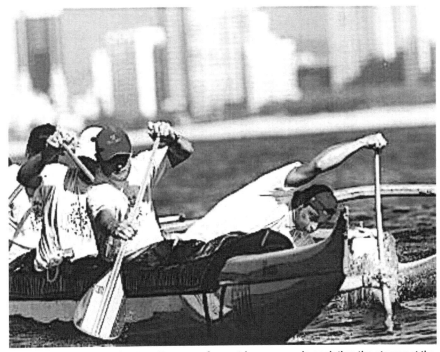

Here's a kahi being used to turn the nose of an outrigger canoe in assisting the steerer at the rear. The advantages of being low down and able to brace against the side walls of the wa`a (canoe) are substantial in being able to apply power to the blade. When stood up, the paddler must lower their centre of gravity to adjust for the pull. *Photo Sue Sheard*

12

Winds, tides, buoyancy aides and various safety issues

Stand up paddle boarding may not be a 'wind-sport' but it has a critical affect on the physical demands of the paddler. For the downwind paddler, the wind is the paddler's best friend, for most other circumstances it can present a variety of problems. Beyond this, tidal flow and various equipment concerns need to be factored into your everyday participation.

Hypothermia

Wind chill is a real concern and therefore consider clothing which lessens this affect. This generally is more of a concern than immersion in water unless you are falling off a great deal into cold water.

Hyperthermia / sunburn

Prolonged hours in the sun can result in heat exhaustion, heat stroke and dehydration. Take precautions against UV rays by covering up. Sunscreens can make paddle and board slippery. Covering up remains the best option, wearing UV protective quality fabrics.

Avoid prolonged periods in the sun prior to paddling and monitor for heat stroke after paddling - nausea, dizziness. During paddling, the wind will have a cooling affect, but this can mask such things as dehydration, so ensure you hydrate and monitor yourself.

Open water distance paddling where support craft are available (and indeed compulsory for long events) permit refreshments to be brought out to the paddler and the logical way for this to happen is to have a swimmer come out to meet you as is common to outrigger canoe races.

Photo Karen Baxter.
Rider: Connor Baxter

Dehydration / energy food / hypoglycaemia
(low blood sugar)

Downwind paddling, racing and training can be thirsty work and the hotter and higher the humidity, the more relevant this becomes, though paddling in a wetsuit can speed up fluid loss in colder climates. If your duration is likely to be greater than an hour, ensure you are hydrated with water prior to paddling (but not over-hydrated) and consider taking a back or waist worn hydration system.

Consumption of around 1lt per hour is the generally accepted amount given warm conditions. New research suggests to drink when you're thirsty, not before.

It is always advisable to carry with you some form of energy food if paddling for over an hour, which will keep you going for a bit longer if you experience low blood sugar which can manifest in the form of the shakes and weakness.

Support

Spontaneous downwind sessions / hydration and energy

If the wind suddenly arrives and you have time on your hands to drop everything and go downwind paddling, given a hot climate and the distance you intend paddling, consider how well hydrated and fuelled up you are? Psychologically you may be fired up to go, physiologically not so.

Planned downwind sessions / hydration and energy

If you have time to plan your downwind session in advance (usually associated with the consistency of trade wind areas) then you can plan to hydrate and eat well, in advance of the session.

Clothing

Freedom of movement is vital, while balancing this out against issues of hypothermia in particular. While in sub and tropical climates, there is perhaps less of an issue, where **board shorts are often worn in combination with no shirt at all, with lightweight rash vest / shirt, thin neoprene top as required.** Temperate and colder climates present a problem.

The greatest concern are areas where there is sometimes a large variance of difference between air temperature (warm) and water temperature (cold). Add to this the affects of wind chill associated with high winds and the issue becomes complex.

A kayak styled cag, is an almost essential item of clothing; 100% windproof and waterproof, sealed around wrist, neck and can be drawn tight around the waist, which may have a neoprene gusset. This protects the torso region of the body from wind chill and even to some degree immersion and can be worn with board shorts or over a wetsuit.

Wetsuits come in a variety of forms. A sleeveless Long John is a very useful item, protecting the legs and torso, over which you can layer, with neoprene or thermals (wool / polypropylene) or kayaking cag.

Full wetsuits are generally a step too far being restrictive and only really applicable for constant immersion. Neoprene gloves and booties are worn when sea temps and or air / wind chill makes it necessary.

Cold hands are painful and make paddle management difficult. Cold feet will lead to discomfort and loosing touch with the board underneath you, which leads to compromised balance.

Accessories
(Not limited to)

GPS
A wrist worn GPS system or similar provides back up where appropriate; poor visibility, use of way points in order to identify progress points, turn points, transits and meeting points. Also a good reference for speed over ground, elapsed time, distance travelled in order to build up an idea of times for different courses given differing conditions of wind, tide, sea states etc.

Digital watch (Tide Watch)
Essential for interval training and for setting alarms so as you can regroup at set times when downwind paddling. Your watch is an essential item, which you can use for working out your progress and allowing for tide times.

A watch is essential for on-water interval training and a guide in relation to changing tides and duration of your session over distance. GPS speedometers can provide important feedback about speed, distance travelled and your progress. A simple LED white light attached to upper shaft of your paddle or peaked cap let's others see you in low light.

Some impact vests now meet the regulation standard 50N and qualify as buoyancy aides / PFDs. They can include pockets and come in many bright colours.

Buoyancy Aide (BA) PersonalFloatation Device (PFD)
Impact Vests (IV) Lifejacket (LJ)

The negatives of wearing buoyancy devices are rarely considered, however the fact remains they are numerous in the context of a variety of water sports and they include; impairment of ability to duck-dive under waves or avoid being hit by the board, impairs the swim back and retrieval of board and remounting can become problematic. The added padding can lead to overheating, limits bio-mechanical movements, can lead to chaffing and all in all can make the stand up paddle boarding experience less of what it should be and at times more dangerous than it need be.

Some of the logic falls within the thinking that boxing gloves makes boxing safer, when they simply allow for harder punches to be made to the head without breaking the hand, which raises the risk of brain damage. The point here, is that floatation devices have their role to play in some circumstances, for some people, but certainly not all circumstances for all people. As a self governing process, if your water confidence is such that you feel the need to wear a BA, PFD or LJ then you should ask yourself if it would not be more pertinent to gain greater water confidence / swimming skills prior. The wearing of such devices to account for your lack is not safe practice in itself, yet advocated by many who fail to see the correlation.

Research and the greater part of the rationale behind the need to wear such devices is associated with the overwhelming number of recreational boat users combining alcohol with their aquatic adventures who benefit from these devices which offer a reduction in cold-water shock on immersion and the slow down of hypothermia. Boats by their nature, being a depression in the water in which you sit, are apt to swamp, turn over and sink, whereas a board is not subject to these critical events. Wearing thermal clothing eliminates the justification as a thermal barrier.

What research fails to account for, is the hindrance such devices cause to the paddler who requires freedom of movement at all times and limited restriction or lessening of the ability to swim, duck dive and re board in the event of a fall - while most importantly being attached to their board through a leg leash, which to all intents and purposes, forms the basis of a life saving device, which is unsinkable and profoundly stable. While the recreational boater aims to avoid being 'overboard' the paddle boarder is in effect, already overboard.

Stand up paddle boarding by nature, is a fall and retrieve sport, where falling is not and should not, be regarded as a critical event as capsizing is to canoeing or kayaking.

Impact vests can be worn in extreme of conditions, many have built in buoyancy and can protect against being winded. In the context of white water paddling, this is highly specialised. Seek professional guidance.

Be aware of the following:
If you fall and are rendered unconscious due to cranial impact - you will need to be wearing at the time of impact, a fully inflated life jacket (which floats you face upwards) because a BA or PFD will not save you, as you will be floating face down and you will drown. Wearing a fully inflated LJ will make participation virtually impossible, limiting your mobility and certainly restrict your ability to swim, duck dive or re-board in the event of a fall.

BAs or PFDs are simply 'aides to floatation' and will not float you face upwards in the event of being rendered unconscious. Your board connected to you with the leash, is your best form of floatation device and should never be abandoned as it provides maximum visibility to rescuers and your best aide to floatation!

Buoyancy aids in the form of an impact vest style garment offer maximum freedom of movement over many conventional styled BAs.

VHF radio / mobile phones / pyrotechnics
A VHF radio is the best commercially available safety communication device. Pre set channels can put you in direct contact with the Coastguard, Lifeguards or other rescue services and may even include an electronic positioning device, which if activated will pin point your position to the Coastguard in the extreme circumstance you need immediate assistance. Use between paddlers is not the idea here, but it could be used in limited cases (you may need a VHF license).

Mobile phones in waterproof bags, in very wet, windy situations are not a suitable alternative as much as you may think it a simple solution. The use of pyrotechnics (flares) is another simple, inexpensive safety device and come in a variety of forms. Consider hand held flares, bright positioning flares, smoke etc. In this regard, the VHF radio is still the better option.

Marine laws

Once you leave the shoreline you must apply the rights of way as per maritime law. Be mindful of any shipping lanes, channels, channel markers, and general marine traffic - ideally avoid shipping and ferry lanes. Educate yourself as to the maritime codes that exist.

An important rule regarding collision is to ensure you make a significant and early change of course to make your intentions clear and if in doubt, give way to everything.

Personal abilities

Downwind paddling is particularly demanding. Arms can become sore and lactated from constant paddling. Legs can become sore from standing and constant adjustment. It is aerobically demanding and therefore it may challenge your fitness. Consider cross training – mountain bike training, cycling, running or swimming considered one of the best cross training exercise for paddle sports. Maintain flexibility through – stretching, yoga movements - yoga boarding. You will need to develop strong legs. Be sure to be confident on and in the water.

Photos Mandy West

Self Reliance

Self rescue

Ideally you would take the path of least resistance (i.e. go with the wind direction) and the shortest path possible to land fall and safety - but these are not always in balance. You will need to consider your best options at the time. Use prone paddling or paddle kneeling technique.

Either of these techniques can be used as part of a self-rescue in the event of a broken / lost paddle, fatigue, head winds, cross winds, strong tidal flow, rough water.

Leg Leash

The single most
important safety
item you will own is
a decent leg leash
in the context of
any off-shore
paddling and
certainly when
downwind
paddling. Putting a
floatation device
ahead of the need
for a decent leash is
to put the cart
before the horse.
OC1 paddlers learnt
this long ago
through first hand
experiences. 14hrs
is the longest I have
heard of someone
floating around in
the Pacific before
hitting land fall,
when a leash would
have saved them
the bother.

Connected

New Experiences

A stranger in a strange land

Whenever you find yourself in a new paddling environment, take time to study the area, talk with the locals, get to know good entry and exit points, areas to avoid, local winds and more **besides.** *Johh Hibbard an Englishman in Hawai`i.*

Environmental conditions

Know the area you're paddling from and to when paddling downwind and consider the affects varying topography may have. Valleys can create strong offshore local winds, while convection winds rising up over high mountains, can suck the air inshore or even take away the wind altogether. Study the pattern of the ocean to see whether there are areas of water, which appear to be behaving differently to all else around them. Consider the underwater topography, reefs, sandbanks, wrecks etc.

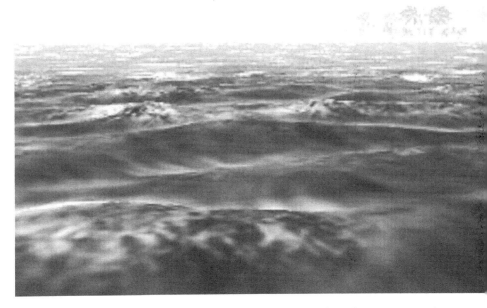

The **underwater topography** can affect the water surface, but importantly if a fall occurs at any speed in shallow water, this raises concerns. In addition obstructions such as submerged logs, rocks, reefs, sandbanks can lead to impact injury. During times of moderate–fresh winds, sandbanks can produce breaking waves in varied form, from pitching to spilling and associated with 'white-water' resulting in potential falls. There's the risk of **falling on or near rocks / reef,** leading to leash entanglement and the paddler suffering impact injury and possible damage to equipment.

Poor visibility caused by haze, dust, fog, rain or misty rain can result in loss of direction. Low light paddling (mornings / evenings) requires white LED lighting to be worn. Possible loss of direction can result. Avoid shipping lanes and potential collisions with people, other water craft.

Marine creature encounters with large marine mammals, such as whales, dolphins and seals are not uncommon in varying parts of the world. Migratory paths of whales in particular should be noted. Shark breeding / feeding areas should be avoided if known. Marine stingers must be noted

Encounters with whales can generally be predicted if you live in a migratory area. Pay careful attention and especially when calves are present as they can be inquisitive and mothers sometimes protective. Fiji Dolphins below.

Photos Steve West

and in areas where present, you will need to consider footwear being compulsory as a precaution and perhaps a 'stinger suit'. Turtles can also be encountered and a collision at speed could very easily result in the loss of a fin or board damage.

Tides and tidal flow

Some areas of the world are relatively unaffected by tidal flow, whereas other areas are profoundly affected.

How will the state of the tide be on your departure, during your session and at your arrival / exit point? Will the flow of water be with or against you and will it alter during the session? How will the high water state be different to that of low water? Will you have enough water throughout or will falling water, expose rocks, oyster beds, mudflats or coral reef, resulting in a long walk making your exit difficult? Will you need to be wearing shoes at the exit point?

Wind over water and wind against tide / current

While not directly related to weather, currents affect the sea state. **"A strong current flowing against the wind causes an enhanced chop and steepness to the seas, whereas a current flowing with the wind diminishes the seas just as dramatically. To recognise the effect, however, requires some experience at sea, since you must be able to conclude that the seas are not consistent with the wind"** (Burch 132).

Therefore, wind travelling counter to the direction of travel of tidal flow, results in water 'standing' and becoming often highly irregular raising potential loss of balance and fatigue. Falling tides can form an extended barrier preventing your exit. While paddling against tidal flow or current can be tiring, there are occasions where it works in your favour as a result of producing steep wave faces - so long as wind strength is sufficient in adding impetus to pushing over and down the wave faces.

Spring and neap Tides

Recognise the variations between Spring (King) and Neap tides how this affects high and low water marks and rate of flow. Tidal ebb and flow are entirely controlled through the gravitational pull of the sun and the moon, hence why full moon and new moon cycles create greater extremes of tidal flow (highs and lows) which falls over an approximate two week period.

Coastal rips and currents can adversely affect the sea state causing paddlers to be dragged off course or experience choppy waters.

Tide charts / table

Purchase a tide chart for your area or view on-line. From the tidal chart understand the rule of twelfths - in general terms, over 24 hours there are 2 high waters and 2 lows. Therefore approximately every 12 hours there is 1 high water and 1 low water period in which it takes approximately 6 hours of flow from high water to low water, during which the water flows hardest within the 3rd and 4th hours. However it is different for different areas, which you will need to investigate. Essentially the first few hours of flow either side of high and low water is slower. This can affect your departure times and how you will be affected during the session.

Fetch and waves (essential knowledge for downwind paddlers)

If paddling 2, 6, 10, 20km – the longer the distance to arrival on an exposed beach, whatever you are seeing at the launch point, will generally be amplified at the arrival point, unless you can find shelter up a river mouth, behind a groin or within a protected area.

In simple terms the size and power of a wave depends on its fetch, fetch being the total distance a wave travels before it finally breaks. Other factors will determine wave size, such as wind strength and water depth. The greater the fetch, the more time waves have to build in size.

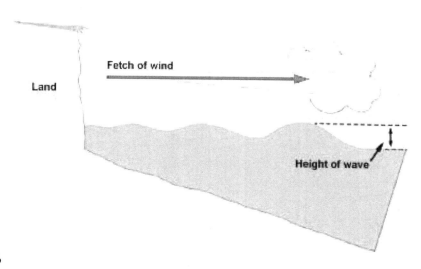

Support craft

The use of a suitable support craft is an ideal companion given certain conditions and situations. Longer downwind racing makes use of a boat often compulsory. With greater distances, greater extremes of conditions, the use of a support craft will eventually become mandatory to ensure the greater guarantee that safety is to hand should the need arise - not withstanding the fact that the boat must be suitable and serviceable and the driver experienced in operating around small craft, towing and rescue.

Driver and Driver Proximity

The driver of the craft will need to be experienced and qualified where local laws dictate. Importantly the driving of a powered craft is one skill, the rescue / pick up / towing and working in close proximity to paddle boarders is another. While there are many good reasons to use a safety craft, there are inherent concerns; safety craft too close to paddlers, can collide with paddlers or paddlers are subjected to fumes and wake.

When following a paddler, sit behind and off to one side. To drop off a relief paddler or refreshments, drop back, turn off to the right (in this instance) and travel at 90 degrees away from the paddler up to 100m, then ahead by up to 200m. Drift across the paddlers line, the relief paddler / support person exits and the boat drifts (using the wind if possible) past the line of the paddler. To pick up swimmer, put ENGINE IN NEUTRAL and have them swim to you, don't attempt to inch your way up them. You could throw a throw line if necessary.

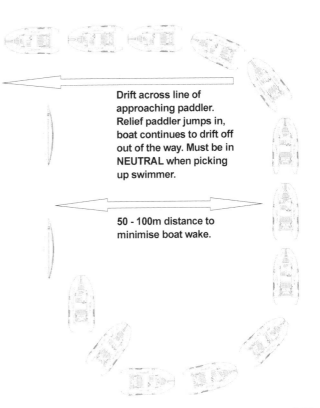

Drift across line of approaching paddler. Relief paddler jumps in, boat continues to drift off out of the way. Must be in NEUTRAL when picking up swimmer.

50 - 100m distance to minimise boat wake.

Consequently drivers should be attentive to; monitor paddlers at all times and all other craft around them. Pay constant attention to boat wake. Consider exhaust fumes and keep downwind of paddlers where possible.

When following a paddler approach from behind and remain adjacent and at a safe distance, perhaps no more than one third of your bow to be past the level of the tail of their board. You can communicate if needs be.

If needing to drop off refreshments or relief paddler, drop back and proceed 90 degrees away from the paddler for a distance of 50-100m minimum and then circle around ahead of them to minimise wake.

Allow for wind drift, tidal flow and wave action. Drift across the paddler's line of travel and have swimmer exit the boat when in alignment with the paddler and ensure engine in neutral, moving off only when they are clear.

When picking up swimmer, ensure engine is in neutral and or switched off and alert the paddler to this 'Engine in Neutral' and have them swim to you in their own time. Don't yank them in by arms. Ideally have them climb in under their own steam where possible.

Photos Mandy West

When towing boards, you will need to create a towing bridal, so as the pull is not from the nose / bow, otherwise the board will oscillate and swerve badly to the point of even flipping over. Ideally a bridal should be pre made to fit over the board.

Winds

High winds can cause the water to become short, steep, confused or choppy presenting the rider with some increased balance issues. Being blown off course can result in being driven out to sea or perhaps shoreward. There is always the risk of encountering adverse winds because of wind shifts or winds generated due to an approaching storm.

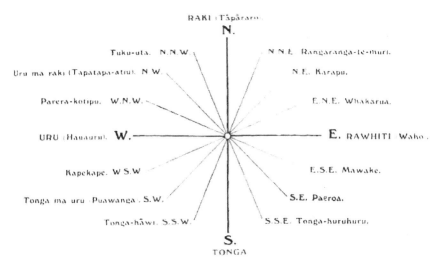

Maori compass, showing specific terms and also wind names, as given by Mohi Turei of the Ngati-Porou tribe.

For the downwind paddler, a relationship with the wind is similar to that of the windsurfer. The more accomplished you become, the greater your need to seek out more challenging and thrilling experiences. You will need to be become knowledgeable about wind dynamics, which will include such things as how wind is created and the nature of differing wind types.

Take time to learn how wind is generated – high and low pressures. Knowledge of local, thermal and convectional winds. Identify trade winds, seasonal prevailing winds and get to grips with the nature of veering and shifting winds, wind shadows and how winds are affected by friction between land and sea.

Wind strength

Generally speaking a wind speed of 12 knots and upwards begins to make downwind paddling possible and enjoyable, but more is better. The greater the wind strength the faster your rate of travel and assistance will be. What

The Beaufort Scale

"Over thousands of years sailors have learnt to estimate the speed of the wind just by looking about. This technique matured into what we now call the Beaufort scale. The universe tells you everything you need to know about it as long as you are prepared to watch, to listen, to smell, in short to observe" ....Howtoons 2006

FORCE 0 — "Calm"
- SPEED: 0 Knots / 0 mph / 0 km/h
- SEA: Sea like a mirror
- LAND: Smoke rises vertically

FORCE 1 — "Light Air"
- SPEED: 1-3 Knots / 1-3 mph / 1-6 km/h
- SEA: Ripples with the appearance of scales are formed, but without foam crests
- LAND: Direction of wind shown by smoke but not by wind vanes

FORCE 2 — "Light Breeze"
- SPEED: 4-6 Knots / 4-7 mph / 7-11 km/h
- SEA: Small wavelets. Crests have a glassy appearance and do not break
- LAND: Wind felt on face; leaves rustle; ordinary vane moved by wind

FORCE 3 — "Gentle Breeze"
- SPEED: 7-10 Knots / 8-12 mph / 12-19 km/h
- SEA: Large wavelets. Crests begin to break. Foam of glassy appearance.
- LAND: Leaves and small twigs in constant motion; wind extends light flag

FORCE 4 — "Moderate Breeze"
- SPEED: 11-16 Knots / 13-18 mph / 20-29 km/h
- SEA: Small waves becoming longer, fairly frequent white horses
- LAND: Raises dust and loose paper; small branches are moved

FORCE 5 — "Fresh Breeze"
- SPEED: 17-21 Knots / 19-24 mph / 30-39 km/h
- SEA: Moderate waves, taking a more pronounced long form; many white horses are formed
- LAND: Small trees in leaf begin to sway; wavelets form on inland waters

FORCE 6 — "Strong Breeze"
- SPEED: 22-27 Knots / 25-31 mph / 40-50 km/h
- SEA: Large waves begin to form; the white foam crests are more extensive everywhere
- LAND: Large branches in motion; whistling heard in telegraph wires; umbrellas use difficult

FORCE 7 — "Near Gale"
- SPEED: 28-33 Knots / 32-38 mph / 51-62 km/h
- SEA: Sea heaps up and white foam from breaking waves begins to be blown in streaks
- LAND: Whole trees in motion; inconvenience felt when walking

FORCE 8 — "Gale"
- SPEED: 34-40 Knots / 39-46 mph / 63-75 km/h
- SEA: Moderately high waves of greater length; edges of crests begin to break into spindrift
- LAND: Breaks twigs off trees; generally impedes progress

FORCE 9 — "Strong Gale"
- SPEED: 41-47 Knots / 47-54 mph / 76-87 km/h
- SEA: High waves. Crests of waves begin to topple and roll over. Spray may affect visibility
- LAND: Slight structural damage occurs; chimney pots and slates removed

FORCE 10 — "Storm"
- SPEED: 48-55 Knots / 55-63 mph / 88-102 km/h
- SEA: Very high waves. Surface of the sea takes on a white appearance. Visibility affected
- LAND: Seldom experienced inland; trees uprooted; considerable structural damage occurs

FORCE 11 — "Violent Storm"
- SPEED: 56-63 Knots / 64-72 mph / 103-117 km/h
- SEA: Exceptionally high waves. The sea is covered with long white patches of foam.
- LAND: Very rarely experienced on land; accompanied by widespread damage

FORCE 12 — "Hurricane"
- SPEED: over 63 Knots / over 72 mph / over 117 km/h
- SEA: Huge waves; air is filled with foam and spray. Sea white with driving spray; visibility very seriously affected
- LAND: Countryside is devastated

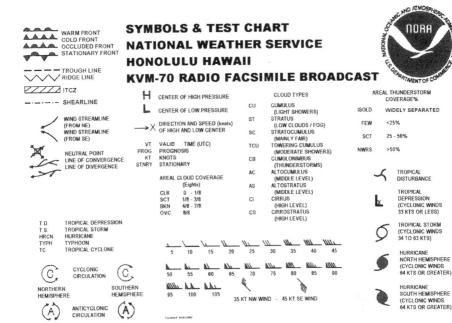

SYMBOLS & TEST CHART
NATIONAL WEATHER SERVICE
HONOLULU HAWAII
KVM-70 RADIO FACSIMILE BROADCAST

WARM FRONT
COLD FRONT
OCCLUDED FRONT
STATIONARY FRONT

TROUGH LINE
RIDGE LINE
ITCZ
SHEARLINE

WIND STREAMLINE (FROM NE)
WIND STREAMLINE (FROM SE)

NEUTRAL POINT
LINE OF CONVERGENCE
LINE OF DIVERGENCE

T.D.   TROPICAL DEPRESSION
T.S.   TROPICAL STORM
HRCN   HURRICANE
TYPH   TYPHOON
TC   TROPICAL CYCLONE

CYCLONIC CIRCULATION

NORTHERN HEMISPHERE   SOUTHERN HEMISPHERE

ANTICYCLONIC CIRCULATION

H   CENTER OF HIGH PRESSURE
L   CENTER OF LOW PRESSURE

→ X   DIRECTION AND SPEED (knots) OF HIGH AND LOW CENTER

VT   VALID TIME (UTC)
PROG   PROGNOSIS
KT   KNOTS
STNRY STATIONARY

AREAL CLOUD COVERAGE (Eights)
CLR   0 - 1/8
SCT   1/8 - 3/8
BKN   4/8 - 7/8
OVC   8/8

5 10 15 20 25 30 35 40 45
50 55 60 65 70 75 80 85 90
95 100 105

35 KT NW WIND - 45 KT SE WIND

Updated 01/03/2007

CLOUD TYPES

CU   CUMULUS (LIGHT SHOWERS)
ST   STRATUS (LOW CLOUDS / FOG)
SC   STRATOCUMULUS (MAINLY FAIR)
TCU   TOWERING CUMULUS (MODERATE SHOWERS)
CB   CUMULONIMBUS (THUNDERSTORMS)
AC   ALTOCUMULUS (MIDDLE LEVEL)
AS   ALTOSTRATUS (MIDDLE LEVEL)
CI   CIRRUS (HIGH LEVEL)
CS   CIRROSTRATUS (HIGH LEVEL)

AREAL THUNDERSTORM COVERAGE%

ISOLD   WIDELY SEPARATED
FEW   <25%
SCT   25 - 50%
NWRS   >50%

TROPICAL DISTURBANCE

TROPICAL DEPRESSION (CYCLONIC WINDS 33 KTS OR LESS)

TROPICAL STORM (CYCLONIC WINDS 34 TO 63 KTS)

HURRICANE NORTH HEMISPHERE (CYCLONIC WINDS 64 KTS OR GREATER)

HURRICANE SOUTH HEMISPHERE (CYCLONIC WINDS 64 KTS OR GREATER)

---

you are setting out to do, is to combine paddling and surfing in harmony so as to enjoy free rides along the way. Increasingly higher wind strength will not necessarily increase the need for greater skill levels, increased water motion and size will however make more demands on your skills.

The determination, identification and classification of wind strength is calculated by use of the Beaufort Wind Scale. Being able to discuss wind strength in these terms with others is an essential element to your relationship with the nature of wind. This skill will enable you to read wind strength simply through observation - observation of the trees and the sea state and the feel of the wind itself. Sailors for example learn this skill very early on. Wind speed can be measured using a simple hand held anemometer.

Hand held anemometers provide simple feedback in determining wind strength. Cupped devices such as the above are excellent as they do not need to be aimed directly into the wind to provide a reading.

351

"In Hawai`i the prevailing ENE wind, called Moa'e or A'eloa, is generated by a high pressure system that is generally located to the N or NE of the islands. Hawai`i is situated toward the bottom edge of this system (called the North Pacific High), where the clockwise winds are blowing easterly. These so-called trade winds average about 14 knots, but may gust well over gale force, particularly when they are funnelled through channels or mountain gaps." http://pvs.kcc.hawaii.edu/ike/hookele/weather_forecasting.html

Wind direction relative to your required line of travel

Identifying wind direction (where it's from and where it's blowing to) will affect the process of determining your session. So far as downwind paddling goes, you must determine to what degree the wind will be 'behind' you (usually no more than 20 degress on your quarter) and suitable 'entry and 'exit' points identified.

Wind direction in relation to land mass can be termed; on-shore, cross-on shore, cross-shore, cross-off shore and off-shore.

Consider how the wind is traveling in relation to where you want to leave from and where you want (or will need to) consider arriving / returning to. If the wind is biased even marginally cross off-shore, this is not ideal. If the wind is cross on-shore, then you have less concern. A simple feasibility sketch of your intended entry and exit points, wind direction, ground swell and sea state (surface runners) and direction of tidal flow can help.

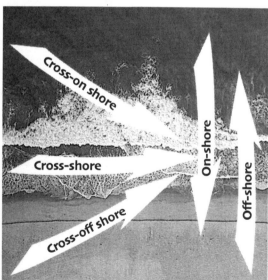

Wind is highly dynamic and can rise, fall, veer or shift often, suddenly and dramatically.

Alignment relative to shoreline / wind direction
While your course may keep you close to shore, it's not uncommon to find yourself a considerable distance off shore when paddling across a crescent shaped bay area. If paddling between islands, this is understood.

13
Downwind paddling, logistics and technical matters.

Often considered the sport's zenith when combining body,
blade and board skills in harmony with the elements, in what can
be a sleigh ride of enjoyment requiring at its peak,
a unique combination of skill sets, often acquired
over many years of experience.

KANU CULTURE

Connor Baxter - a prodigy of the stand up paddling evolutionary process, enjoying the sleigh ride, dropping in with poise, purity of focus and purpose. Out here in a world without roadsigns, you can find the essence of the sport in a culmination of all that you've ever learnt, but where you quickly learn there's more to know, a place where the feeling of accomplishment may pass, but where the sense of exhilaration never does.

Photo Karen Baxter

Torque, rotation, compression, tension, flexion, drive, commitment, leverage, pressure, digging deep into a sapphire ocean in search of gold at the finishing line. Racing of this nature is a state of mind, demanding you stay focused on extracting all that you can from the elements in the, here and now, without side-lining your thoughts elsewhere. The more rides you miss out on, the more paddling you'll need to do. In some respects the mantra here might read, 'He who takes the least strokes wins.'

Photo Karen Baxter
Rider Connor Baxter

Stand up paddle surfers for the most part, surf ocean ground swells generated by distant storms which pitch and break over shallow water. Downwind stand up paddle boarders pursue a completely different ocean energy; wind generated surface waves or wind swell often referred to simply as the, 'sea' hence descriptive terms such as, 'sea state'.

Stand up paddle boarding at its zenith?

Those who hail from an ocean paddling background, tend to bring this knowledge of paddling to the sport with them. Many who are fanatical 'downwind' paddlers, often possess years of uniquely acquired paddling skills and a passion for chasing 'runners', connecting the dots, knowing the rush one gets from combining the energy of wind and water.

This particular form of stand up paddling is gathering momentum rapidly. Of the three essential disciplines of the sport; surf, flat water cruising (limited breeze) and downwind paddling (strong winds) it is the latter which truly tests the rider's combined surfing and paddling skills; dependant on endurance and an entire repertoire of ocean skills and physicality honed over many years of a devotion to an ocean sports lifestyle.

Overview

You can surf, without a paddle, potter around on flat water with minimal fitness levels or ocean skills. But to take on the might of wind and water, paddling significant distances downwind between two islands separated by deepwater channels or from one land point to another, travelling at high speeds, is to take the sport to a place which truly reflects its zenith in combining the melding of mind, body, board, blade and the elements.

In this ocean environment, there are no road signs, no rules and no crowds. It is in short the ultimate testing ground, where sensory perceptions are tested to the limit. Here bodies can be brutalised, combining paddle skills with poise, balance, stealth, speed, endurance and tenacity. With each drop-in, the rider constantly scans the ocean for holes and powers up and down between sets, chasing 'runners' and looking to squeeze every drop of energy from its movement, searching for speed and a trade off between surfing (relaxing) and paddling hard.

While mastery can take years, initial practise can be on sheltered waters, but the biggest thrills are to be had in deep ocean waters. Here the sport is unparalleled to which no casual participant can randomly subscribe to. This is hardcore stand up paddle boarding in the purest sense, where specificity of training and equipment, passion and drive are paramount.

Defined

Downwind paddling is characterised by the rider using the wind to their advantage and enjoyment, in combing paddling and surfing skills so as to travel in a near direct line of travel of the wind (usually up to 20 degrees either side) harnessed through appropriate equipment, skills and physicality and an understanding of the required logistics, ocean and wind dynamics, central to the discipline. Specialised boards, fit for purpose, provide the best performance needs of the downwind paddler.

This form of paddling can at times be an extreme element of the sport where elite participants seek strong winds and fast moving seas or waters of undetermined size. Locations are varied and defined as exposed coastal waters and protected bays, lakes, lagoons; wherever a wide open exposed body of water can be found and used safely and legally.

Downwind water locations are often characterised by open stretches of water, generally exposed to prevailing winds, which may be 'trades' as associated with tropical and sub tropical regions of the world, or simply 'prevailing' winds. In either case, winds of this nature tend to be seasonal and have some degree of consistency of direction and velocity relative to the time of year, though any wind may be harnessed.

Many stand up paddle boarders go downwind paddling on their own purely for the fun of it and the unique challenges it presents. It combines a great sense of timing, anticipation, heightened levels of paddle skills, elements akin to surfing which are best learnt through discovery and a good sense of balance and confidence, both of which are not teachable in the true sense of the word. Most of what you learn is experiential and only acquired after a considerable amount of time - in effect you never stop learning.

Downwind paddling is arguably the pinnacle of the stand up paddle boarding experience, combining the power of the wind and waves and the skill of the rider on all levels, requiring stamina, concentration and the melding of sound maritime skills and logistical knowledge.

On a good day, downwind paddling should mean that everything worth catching is ahead of you, not behind.

Downwind solo paddle craft - the evolutionary tree. The wonder years when the sports blossomed . . .

Paddle Boarding 1930s Hawai`i

Tom Blake had been working on his new hollow prone paddle board designs which he first introduced to the racing scene in 1929 in Hawai`i, which between 1932 and 1938 became very popular. The Catalina Classic paddle board first ran in 1955 and became a focal point for prone distance racing. It could be considered that the craft itself runs closest to the stand up paddle board in terms of design parameters.

Surf Ski - 1970s South Africans / Australians

The original surf ski has been accredited to several but the most likely seems to be Australian Harry McLaren, who started dabbling with the ideas in 1912. Through the 1930s and 50s the craft underwent many changes in the hands of the Australians. In 1956 footwells were added and soon a recessed seat as widths were narrowed. In 1971 the first rounded fibreglass hull was designed by Australian's, George and Gordon Jeffery, subsequently built at Hayden Surf Skis Maroochydore and in 1972 hollow fibreglass paddle shafts appeared. In the early 1970s the South Africans began to pioneer ocean surf ski racing and the craft to suit.

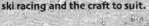

Todd Cohen. Photo Steve West

OC1 1990s Hawai`i

Conceptually, a very ancient craft most prevalent throughout cultures of Oceania but with traces as far back to cultures of East Africa, India and SE Asia, back over thousands of years. Ocean racing OC1 evolution commenced in 1986 with the modification of an imported rudderless open decked va'a hoe from Tahiti into Hawai`i, which led to open water OC1 downwind paddling as a niche area of interest. The first Moloka'i to Oahu race was held in 1989 (Kaiwi Challenge) with 3 entrants.

Stand Up Paddle Boarding 2000 Hawai`i

For a sport currently relishing such universal growth and development, it has to be said that the long, latent gestation period from the 1960s through to the 1990s seems somewhat incredulous. Now that the sport has rocketed to popularity, the varying niche interests are manifesting. Downwind paddling on any craft can be a buzz, but on purpose made boards in ideal conditions and honed skill-sets, it represents in the context of paddle sports a unique combination of paddling and surfing skills. Archie Kalepa first entered the 2004 Moloka'i to O`ahu prone paddle board race in 2004. Just yesterday in chronological / historical terms.

Connor Baxter Maui to Moloka`i crossing. Photo Karen Baxter

Historically, South Africans, New Zealanders, Australians and Hawaiians in particular, make up the bulk of the worlds best downwind paddlers across a number of paddle sport disciplines, be it surf ski, outrigger canoe or prone paddle boarding. LIving in areas of the world where predominant winds, ocean conditions, mindset and cultural affinity for hardcore paddling prevail, they are free to develop equipment and skills to suit.

Bumps and runners

The term paddling 'downwind' is commonly used by the ocean paddler to describe paddling with the wind behind, chasing fast moving, wind generated surface water, which can of course be termed for any body of water where the paddler is following wind direction.

The experienced paddler reads the ocean or water as a series of ever rising and falling peaks and troughs collectively known as 'bumps' into which they steer their boards, attempting to remain on the 'fastest' sections which provide the most assistance - the downward slope or forward face.

While there can be many bumps, not all bumps are 'runners', a term which more accurately defines the waves as being able to deliver speed and assistance to the board's momentum. There can be many bumps, but some are better 'runners' than others and this you learn by attempting, often fruitlessly, to chase and paddle hard for everything. The art is in selection.

As a snow skier moves left and right to carve a path between bumps, so too, the ocean paddler seeks a similar path between the waves. In response to this particular skill, designers have created boards specific to the purpose of ocean paddling, more specifically, chasing runners downwind.

The art of selecting and remaining in the fast section of these runners requires the paddler to remain alert, anticipating or seeing where one section is diminishing and another is forming. The goal is to ultimately 'connect' or 'link' these newly forming sections to maximise assistance and speed, sometimes referred to as 'connecting the dots'.

As a consequence, in the case of downwind paddling, the fastest direction between two points is rarely in a straight line. Importantly, when moving at speed it's not so much what's behind you that matters, but what's in front. This is in contrast to free-surfing, where for want of a better term, you are 'pushed' from behind. This represents a paradigm shift in thinking for surfers in particular.

Ground swells or wind generated waves and swell

While surface generated wind waves and swells are a localised phenomenon, a larger ground swell can reside below and between. Ground swells, are caused by distant powerful storms and are often mere decoys in terms of where real gains in speed can be found when paddling offshore.

Though the ground swell encountered far from shore in deep water will often be moving at a greater speed than that of the surface waves, they are generally difficult to catch because they are not as steep as the surface waves and not always travelling in the direction of the wind. However, if the distance between the ground swells is short and the incline steep and following the direction of the wind, this could change your tactics.

Navigator Nainoa Thompson explains the difference between swells and seas, or locally-generated waves: **"Swells are big waves generated by pressure systems far beyond the horizon, and they maintain their direction for long periods of time (and travel in the general direction of the winds generating them). Seas are generated by local winds. Seas generally come downwind, but they may vary by as much as 30° on either side of the wind. When the wind changes, seas become more of a mish-mash"**
(Kyselka 167-8)

Safety first - involve others

Downwind paddling often elevates the need to take safety to another level. This includes advising others of your intentions and your intended course and duration, especially if paddling on your own. Whenever possible, paddle with others, but be aware of each other's abilities and stay within them.

When paddling with buddies, you may often be only as fast (or as safe) as your weakest paddler - some paddling buddies can be more of a liability than an asset.

Notify someone you can trust and understands what you are doing. Consider notifying the Coast Guard of your intended departure time and more importantly, notify them of your arrival. This is important when you have a larger group of people or where the conditions are do-able but perhaps technically difficult. If your course takes you past a Coast Guard Station or Surf Lifesaving Club, it's sometimes common courtesy to let them know what you're up to. Sometimes 'do-gooders' will ring the Coast

Guard thinking you're in trouble, but if authorities know you're out there, then you are covered. To quote a famous movie line 'A good man knows his limitations' and while it's important to push the boundaries in having fun, the question you should ask yourself is, 'If things go bad, am I covered and how will I respond?'.

Logistical issues

Central to downwind paddling is good planning and becoming accomplished in dealing with the logistics required. 'If you fail to plan, you plan to fail' as the saying goes. Whilst this may become second nature over time in your local waters, any move away to take on new areas of water will lead to logistical challenges.

It can be beneficial to document and plan out your session using a note book or white board, drawing in the wind direction, course to be taken, areas to avoid, exit points and final destination.

Connor Baxter Maui to Moloka`i crossing. Photo Karen Baxter

Try to estimate how long the journey will take and factor in when paddling with others, that 'You are only going to be as fast as your slowest paddler' - avoid paddling off into the distance, leaving your slower (weaker) paddlers behind - stop at regular intervals if required.

In the learning stages, you should paddle in sheltered (enclosed) waters where the waters are relatively calm. Practice over short distances of 1 - 2 miles and learn to time yourself to get to know your approximate duration over any given distance, though take into account any random factors that will affect this - wind strength, wave assistance, board design, paddling skills, fitness levels, tidal flow, all of which you need learn to factor into your calculations.

Transportation Issues

At your arrival point you will need to consider some form of transportation unless you have paddled back to a safe haven, such as back to your home, or a club ground or similar.

There are a few approaches to this. **Taxi ride.** Drop off a sufficient number of vehicles at finish point, to take paddlers and their boards (some or all) back to their vehicles at the start point. **Taxi ride and trailer.** Drop off a vehicle with trailer at finish point plus enough vehicles to return paddlers and their boards back to the start point. **Designated driver.** Have designated driver/s after your departure, drive your vehicle/s to the finish point. **Paddle home, ride back.** Here you drive to your entry point, set off and on arrival you leave your board somewhere safe and you could ride a push bike back to your car or if your lucky enough, get a lift back using your second vehicle with the help of immediately family / friend.

Carrying and managing your downwind board on land

Have help on windy days when loading / unloading and in carrying, as boards of any size can be a handful in fresh winds – the larger the board the greater the windage, the more likelihood of loosing control. Ideally you can call on the assistance of a buddy or passing stranger if the situation warrants it. Managing long boards safely in fresh winds can be very demanding, both in terms of securing and removing from a roof rack (especially high sided vehicles) through to placement on the ground and carrying in general.

Boards are easily lifted and blown off the roof of your car and can easily roll down the beach if left unattended. When being carried, they can swing around violently through wind pressure and impact against people or solid items. All of these scenarios can lead to injury to self or others, damage of board or other valuable items.

Never leave your board side on to the wind; usually upside down with the tail into the wind offers the safest option. When carrying in a cross-wind, carry board on the downwind side to avoid board compressing against you and spinning you around. You can let the board lift up and

In this situation the wind is blowing right to left (side shore) and the shore break is confused and messy. Keeping upwind of the board, the wind gets under the board and lifts it in your favour. When the board is placed in the water, you want to be upwind of it in this situation.

This is hardly a text book launch, but faced with freezing cold, dumping waves directly onto shingle, strong cross-shore winds as in this instance, you end up having to muscle your way out - not that you shouldn't still time your entry!

16' downwind boards do not cope well with shore breaks and neither are they easy to manage. These often, lighter, longer constructed boards, have greater longitudinal flex and could snap if impacted hard enough.

Loss of control on the way out could be expensive as they are not designed to get 'worked' in the surf.

away from the side of the body so as the wind passes under and over it. Carry it so as aerodynamically, it is working with you, not against you.

Launching and exiting the water

Launching and exiting the water in high winds can be problematic, more especially launching. The degree of difficulty will depend on the wind direction, relative to the board's angle of placement in the water. Strong cross-shore winds for example may threaten to roll the board in which case, stay upwind of the board, ensure you keep pressure on the deck when you place it, to keep it steady and flat on the water. Mount the board with minimal delay and set off as the shore break allows - you may need to be paddle kneeling to clear the shore break. Consider securing leash to either leg for ease of launching (leash should attach to rear leg in relation to the side you are mounting the board - left if from the right and vice-versa).

Learning days in brief

While it is possible to paddle downwind in extremes of wind on flat water, knowing your limitations is a good maxim to live by. Ensure the wind is moving in a suitable direction and ideally, no more than 20 degrees either side of (directly behind) your intended line of travel. Check weather forecast for changes in wind direction or velocity. Ensure you are confident to the task as is your fitness. How is your confidence in deep water? Ensure your equipment is up to the task and suitable for the conditions. Calculate your approximate departure and arrival time and inform others. Notify appropriate authorities / persons. Ensure you're suitably hydrated and have sufficient energy levels.

Entry and exit points

Wind direction will have a profound affect in determining your entry and exit points. You must establish safe and suitable exit points for your downwind run. The longer the distance to be traveled, you should consider additional exit points along the way if the need arises. If there are non available, you will need to implement additional safety measures. A common error is to fail to account for the exit points changed state over time due to rising or falling waters (tide) or increased swell / wave action accompanying this and the effects of 'fetch'.

Get to know your local area, prevailing wind directions and water conditions. Familiarize yourself with your surrounds in all conditions and always carry out some reconnaissance before each session. In unfamiliar areas, seek out local advice, study maps and get informed. Not uncommonly the entry point is often calm or in the lee of the land, whereas the exit point can often be rougher and more exposed unless a safe haven can be reached.

When the wind is very high and cross-shore, a second pair of hands can be a great help. 14' boards upwards are a handful to carry in strong winds. Where shore break is present, patience is a virtue and timing is everything. Check the wave pattern / regularity and launch when there is a surge back out to sea and a lull in the waves.

Entry points

This will be your 'upwind' point from which you will launch and proceed to paddle to your 'downwind' exit point. Entry points take on many differing types; river mouth, harbour entrance, exposed beach. In all cases exercise due caution.

With windy conditions, a shore break is more likely. On-shore winds can create dumping waves and make launching challenging. Don't break any access laws, respect private property, check for any signage associated with that particular stretch of beach. Ensure beach break is manageable.

Exit points

Changing weather, wind and tide conditions can affect the exit location and make exit difficult or unsafe. If you know your exit point is consistently safe and free of hazards then there may be no reason to check this prior to departure.

Due to the logistics involved it is commonplace for vehicles / trailer to be left at the finish point and therefore the finish / exit point will often be seen prior to departure. You could ask a friend who lives in that direction to provide feedback or if available, check out a web cam, view any maritime / surf information.

Things are never static, in 2 hours time, the tide may have come up and

Leaving a beach where there is a shore break, you may need to push off and launch with a bit of inertia to get the board stable and to push through any oncoming waves. Some longer downwind boards, are not designed to punch out through shore break and prone to stress so paddling out from the shore break, paddle kneeling, is a sound option.

373

wind increased 10 knots. You wouldn't just check out that one exit point over a distance of say 10km, you should allow for additional exit points along the way – in the event you have to abort.

Equipment

Check your paddle for signs of stress and replace / repair accordingly. Paddle failure once under way can have dramatic consequences. A 2 or 3 part spare paddle can be fitted to longer boards if deemed necessary in more extreme circumstances. Check your board for sharp edged dings, decking, tiller arm set up if included, fin fitment and security. Ensure your leash is not showing signs of fraying or fatigue. Checking your equipment, allows you to form a better relationship with your kit - many paddlers fail to maintain or look at their equipment in any detail.

Downwind boards

Inappropriate board sizes and designs for downwind paddling, will affect performance, enjoyment, speed and time over distance travelled, often resulting in greater energy expenditure for less return. Open water paddling requires good balance, paddle skills and anticipation. Typically shorter (12'6") entry level boards, tend to be wide, flat and stable - not a recipe for speed. As you improve, you will lean towards, narrower, longer, sleeker boards, which will provide added stability through speed gains.

This is a specialist discipline and there are currently a limited number of purpose made boards, designed with no other consideration in mind other than excelling at this one task. Many non specialised boards, still provide a great deal of fun in a downwind paddling environment.

The fastest downwind boards in their purest form are between 14' and 18' in length and at the upper length limits foot operated tiller arms which transforms the fin into being a rudder, are almost always fitted. Many of

these are custom made for the paddler. 14' boards are more common place for downwind paddling (and the racing scene) while there are also a limited number of 12'6" boards which also perform reasonably well and often provide entry level to this discipline.

These boards are at the upper end of the price range, but represent the pinnacle in form and function. Downwind boards generally have large flat areas for planing or feature concaves, soft rails for most of their length to avoid 'tripping' and harder towards the rear. They are often narrower than many conventional boards; often 28" and under and have recessed deck levels to lower the rider's centre of gravity. They may feature pin tails (similar to the gun shapes of big wave boards) or rounded pin shaped tails, though some are squash tailed (squared off).

14' without tiller arm rudder for higher performance downwind paddling.
14' with tiller arm for improved versatility and higher performance.
16 – 18' boards with tiller arm for pure specificity. (See chapters regarding board design)

Jamie Mitchell paddling with the essential bare minimum in a tropical climate. Coiled knee worn leash. Waist worn hydration pack, with tube clipped to shirt for ease of reach to bite valve.

Photo Dana Edmunds Courtesy of Ocean Promotions

Paddles

Heavy, overly long paddle lengths and oversized blade faces can cause extra effort and therefore fatigue. High wind, specialist downwind paddlers often prefer smaller blade sizes in order to permit high stroke rates being as downwind paddling is aerobically demanding, sometimes only 7.25" in width. The smaller blade permits faster turn over and better handling, together with the shortened total length of paddle.

Larger, rougher water will demand the paddler is constantly lowering their centre of gravity through crouching and the shorter paddle assists in this regard and shortens the lever arm giving the paddler greater direct control and power to the blade with the lower arm.

Leg leash

Knee worn coiled leashes are popular for avoiding drag and de-cluttering the deck. Be careful when paddling over breaking waves if you fall, because of the potential for recoil. Popular for racing and learning in non-surf environments being as the leash is raised from the deck and does not drag over board. The leash can also be removed quickly and easily.

While it's possible to paddle any board downwind, it's all a matter of specificity and ultimately how much fun the board will deliver as a result of speed and responsiveness. Downwind paddlers love to go fast and anything that limits that enjoyment tends to get replaced!

Some shapes remain iconic. Simple, enduring, pleasing to the eye and will forevermore be with us as classic embodiments of form and function. 14' V1 C4 Dave Parmenter semi-displacement high volume board for smaller moderate days. SIC F16 purpose made downwind board and a 14'8" Starboard Point, both Mark Raaphorst designs, which come alive at the higher ends of the wind spectrum.

Form and function

"Free riding wind and water in harmony, puts downwind paddling into the realms of addiction."

During the mid 90s on a flight from Honolulu to LA to compete at the Catalina Classic, I was discussing with Todd Bradley some of the many skills required to become a world class OC steerer. Naturally the subject turned to paddles, a favourite topic of mine and Todd's. He made the analogy that for the steerer they must be able to wield their paddle from side to side of the canoe like a swordsman or warrior. This has long since remained with me as a classic way to describe your association with the paddle. Downwind paddling places this same need upon the paddler to quickly move the paddle from left to right in response to the nuances of the water around them in making correctional strokes and in powering up.

An alternate way of switching paddling sides. When the board is 'running' at speed, reverse the lower hand to an under-hand grip and direct the blade upwards using the lower. Literally flick the blade up and over and switch hands on the new side.

Paddling techniques

Variance of Stroke Rate Relative to Rate of Travel of the Board

When paddling downwind following a 'running' sea, knowing when to paddle hard and when to back off are key skill elements. The ability to deliver varying power, increased stroke rates and different technique to achieve effective speed gains, is a true skill.

The trigger to change any single or multiple aspect of technique or application, can either be a visual response in seeing the runner forming ahead in the form of a trough or a 'feeling' when the craft begins to drop at the nose and lift at the tail.

Your focus needs to be on what's ahead of you, reading and interpreting the constantly changing shape of the ocean and anticipating how your board is going to react. These skills transcend true explanation and must be learned by experience.

You must remain resolute and confident, continually biting away at the ocean, reading its nuances immediately in front and below the blade, keeping the board steady between the curvatures of the ocean, keeping a broader view and continually setting up to take advantage of the ocean's energy. Avoid 'switching off' and simply swinging away without thought.

Knowing when to vary the stroke rate, how much power to deliver to the blade, and your optimum length of reach, is only acquired by paddling all points of the ocean; across, into and with, so you learn to vary your stroke

The wind can be as much as 20 degrees on your 'quarter' relative to your downwind destination, compensated for by engaging the rails and or use of a tiller arm to bring you back on line.

to get the most out of the ocean and your board. This knowledge is paramount in remaining in harmony with a constantly shifting ocean.

The faster the board travels, the higher your potential stroke rate will be, indeed it should increase and in addition your stroke rate can also be shortened. Stroke rate can be measured by strokes per minute. Some paddlers fail to vary their stroke rate, creating retarding forces countering the board's progress.

Mental picture: Think in terms of powering a scooter, using long and strong leg pushes on flat ground using a regular steady cadence. As you progress up a hill, your leg action will shorten and slow on account of the added forces working against you, then as you reach the crest and drop down the hill, your leg action speeds and length of reach will increase momentarily, then shorten as you reach maximum speed, at which point you can stop altogether as you enjoy the ride. As the scooter begins to slow, you bring your leg back into action to provide direct power where gravity has left off.

Vary your stroke rates, relative to your position on each wave. This variance will alter your paddling between anaerobic and aerobic

states. Slower equates more anaerobic. Faster equates, more aerobic (more oxygen dependant). Essentially chasing runners consists of a series of short sprints followed by periods of relaxation (recovery).

Variance of Stroke Rate Relative to Position of Board on Wave

When you are in the trough of a wave, between wave sets, your stroke rate will tend to slow as the surface water particles are revolving counter to your direction of flow, which tends to bring about a longer, deeper, stronger stroke. Long and strong is the maxim here generally. By adopting this technique, you conserve some aerobic energy and prime the board keeping the power on the blade.

Water particles within waves, rotate forward at the crest and backward at the trough. This results in (approximately) no net motion of the water as the wave passes. Within the wave trough the water particles are revolving against you. As you approach the back of the wave the water particles tend to be revolving in your favour, assisting in 'pulling' you up to the crest. Once you reach the crest (peak) the rotational forces increasingly act against you as you begin to move down the wave. At the crest, you will need to 'push-over' this section by paddling over the crest and onto the wave face until such time as the net rotational hydrodynamical forces of

On marginal days, this seesawing is common on account of the board stalling between sets.

Stalling

The board begins to stall as the nose angles upwards and the revolving water particles within the trough, work in the opposite direction of travel to pull the board back. This is a good time to change arms and prime the board for take off.

Take-Off

The wave then reforms and lifts the tail and the paddler powers up as the nose drops and the board 'takes off' - the water particles now assisting the board as it now sits in a newly reformed section. Ideally you want to avoid 'stalling' but many factors can work against you - a tidal flow moving in the other direction is a classic example.

the water moving up the wave face due to the board's speed are sufficient so as the buoyancy of the board and the gravity of your weight acting downwards, reach a point of negating each other (net zero force) which frees the board up so as it is 'surfing' and you can partially relax.

This will tend to lead you to initially weight the board towards the nose, then step back as the board gathers speed down the face.

Either the nose of the board will drop, as the tail lifts as the wave behind catches you up if you have slowed dramatically, or if you have maintained speed (ideal) you will steer the board over and into the next trough (hole) - both can result in the board beginning to surf the wave at near planing speed and as this transition happens, the board will gain speed and momentum and your stroke rate should increase in direct proportion to the point where you can cease paddling and enjoy the ride. At this point you can stand up tall and stretch and relax or adopt a crouched stance in order to apply pressure to the rails and gain increased stability.

Once you get into a rhythm of the board's nuances and interaction with the waves you will be better able to alter your stroke rate to suit and in time it will become instinctual. What you want to achieve is priming the board up (going deep, going hard), increasing stroke rate as you drop into the wave, ultimately stopping as you catch the wave and ride it out, coupled with a skill known by many as 'connecting the dots'.

Common mistakes

Failing to vary stroke rates. Failing to vary stroke lengths. Failing to combine these in harmony. Tending to follow a straight line. Not eyeballing water around you, looking at feet or board. Chasing poor quality waves. Chasing every bump (not every bump is a 'runner'). Lack of concentration.

Switching paddling sides

Canoeing incorporates a 'sit and switch' style of paddling while stand up paddling incorporates a 'stand and switch' technique. The fundamental principal here is to ensure your arms remain fresh, so your aim is to change sides before you fatigue. In the context of downwind paddling, where there are runners to be had, there is a time to change sides and a time not to.

A good time to change sides, is if you feel fatigue building up, but if you're just about to drop in on a runner, this could jeopardise your success. Ideally, change sides before you fatigue. When the board stalls and its forward momentum has slowed between waves, usually because of the retarding forces of water flow in the opposite direction of your travel, this is a good time to switch sides so as you can grind hard and deep to get momentum.

Just as the board begins to take off, your stroke rate will increase. This is not a good time to change sides if you haven't quite got the momentum you need to drop in. Once you are actually surfing down the face, this is a good time to change sides. Change to avoid fatigue and to maintain momentum in relation to your board's rate of travel, whether stalling or accelerating. This skill applies even when chasing small runners.

The very idea of downwind paddling is in taking time out to enjoy the ride. Novices often 'spin the wheels' with high and consistent stroke rates - without taking time out to take stock of what's going on around them in figuring out when to 'go hard' and when to 'back off'. If you're paddling with buddies who are pulling away from you dramatically (given same / similar boards) then you need figure out which part of the puzzle they have figured out.

Going long or going short

While keeping a 'long out-front' paddling style is essential, there are times when you will want to shorten up. This is a 'feel' orientated skill which takes time to develop.

Going short, is demanding in terms of its application. A shortening of the reach provides you with a brief opportunity to; increase board speed through increased stroke rate; maintain speed in adverse situations such as paddling against strong tides and shallow water (where the hull is sucked down - known as 'interaction') or when you need to push over the face of a swell. It can also be used in short bursts to catch up and overtake another board when racing.

Perhaps the most common example of its application is from a standing start where the stroke-length is initially short and deep, progressively lengthening out as a steadier pace is established. The skill here is in having excellent paddle control so the blade is buried cleanly, ensuring it 'bites' before power is applied and that the exit is clean. 'Rooster tail' starts may look good, but are generally inefficient.

While the longer stroke is appropriate for consistent distance pace paddling, when a short burst of speed or additional power is required, marginally shortening the reach and depth-charging the paddle can effectively provide acceleration. Working within a burst of six to ten strokes seems most effective.

Adding variety to your stroke

The most common time to vary long and short reach is when chasing runners. A following sea continually accelerates and decelerates the progress of the board as it travels between waves and at times 'stalls' in the trough when it buries into the back of the wave ahead. During the 'lull', when the board falls off the runner and labours in the trough, it's a good time to 'shorten up'.

You want to apply plenty of power, driving deep, 'depth- charging' your stroke for a short period of time, to 'prime' the board for the next drop in. Naturally your stroke rate slows marginally, proportional to the board's speed, so you compensate for this by pouring on the power. As the board drops in and gathers speed, the stroke is 'lengthened' out and the stroke rate increased proportionally to match board speed.

Flat water paddling calls for a consistency of stroke length and rate. But even in this situation, variation will break the monotony and provide bursts of speed in between the 'distance pace'.

Power up / power down

Relates back to our stroke rate and length. Powering up means you are applying maximum power to the blade. Pulling / rotating as hard as you can. Often used in the trough or when wanting to drop in on a wave or when board is stalling. Here you are priming the board, putting a lot of power to the blade. Whenever you find the board is slowing, apply lots of power and consider switching sides to use fresh arms.

When you feel you are about to surge on to a wave, the faster you begin to go, the less leverage or power required to the blade being as you are transitioning from paddle power to wave power - in effect, going from muscling the board into position to allowing nature's power to take over.

When switching paddling sides, avoid doing so when totally fatigued. Do so before this happens in order to maintain a higher overall level of power and consistency. Having changed sides, power up straight away. Changing sides is not a time to rest, but a chance to power up with fresh arms.

Use of paddle as a brace

Used often when the board is up and riding a wave. Learn to throw the paddle around and use it in the same way as a tight ropewalker uses a pole.

Put the paddle out to one side, blade face skyward, extending out from board, crouch down and over the board for improved balance.

When bracing, instinctively bend at the knees and allow the blade to be kissing surface of water. Use this when you feel any sense of instability in choppy or uneven water or with big, fast, steep drop-ins. Use also when stationary, with paddle over one side of board and just tapping it on the surface, slight pressure acts as a tripod in effect and transfers pressure to the feet.

Lowering your centre of gravity (CG)

It becomes increasingly important to lower your centre of gravity to bring it closer to the board's centre of buoyancy. By doing this, you increase your stability. Riders bend their knees to lower centre of gravity.

Assuming an offset (diagonal) bent knee stance, lowers the body's centre of gravity assisting balance. In addition a low arched recovery of the blade allows for quick and smooth bracing to be made when required.

Paddling variations simplified

1. Long and strong when the board is 'running' along larger wave face, when cruising in flatter water keeping lots of power to the blade. Avoid pulling too far past the hip.

2. Short and deep. Shorten length out front, but go deeper. Use when in trough of wave. When powering up, or just before you drop into the wave. Shorten stroke and go deep.

3. Quick 'n light. Stroke rate increases, power to the blade lessened and not driven so deep. Use when on wave, moving quickly. Board travelling very fast at speed, maintain momentum, quick and light to keep board moving. Think also in terms of exiting paddle early.

Generate mental pictures of varying paddling rates and how much power to apply to the blade. Going deep gives you power but is fatiguing so vary it and know when to use it. Varying stroke rate and length is to work with the movement of the water not against it.

Foot placement

Where you are stood on the board relative to the wave under you and relative to the board's variance of 'sweet spot' will maximise the board's efficiency in hull speed. If you maintain same stroke rates and lengths and fail to move around the board, fore and aft to some degree (longer the board, the more you will need to move around) it doesn't acknowledge the changing dynamics of the water's movement underneath.

Don't stand in the same spot all the time. Move around in order to keep the board planing as much as possible. Maintain momentum at optimal speeds. Downwind paddling requires you avoid standing in a neutral stance but have an engaged foot placement, one leading leg and one behind ie Goofy or regular. Understand your preference. As soon as you drop in on wave, you are ready for it. This allows you to lower your centre of gravity and use rail steering when required.

Rail steering

Use the rails to make transitions; apply your weight to left / right rail to alter direction of travel. This is the smoothest way to make direction changes at speed. Rail steering only becomes effective when you step back as it does not work so well from the middle of the board. Apply weight to

rails under speed. As board slows, step forward again.

Downwind boards don't require radical variance of direction change, only maybe 20 degrees either way and therefore rails are generally softer (rounder) for most of their length so as the board doesn't trip, track or dig in towards the front as it drops in and tend to be harder / sharper toward the tail to provide added directional tracking at speed.

Tiller arm rudder steering

If you have a board with tiller arm steering, you will need to learn how to use it. This can be used if the wind or waves are on your quarter, or wind pushing you in adverse direction counter to where you need

Dropping into a runner may take on a different approach from conventional surfing, however it is important to learn to trim your board down the wave face rather than straight lining your travel so as you bottom-out into the back of the wave ahead of you. Trimming the board gives you added control and speed at critical moments. This will provide for the longest 'runs' to be had - and the most fun.

to go. The idea is to use the tiller arm as little as possible, being when you turn the fin too far; this creates drag and slows you down.

It is a very useful device which can elevate your paddling experience and the range of conditions you can enjoy and safely manage. If the wind alters adversely the tiller arm can be a employed and become a useful 'safety feature'. You can keep fresher arms as it can negate the need to paddle on one predominant side so as you can keep power to both sides of the board. While specialist 'unlimited' boards tend to have tiller arms, many do not.

The main benefit is to offset any bias of travel – going between two points, countering any wind, tidal or wave action taking you off line, enabling you to concentrate on paddling without having to paddle on one side all the time. In some regard it is a safety device and in time, they will no doubt gain greater prominence. For boards of 16ft upwards it makes the board far easier to manage given their length.

Note: Avoid over reliance of the steering mechanism and being fixated by it. This will tend to limit advancement of your paddle and board skills. Think of it almost as a safety device, which you use only when you need to offset adverse conditions. Nevertheless, a very useful device to have.

Continued board run

An ability to maintain good board run is due in part to the combining of all factors. Your ability to maintain stroke rate, stroke length, changing sides at appropriate times, moving your feet correctly, keeping the board on its sweet spot, making rail transitions only when required, switching onto the environment and working with the water and not against it, sourcing out the waves and holes when present, in order to maintain a high average speed. Combining all these abilities will reduce the amount of time you spend stalling. The Idea is to keep momentum as much as possible.

Sweet spot variance between boards

The shorter the board, the narrower the 'sweet spot' band will tend to be, in contrast to a longer design. A 14ft board will have a greater range of sweet spots and therefore a greater range of water conditions, in which it will perform well. Short boards lack board run (glide) - under 12'6" and this performance diminishes noticeably. Short boards will constantly stall and rock back and forth between waves and lack momentum and hull speed inherent in a longer design. The constant shifting of the undersides foot print relative to where it is on the wave, requires that added 'rocker' designed into the board, keeps the footprint more constant and conforms better to the natural curvature of the waves. Straighter boards can struggle in nose diving and overall general handling.

Observation and anticipation

An ability to identify runners and knowing which ones to chase is a skill. You need constantly be eyeballing the water and looking to put yourself into a position in order to stand a chance of connecting with it. Remember these runners are all ahead of you (on a good day).

Change paddling sides frequently to keep fresh arms and to keep in sync with the ocean's movements. When you drop in, alter foot placement to suit, alter your centre of gravity. Enjoy the ride, but it's important not to switch off, as you need to keep looking for the next.

One way to identify a runner forming ahead of you, is to observe the ocean tearing itself apart, creating a hole. You're looking to put yourself there by steering the nose of the board in the hole.

On light wind days, just go out and paddle in the direction of travel of small bumps. Try and catch up to them and connect with them to enjoy short assisted runs - learn the benefits of powering up and down and the nuances of your board. You don't need lots of wind to learn some downwind paddling skills.

Not every bump is a runner. Every time you see an opportunity, work out if it is worth chasing. You're looking for the steepest and fastest moving section, traveling more or less in the direction you want to go. After 3-4 hard strokes, if you're not on it, save your energy and look elsewhere. As you begin to fatigue it's not uncommon to begin to make judgment errors and get caught out.

The surface generated waves - the fast moving surface water, is generally what the downwind paddler seeks. Ground swell can be caught only with this assistance, but are not the primary provider of speed gains. The primary distinction between surfing and downwind paddling, is that the surfer is concerned with waves behind him. For the downwind paddler everything is generally ahead of you, traveling at speed, looking to drop into the wave ahead of you. Looking ahead of you. A bit like downhill skiing, looking at dropping into depressions and putting yourself into a series of holes. Don't look over your shoulder – look in front of you.

Developing a sense of anticipation is an essential skill only learned with lots of time spent on the water chasing runners. Anticipating how the waves are forming ahead and around you and determining where you need to be, even before it happens, is a sixth sense, which the best downwind paddlers develop in putting themselves with consistency into the fastest sections of water which pay off in speed.

Dangers of falling at speed

When you fall at speed things are naturally accelerated and can become chaotic, but you need to learn to fall under control. Avoid show-boating and trying to get style points. Falling onto your stomach can lead to being winded, falling near other paddlers can result in making contact with other boards / paddles or cause others to fall and falling without thought can lead to injury.

When you fall at speed on a longer board, because there's lot of impetus, fall relaxed while maintaining some control over board as you are falling. As with surfing, don't become over reliant on your leg leash, its only there as a back up. Attempt to slow the board's run as you fall - brace the paddle in the water to slow its progress, fall with eyes wide open so as you are aware of what's around you (and under you). Don't fall head first, ideally feet first in deep water. Because the board will generally be traveling away from you, attempt to fall just behind or to one side of the board. Allow for any possible recoil if wearing a coiled leash. Paddle should be held above head or to one side of you and avoid contact with the board.

Hold onto the paddle as it could get blown away from you. Don't throw paddle away and then attempt to land on the board. The board's momentum will carry it away from you anyway. The winder it is, consider going under water to protect yourself.

Wind affect on board when you fall.

If you fall in extremely windy conditions, there is a likelihood, if the board becomes side on to the wind, that it can be picked up and rolled over. Though you're wearing a leash, under extremes, the leash could break, which may be better than a dislocated knee or ankle. Recover board as soon as possible and point it downwind to avoid wind getting under it. Consider remounting board upwind.

Physiological aspects

Chasing runners is essentially a series of sprints or efforts followed by recovery periods culminating with the set distance or marathon pace. While it would be easy to think of the Moloka`i to Oahu as a marathon event, in ideal conditions, it's really a series of sprints, with brief rest periods in-between.

In such conditions, it's important to remember that bursts of effort for long periods of time are neither possible nor profitable. Rest periods, or at least periods at a steady pace must be balanced between these bursts and surges in power and effort.

During these bursts of effort, heart rates increase and the lungs may scream for air, placing high cardiovascular demands on the body, as opposed to the slower, more sustainable rate. Downwind paddlers must develop strong cardiovascular fitness because there are high aerobic demands placed on their bodies. Running, bike riding and swimming are activities which complement this fitness, delivering higher maximum heart rates than perhaps achievable when paddling.

Downwind paddling does not mean you stick to a straight line simply following the procession of waves ahead of you. As you drop in think about trimming the board along the wave face as with conventional surfing for longer rides, gains in control and speed. Get low and enjoy the free ride.

Summary

Like surfing, downwind paddling is something of an art which cannot be taught per se, but must be learned through time on the water - lots of it. Observe those more proficient than you and don't be surprised that even paddlers very much older and wiser than you, but not as fit, can still leave you way behind, purely on account of how they read the water and apply body, blade and board to the task.

The sense of isolation, self-reliance, application of acquired skills learned over many years, may mean the sense of achievement diminishes, but the sense of exhilaration never goes away to the point where it becomes an addiction of the best kind, reaffirming perhaps the more primal instincts of survival which lingers just below the surface in us all. Out here, there is a rawness which allows you to experience something out of the ordinary, which you can carry with you during the mundane grind of daily life.

The rest element, both mental and physical, is that point when you've worked hard enough for that free ride, when you can stand tall, suck in some air and take stock of the fact there's nothing you would rather be doing.

Photo Karen Baxter
Rider Connor Baxter

As the expression goes, 'It's not the size of the dog in the fight, but the size of the fight in the dog.' So too, it's not the size of the swell over your course that matters so much as the size, speed and steepness of the wind generated surface 'runners' following the wind's direction. This is where real speed gains are to be found. Distant generated ground swells, may be running to places unknown and contrary to your desired direction of travel.

Photo Karen Baxter
Rider Connor Baxter

Weighted forward, Connor anticipates the drop in,
body aligned diagonally and 'goofy' style, blade
placement will be into the wave face, so as to 'push-
over' and drop down into the steep section,
followed by trimming the board along the wave.
Travelling faster than the surface runners, is
achieved by paddling over the back of the wave in
front and down its face, thereby avoiding 'stalling'
between sets and making big speed gains.'

14

Racing

Racing may not appeal to all, but it remains the cauldron and chalice from which designers and paddlers alike forge advancements of equipment through a need to go faster and ever further. As paddlers' abilities out strip that of their equipment, this sets about a response to advance designs of both board and paddle.

'Stand up paddle board racing, consists of specially adapted boards that are paddled standing up in either short or long distance races. Maui waterman Archie Kalepa confirmed the possibilities when, as an unofficial entrant in the 2004 Quiksilver Moloka`i to O`ahu paddle board race, he made a strong solo crossing on his custom-made 12-foot EPS/epoxy board. His endeavour lead me to lobby organizers of the local Hawaiian paddle board races to include stand up paddle board divisions, thereby officially introducing the new sport into the traditional ocean regatta races already such a part of life in the Islands. The sponsorship of the first-ever official stand-up divisions in the 2005 Hennessey International Championships and the 2005 Quiksilver Moloka`i to O`ahu Paddleboard Race, the revolution caught fire: in both these events stand-up racers showed that they could compete head-to-head with the world's top paddle boarders in the most prestigious races in the world. ' *Todd Bradley*

It is said, training is a 20% mental - 80% physical state, racing an 80% mental - 20% physical state.

Photo Steve West

The ocean paddle sports athlete

Throughout my outrigger canoeing career, I have been very fortunate to have been coached by, raced with and alongside many Olympians, predominantly from the USA and Australia, most hailing from swimming, gymnastics and kayaking backgrounds, including world class surf ski paddlers and Australian Ironman such as Darren Mercer, Martin and Grant Kenny, Danny Sheard and Chris Maynard to name but a few. One thing is abundantly clear. Most all Olympic sports, have been narrowed down to a science. To be an Olympian is to become a part of a culture which is strict, regimented and fundamentally obsessive in the pursuit of excellence, carefully structured around the science of perfection which in turn demands that the athlete adhere to their commitment with military rigidness.

In contrast and in general terms, the ocean athlete is by comparison, undisciplined and instinctual yet no less physically or mentally tough or capable than the Olympian. The ocean athlete is more often than not unable (unwilling) to adhere to strict regimes on account of being very much in tune with nature and the moods of the ocean and the weather around them. They are in short, easily distracted and have poor attention spans, where the moods of the ocean and the winds are their temptress.

Hamilton Island Australia

405

Their passion is a lifestyle, which at times tests their bodies and minds to the limit and on occasion, their levels of competence and ocean skills, are called upon as a matter of survival in adverse conditions. They are in essence pleasure driven, thrill seeking adventurers.

The rower, K1 or C1 paddler's world relies upon relatively static conditions, in a controlled sheltered environment. Much like the thin black line that the swimmer must follow, so too the rower, kayaker and canoeist must stick to their lane, to which end the ocean athlete, metaphorically speaking, would struggle to stay within the construct of a defined course - it is if you like, not a part of their nature.

This being said, this is not to suggest that the elite stand up paddler, outrigger canoe paddler, surf ski paddler, prone paddle boarder or surfer does not work to training programmes, as many do. They embrace the notion of periodisation plans, interval training and phases of the training year relative to minor and major competition, but within this context, they are highly flexible and tend to be opportunists constantly aware of what's going on around them in the context of the elements. Rather than choose to ignore them on account of not missing a scheduled 'session', if the phone rings with a better offer, chances are they will leap at it.

Photo Sue Sheard

Race strategies and preparation

The concept of race strategy and preparation is a complex issue, it is however what sets apart those who take their racing seriously from those who 'also raced'. Ultimately it is a form of management.

Preparation is primarily a pre-race strategy for success. A race strategy is the bringing together of all the facets of that pre-race preparation when on the start line and once the race begins, to ensure the greatest success.

Preparing a number of weeks out from an event, even months, constitutes good planning, whereas planning when on the start line could be considered a strategy for disaster. Generally the longer the race, the greater the importance of planning and amount of preparation needed.

Writing a training plan for a major event, is often written backwards, not forwards, being as you know the condition you will need to be in on a particular date, therefore it's easier to consider progression, back to front, accounting for where you are now.

Pre-race preparations

Over the course of time leading up to an event, months, weeks and days, various pre-race preparations will need to be considered as part of your strategy for success.

Selection of a training regime, hydration, food, selection of equipment to be used, checking and carrying out maintenance. Payment issues, registration, travel, accommodation, food, medications, eligibility, divisions, pre-race food, briefing times, travel arrangements - the list is exhaustive and if you're using a support boat, the logistics increase and if paddling as part of a team, you will need to establish a basic change-chart of who paddles when.

Pre-Race Analytical Considerations

Various pre-race analytical considerations will help form the basis for success. For many races, the course is decided upon only a few days out and there are often alternate courses in place to allow for poor weather conditions. However, having some idea of the race area is at least a greater benefit than having no idea.

Analyse the race course, use charts and maps, consider tide states and direction, prevailing winds, sea states, prevailing swells, currents, length of race, expected duration. Analyse the start line, noting the time of race and 'expected' conditions, reading weather charts, listening to local forecast. Use web-based weather prediction sites. View the race course and travel over it by boat beforehand if required.

All these considerations help to build a picture of the nature of the race so you can begin considering your preferred race strategy - course to take, change over points, starting line position, etc.

Race day preparation
Check actual conditions against predicted, ensuring the course is the same and has not been altered. Check all equipment is appropriate to conditions. Know the start procedure. Ensure registration, support boat checks (if needed) attend briefing, hydration systems in place, food if required, team talk or meeting (change race) speak with individual paddlers to motivate.

Photo Sue Sheard

Race strategy

Your race strategy is putting into practice the pre-race analysis which you have formulated. Having confirmed the course and checked the actual conditions, you can now put into place your plan; position on start line, course to take and the manner in which you will run your race, etc.

The three basic strategies
Three basic strategies include; lead and pace, even pace and negative split.

Because stand up paddle board races may sometimes be practised in adverse weather and sea conditions, it is important to be adaptable. A relatively static, flat water course provides for a number of strategies, but as conditions deteriorate, options tend to be limited as the event turns into a matter of survival of the fittest. Each requires a different strategy. For shorter races, the more turns, the more technical the race becomes.

Lead and pace

Used for short sprint racing in particular, where the object is to establish an early lead and to hold on until the end, putting psychological pressure on the opposition. Training for this race strategy must be specific, as it requires paddling at maximum pace for as long as possible.

The lead and pace method requires maximum pace at the outset and you must be well disciplined to rate high and be able to make a transition to a longer slower sub-maximal rate in a smooth and efficient manner. The first strokes of the race are crucial with minimal blade slippage, therefore good paddle skills and a high degree of strength are required.

Even pace

Essentially this requires the race to be broken up into two equal parts. The intention here is to attempt to cover the first section of the race at a pace which is less than maximum, finishing the second half of the race with greater intensity and pace. This requires a high degree of discipline, it means being behind at the start and saving energy for the second half of the race. Even pace may work fine in calm conditions; if conditions deteriorate the plan could be affected.

Negative split

More suited to longer races, the concept relies upon constantly improved upon intermediate times, i.e. progressive build up of speed to the finish. Technically very difficult to implement.

Strategies over distance

Most successful paddlers have fast starts and an ability to maintain a high average speed throughout the race, having enough in reserve for a fast finish. In many respects it is the lead and pace strategy which most top paddlers adopt.

A fast start is crucial to avoid collisions and adverse wake and in many respects the lead and pace approach seems to bring big benefits in this regard. High intensity off the start line, employing a high stroke rate, which lengthens and slows with only a marginal drop in intensity over the first few minutes is the key.

Dominating the start of a long race and establishing a good position within the first 15 minutes of a distance race is important, as it seems that there comes a point where positions often remain relatively unchanged within any given race. There are many ways to break this 15 minutes down; the first 30 seconds, the next 60, the next 2 minutes...

Top paddlers tend to mix a blend of near maximal and sub-maximal paddling throughout the race, i.e. 75% - 90% effort. This is particularly true where a race course includes following sea and wind conditions. Additionally, some paddlers will have an advantage depending on their preference for rough or smooth water, upwind or downwind paddling. Knowing your own abilities (and limitations) and optimum performance conditions will play a big part in your race strategy.

The start

It's essential that you take the initiative to ensure a good start of any race. You must take control of the situation and position yourself in a good spot early on the start line; beach, shore or water based.

Photo: Steve West

Typically, the start of any race, tends to constitute the most intense period of time - and this may vary from just a few minutes to upwards of 15 minutes over longer courses when establishing your position. Practicing similar levels of intensity in training is essential. In big races, where there are many boards on the start line and when conditions are adverse, collisions are common and you will want to avoid these - however you cannot account for others losing control of their boards or those who are aggressive in nature and use ramming tactics.

Some paddlers will try to line up beside fast paddlers who know what they are doing - but then you are more likely to end up log jammed. If you are relatively slow, it may be a good idea to line up behind a fast paddler, not beside them, so you have a clean run behind in their wake. It does pay to know your limitations at times.

After the start

After a few minutes into the race, you will be jostling for position, eyeballing the best line, seeing where the top paddlers are headed or if you are out in front, you will have to begin putting your own stamp on the race as leader.

Avoiding collisions with others is still a priority; out-paddle, out-steer but avoid actual physical contact with others if at all possible. Settle yourself, find your pace and line.

Remember to look over your shoulder, don't get tunnel vision. It's OK to cover an overtaking board from behind, ie move left or right to prevent a board from passing, but once it has established an overlap you should give way (assume nose passes the mid section of your own board). This can be detrimental however to your own game plan and ultimately an exercise in folly. Realistically, if you're being out paddled, it's smart to let them go as it's fairly inevitable that they'll get past at some point, don't make it to your detriment. Choose your battles carefully.

Though you have your race plan, be flexible. Keep your options open as many things can occur during the course of a race - the longer the race, the greater the number of variables which occur. You will have to make judgement calls at some stage and this may mean being bold and courageous in order to counter a situation and improve your position.

Collisions, T-bones and rounding markers

Accidental collisions occur, no doubt. Yet many could be avoided. If you believe that as a genuine part of your race strategy, you should set out to deliberately collide with others, then you need seriously rethink this approach. Above all other considerations, it's dangerous, reckless and irresponsible behaviour that can injure people and damage valuable equipment. This is not a bonafide race strategy if you want to gain respect.

Photo Steve West / London River Thames

Regrettably many race rules do not cater for issues of rounding marks and buoys, overtaking situations, rights of way and so on and as a consequence some paddlers figure that it's open season on anything in their way.

'Interaction' - what is it?

Interaction is that spooky thing that happens when your board travels over shallow water of less than around 3' (1m) so it feels as if it's moving through mud. The shallower it is, the slower you seem to go. This is one level at which interaction can occur. It can also occur when two boards are close at speed, so as they are attracted and collide due to pressure waves.

Over shallow water, the hull and the sea bed act to squeeze the water between, creating pressure which pulls them together. The board is actually being pulled downwards and the faster you are travelling the greater the effect. Cutting corners and travelling over shallows and experiencing interaction is often a poor trade off, as you will suffer in having to work hard to deal with this added resistance.

Psychological issues

In the lead up to race day, the night before and actual race day, paddlers will deal with the build up in differing ways. Paddlers may talk in terms of 'psyching' oneself up - but this can often have the reverse affect in 'freaking' oneself out'. Creative visualisation remains one of the more positive ways of dealing with the pressures of race day; visualising the race, considering your strategy and generally giving yourself a good talking to.

Closure

Paddlers cannot compete in the past or paddle too far into the future. Therefore, to maximise the likelihood of success, individuals must paddle focusing on the task at hand and the current stretch of water.

The paddler should consider what has been done well and where improvements can be made and then focus the rest of the time on what they will be doing next and how to achieve it. Unfortunately, not everything is under the athlete's control (head winds, the opposition).

These uncontrollable events can distract the athlete's focus away from the relevant thoughts about achieving the pre-race goals. A useful phrase athletes mantra is 'right here, right now'. This also works as a distraction technique which will block out anything that has happened in the past and stops you from getting too worried or focused on sections of the race which are far ahead.

One way of dealing with these issues is to use a technique called, 'Parking thoughts'. Just as the thought suggests, having a mental location where problems can be left and dealt with at a later date. The reality is that energy spent dwelling on an incident is a waste, so by using the black box and bringing closure, you can focus back on the, 'Here and now'.

Arousal levels

Paddlers need to maintain a level of physical and mental arousal that allows for calm, clear thinking and be energetic enough to maximise their performance. These energy levels, need to be most focused and ready to exert maximum performance in an energised state.

Many different techniques exist for controlling arousal. Relaxation (controlled slow deep breathing) can be used to calm down an over aroused state, whereas, increased arousal can be generated by sharply

Photo Mandy West

increasing physical activity (push ups). When paddlers have reached a state of optimal arousal (or activation) then they should begin to consider their goals for the next paddling session.

Concentration

Athletes are usually always thinking, however, they're not always concentrating! The key is to be able to focus and concentrate on the right thing at the right moment. Paddlers can optimise their concentration by knowing from the outset what has to be done and by being able to focus whether they are working towards that goal, or whether the plan needs to be modified.

Keeping in touch with your personal goals for the race is often a useful strategy to achieve utmost concentration. Paddlers who have planned their goals for the race, written them down and kept them specific, measurable, and realistic, are setting themselves up for success.

Creative visualisation

Paddlers can visualise exactly what and how they are going to achieve the goal of their next paddling session. Visualisation allows an athlete to experience success in their mind, by preparing the body for its next activity.

Visualisation is the result of 'what you see is what you get'. An athlete who thinks about failure is setting themselves up to achieve it. Therefore, the successful athlete is the one who not only wants to achieve success, but can see themselves achieving it.

Positive thinking and communication

The key to any self-talk by the athlete is to remain positive. This is probably one of the greatest skills an athlete can develop. When an athlete is positive, their self-esteem and confidence will increase, allowing them to best maximise their potential.

Using cue words is a useful strategy for helping a paddler to develop a desired mind-set. If you are feeling like you need to relax, 'Calm' may be the word you need. If you need to get energised, 'Fire up' may be the phrase you need. The mind and body are highly responsive to the words we use, so in your pre-race preparation and training, experiment with words which will lift you to the level you need.

Change races

Change-over races bring an interesting component as experienced in the Team Divisions of the Moloka`i to O`ahu race.

Time off of the board during competition.

Typically in long distance races, individual paddlers will spend some proportion of the race off of the board and in a support boat. Clearly this provides an opportunity for the physiological needs of the body to re-hydrate and replenish vital energy sources. What some paddlers fail to recognise, is that this time is also a good opportunity to re-focus the mind.

In land-based sports such as tennis and volleyball, the suggestion has been made that winning or losing the next point is largely influenced by what the athlete does in between points (both physically and psychologically). Similarly when given a break during a stand up paddle board race, how that time is spent will greatly influence the energy and determination a paddler takes back with them onto the board.

Photo Mandy Wood / England

The mindset of the paddler is an important concern. For example, p[...] in the support boat realising the team is not doing as well as they e[...] may spend the change-over time with thoughts of, 'it could have b[...] different' and 'we're not going to do it'. Such a mindset is likely to leave the paddlers feeling negative, perhaps causing them to develop a self-fulfilling prophecy where their diminished effort results in the unsatisfactory placing they knew they were going to get!

Compare that example with the paddlers who use the change-over period to create the ideal mental platform for the next stretch of paddling. These athletes appear confident, in control, and portray an image of composure to their team mates. Success thrives on success and a successful team generally consists of athletes who believe in their own ability. To maximise your efficiency during a change-over you must give yourself the best possible chance of preparing for the next session on the board.

Summary
Psychological skills are like any other skills, they need to be developed and practiced so they become an integral part of performance. Practice these techniques in your training so you can utilise them during competition.

The training year
The training year assesses the entire season, over a one-year period and will need to include phases which embrace off-season and pre-season training considerations in respect of training and preparing for competition.

Season planning
The first step in developing a seasonal plan is identifying the dates of the major (and minor) races well in advance and then choosing which of these events you will attend.

Periodisation
Periodisation has become a term that can cause confusion amongst paddlers and coaches alike. In its most simple form, is it simply, planning your season around different phases of time, each phase targeting specific goals appropriate for that stage of the season.

KANU
CULTURE

Ocean paddlers tend to ensure they play and train on a variety of craft in order to work the body in differing ways, honing new skills and above all, keeping themselves connected with the nuances of the ocean in all states, whilst avoiding boredom in repetition.

Photo Steve West / Queen Lili`uokalani Race Hawai`i

Photo Mandy West
Padder Steve West / England

Training phases of the year

General preparations 6-8 weeks
Specific preparations 10-12 weeks
Pre Competition 6-8 weeks
Taper 1-3 weeks
Transition phase
Off season

General and specific preparation phases usually comprise the majority of the season and are used to develop the qualities that are fundamental to performance later in the season in developing a sound base.

Interval training

Competitive ocean paddlers rely heavily upon interval training. It is the singular most important training regime you can use and the easiest in using your board, paddle, water and body toward increased levels of fitness and skill levels. In simple terms the basis of interval training is centred on time (mins) x % of perceived effort (usually 50-100%). So this may look like;

10 x 1 min @ 100% (30 second active rest period @ 50%)
So that's paddling flat out 10 times for 1 min with a 30 second break between each set, at 50% effort, as part of an active rest period.

4 x 20 min @ 75% (5 minute passive rest period between sets)
So that's paddling 4 lots of 20 minute sets, at 75% effort, with a 5 minute rest between each set of 20.

Importantly you will note that distance per se, is not factored in. Time is the key as this alludes to duration / endurance / developing strength of mind. The miles will take care of themselves!

General preparation

Pre-season training

Volume (kms). Long slow paddling sessions, gradually emphasising endurance, fitness and technique. Intensity will vary from low to medium. Paddling specific drills, including learning new skills, paddling in different conditions. **So your interval training session may simply be 1 x 90 min at 65% - ie a continuous aerobic based / low intensity / skill session to work on base fitness.**

Specific race preparation

Developing race or stroke specific performance and technique. Volume (kms) are gradually increased then decreased. Intensity is increased as volume decreases. Paddling becomes stroke and or event specific. Technique is still emphasised. Resistance training is introduced (on and off the water). Anaerobic threshold work introduced, more sprint sets. Longer time trials, one per week. **Your interval training will become more complex as you factor in more intense sessions, but as suggested, long continuous sessions are replaced with shorter sets at higher levels of intensity as competition day approaches.**

Pre-competition phase

The primary aim being to gradually increase intensity to race specific pace. Some anaerobic threshold work will have been introduced in the **specific preparations phase** and the pre competition phase will act as a bridge between this work and the higher intensity race pace work.

Prepare the body to start doing race pace work. Increased anaerobic threshold training. Increase intensity as volume (time/distance) decreases. Develop psychological skills. Small tapers are made for sprint events, less so for longer races. Competitive experience is gained through attendance.

Paddling specific examples of work here include;

Lactate tolerance sets, quality anaerobic threshold sets, race pace work, long sprints sets while allowing for recovery with easy paddles and stroke drills all of which can be accomplished using interval training.

Photo Steve ... London River Thames

STARBOARD

Competition phase

The final stage leading up to major championships. This stage contains as much high rating, high intensity work to ensure that the body is prepared physically, technically and psychologically on race days. The general principles of this phase are;

Long recoveries between quality sessions. Race specific work, including warm up practices. Volume is decreased, intensity maintained / increased due to recovery time.

Taper

The final stage of the training program focuses on tactical and psychological aspects and incorporates tapering of the training load to allow for peaking to occur in the final week or two. The general principles of this phase are;

Most paddlers who are larger muscled will need long tapers. The older the paddler, the longer the taper. The longer the build up, the longer the taper The shorter the race, the longer the taper, the longer the race the shorter the taper.

NOTES: Rest intervals are increased during and between. Intensity is to be maintained or increased due to feeling good as a result of increased rest. Very important that nutrition is controlled to account for the drop in kms paddling / training etc.

Transition phase

This usually follows the last race and is is characterised by resting or low intensity paddling and or cross training. It is a good idea to stay off of the board for a while and do an alternative activity, but not too much, to allow mind and body a chance to relax.

Photo Dana Edmunds Courtesy of Ocean Promotion

KANU CULTURE

Paddling upwind

There's no escaping the fact, upwind paddling requires not only good technique, but strength. Not surprisingly, the greater the wind strength the tougher it will be to make head-way. There is no better form of resistance training. Avoiding paddling upwind will only mean that when you have to, you will struggle which could compromise your safety and your race preparedness. Typically, shoulder fatigue, wrist and or hand pain can result from extended periods paddling against the wind and often paddlers take steps to deal with this in a variety of ways.

Stroke rate and length

Your upwind stroke rate naturally diminishes as a result of wind resistance against your body and board and having to push against oncoming waves. The preferred technique is to ensure a long reach, keeping technique smooth, maximising blade time in the water, pouring on the power and maintaining a quick recovery and ensuring importantly, that the paddle is exited very early. Stronger, heavier paddlers often benefit from this approach.

Lighter paddlers, including women and juniors, often apply a long reach, short pull back and fast recovery, keeping the stroke rate quite high. This is done because of a general lack of strength endurance and if the stroke is 'laboured' combined with a slow recovery phase of the stroke, the board is more likely to stall before re-entry of the blade.

One technique when paddling upwind is to avoid paddling directly into the wind and to take a zig-zag course much like a sail powered craft tacking upwind. Angling the nose of the board by about 10 to 15 degrees either side of the wind, will make paddling more comfortable and reduce some of the direct affects of windage against the body, while also diminishing the pounding of the nose into oncoming waves. The same technique can be used when paddling into strong tidal flows.

Paddles with a marginal degree of flex, tend to cushion some of the body stresses associated with upwind paddling.

Choking down

In order to deal with added resistance and therefore load on the body, it's not uncommon for paddlers to either choke down with the lower hand to shorten the lever arm or to take the top hand and place around the upper shaft in order to take some of the pressure away from top shoulder. In all cases your reach will be shortened as will power and control of the blade face, but you will be able to increase your stroke rate and lessen some of the load on the body.

Notes on strength to weight ratio upwind

Two paddlers in the gym, one weighs 75kg the other 95kg. The 75kg paddler is not as strong as the 95kg paddler in terms of 'raw strength' ie the 75kg paddle cannot lift or pull as much as the 95kg paddler and therefore he is deemed weaker. The two paddlers then see how many chin ups they can do in 60 seconds. The 75kg paddler manages to do 35 which totals 2625kg the 95kg paddler 25 which amounts to 2375Kg. What this tells us, is that the lighter paddler has greater strength to weight ratio and greater strength endurance.

Paddling is not about who is stronger than the next guy, it's who has greater strength endurance (strength to weight ratio) and ultimately the better technique. Within this mix is the paddle itself and universally most all elite paddlers seek to use the smallest blade they can get away with, not the biggest, as bigger means greater drag and residual resistance surplus to requirements, which leads to loss of energy

Paddling crosswind

Paddling cross-wind can be one of the most challenging skills to master. As referenced in the chapter regarding stance, how you offset your feet can make a huge difference to gaining some control over the boards direction of travel and how you can offset the force of the wind, through transferring drive through your leading foot in particular (when stood offset).

You can employ a kahi or reverse kahi stroke in order to counter the push of wind, added in between your regular stroke or you could use a 'C' stroke which enters on the lee-side (downwind side) towards the nose and sweeps progressively away in a semi-circle back in towards your feet or just past the level of the hips. This pushes the board away from your paddling side and counters the cross-wind.

Regardless of what you do, the chances are you will fatigue if you stay paddling on one side too long and therefore you must learn to counter this. Don't obsess with going in a straight line to a given destination. If you wander upwind then downwind from time to time this can ease the load. Look for sheltered areas behind headlands, boats, houses, shorelines. When racing in such conditions it's essential to be alert to how you can minimise the wind's negative effects, yet maximise its positive effects when the opportunity arises over the race course.

Blade depth

The depth at which you bury the blade should vary in certain circumstances. When the board is 'bogged' or when you want to power-up in flat water, burying the blade deep and clean is vital to maximise blade grip, creating potential for maximum effectiveness during the 'power phase' of the stroke.

In this instance, you can 'choke down' on the shaft of the paddle roughly one hand span down from your usual grip. When the board 'breaks free' from the current or begins to surf down a wave, 'choke up' on the shaft. When the board begins to 'surf' you can simply 'tap' the board along, burying the blade so the upper shoulders of the blade are visible. This enables a higher stroke rate with less 'effort' and constitutes a 'rest period'.

Quick 'n light strokes

You can bury your blade less deeply and resort to a quick, light 'tap' keeping it from dropping off in speed. A 'quick 'n light' technique is often very effective and associated with a decrease in power application, length of pull-back and blade depth and increased stroke rate.

Varying your stroke rate

Many things dictate stroke rate. You will have your established 'base rate' or the rate at which you feel most comfortable for extended periods of time, then everything in between. Given 'clean' water, without the influence of adverse wind, waves/swell, current or shallow water, the 'base' rate is easily established. Once external factors come into play, your stroke-rate is directly affected by them.

Shallow water will slow your rating, as will adverse wind, while chasing a runner or travelling with the flow of a strong current, will increase your rating as hull speed increases with the assistance. On many occasions, just staying in touch with what you feel through your feet, is as good a way as any. Listen with your head too much and you can loose the 'feel'.

When a paddler threatens to overtake during a race situation, maintain composure, deliver good reach and rating and consider how to best deal with it. Going that few extra inches in the reach out front will help, while increasing your stroke rate, must ensure continuance of good technique as this is often when it will fall apart and inefficiencies creep in. Lots of splashing and thrashing often means a loss of composure. Ultimately racing for the most part, is a battle of wills.

Don't be distracted by other paddlers in close and tight racing situations, or be distracted by the cadence of their stroke rate. Keep your head space focused on you, your board and the water and think your way to better paddling rather than resorting to muscle power only.

Wake riding

Generally accepted as part of canoe and kayak marathon racing, so it is with stand up paddle boarding. There's an art to it and not entirely a 'free ride' as some might imagine. The principal is to use the wave generated by the depression in the water formed by the board ahead of you, to essentially pull you along. I will leave this subject open-ended.

Photo Dana Edmunds Courtesy of Ocean Promotion

15

Into the Surf

Venturing through shore break or playing in the waves is best
learned through other more manageable means than
necessarily on a stand up paddle board. If your first time
encounters are on a stand up board, be very aware of
your limitations, the dangers involved and how best to
approach the learning phases. The sport should not be
seen as a 'surf sport' with no right of passage.

Poise

So, if you're going to have to play in the shore break, an inflatable board can provide a solution to limiting impact injury. But it's not a practice to be encouraged.

First time in the waves – safety first

A right of passage within the waterman community means a great deal. It's born out of respect, out of doing your time and earning your place within the context of knowing your limitations, while advancing your abilities and knowledge, in a manner which respects others and safeguards you and those around you, while showing respect for the ocean's immense power and indifference to your well-being.

Learning surf skills on a stand up paddle board represents one of the most hazardous rights of passage into the surf environment possible. In truth, the best way to learn to surf, is to free-surf first, learning the ropes at grass-roots level. Hone your paddling skills in the flat, then ultimately combine the two. This hasn't been happening and consequently surfers are rightly not happy about the lack of respect given. The world's best stand up paddle surfers are so, not through divine intervention, but on account of having followed a natural path of progression.

Basic surf etiquette

Knowledge of accepted surf etiquette, or simply translated, how to safely share waves in the surf zone is vital if you are to make friends and influence rather than make enemies. Make no mistake, 'agro' exists amongst the more narrow minded tribal members of surf, though its fair to say many have the right to get 'upset' given the behaviour of some stand up paddle surfers. Learn to catch your first waves in the absence of crowds. Give yourself as much space as possible. Drive that extra mile, paddle that bit further or simply paddle away from the primary action.

'Body Boarders will kick you out of the line-up. Groms will wax your rental car windows. Old long boarders will drop in on you. Chicks will hassle you for set waves. Hawai`i is the only place in the world of surfing where it is still cool to be a local. Localism in California is seen as a Cro-Magnon

throwback to the burn out hippie days. In Hawai`i 'respect' and 'waterman' are big words that hide the strong arm of incestuous jingoism. Veneration is demanded, obedience required. Chasing out travellers and bullying the weak is seen as honourable rather than cowardly.' Sandow Birk

For the most part, experienced short board surfers like hollow plunging fast moving waves, the long boarder fuller, spilling waves. These are more along the lines of what you will be seeking out as a newbie and as a stand up paddle surfer.

Avoid crowds when possible
Stand up paddle boards do not play well with other surf craft or evoke warm gushy feelings of brotherhood between users. The sight of a stand up paddle board in the line-up generally evokes contempt and a primal evolutionary surge in emotion amongst regular surfers who contest they were here first; not an unreasonable feeling.

Patrolled beaches
Where there are lifeguards on duty, red and yellow flags will indicate a designated swimming area. Do not launch between these flags, look for the black and white flags or check with the lifeguards where you can launch.

Lifeguards will enforce any bans imposed on the use of stand up paddle boards where applicable. The US Coast Guard originally classified SU boards as, '. . . vessels capable of travelling offshore' which they have since modified to being simply a '. . . floatation device.' About as vague a classification as is imaginable.

Paddling out
Be mindful not to obstruct the path of other riders. Take a round-about path back out if needs be or stall and wait for the sets to dissipate before paddling back out.

The line up
The line-up (out the back) is the area in which you hang-out and prepare for take-off once you select the wave you want to ride. Because your board is powered by a paddle, you can catch waves often long before they are fully formed and in addition larger boards, will catch small slow moving waves with relative ease as in the case of all long board styled surfboards, which provide a wide stable platform on which to ride in graceful form along the wave.

Being bigger than most regular surfboards and powered by a paddle may give you an advantage, but not a license to upset those around you by intimidation. Share the waves and be mindful. Don't push in, try and see order in what's going on. Spread some Aloha, not grief, as it will not only reflect on you, but the sport in general.

If there are others around you, observe where they are taking-off from to catch the waves and note where you are relative to shore by taking a few transit points, ie fixed points on land. Again be courteous. Take-off points will shift with the tide, wind changes or swell movements.

Dropping-In
Dropping into a wave already being ridden by someone will lead to all sorts of negative consequences. The rule applies to all surf craft. Don't even think of it, let alone do it. If you do, consider pulling-out.

Bailing out
Before being bailed off your board, or voluntarily bailing, be observant as to who is around you. Don't just randomly fall and push your board from under your feet, consider if you need to attempt to limit the board's travel to avoid contact with other water users. The practice of grabbing your leash to shorten the boards travel is advocated by some however larger boards can be too much to hang on to. Don't over-rely on your leash.

Photo Steve West / Mallorca Spain

Falling close to shore in shallow water is not without its dangers. Calculate your falling technique in relation to the water depth and seabed type.

Stephane Robin wrote in his Surftime #21 editorial: **'When people tell me that the future of surfing will consist of rotations above the wave with incredible speed on a 5'10", I'm sceptical. The vast majority of us are not concerned with this progression. So what is the future of surfing? If we listen to Laird Hamilton, SUP will take pride of place in line-ups without damaging any other discipline. It's a question of accessibility, fun and optimising everyday surfing conditions.'**

Wave etiquette is a question of education and up to now the sport is unusual in the line-up. The hierarchy of certain spots was shaken up by the arrival of the big boards. Many are united against this discipline.

Laird Hamilton sums it up. **"It's all a question of education. SUP is a natural evolution of surfing in the same way that long-boarding and short-boarding are. Respect for other surfers in the water remains at the centre of it all, whatever board they're surfing on. On a SUP, we should behave as anyone else, share and respect the rules.'**

Surfing safety (etiquette) *by John Hibbard*

Picture the scene. The surf is clean and about 2 to 3-foot. It's the first day of waves in a while. Everybody and anybody are in the surf. Every conceivable surf craft is in the line-up - short boarders, long boarders, body borders, kayakers - and now here comes a 'wanna be' stand up paddle surfer down the beach with their 10' or 12' board.

There are no lanes or give way signs in the surf so it can turn into total carnage if people don't know what they're doing. A 12' board is a lethal weapon in the wrong hands. Even when used correctly with a leash you still have to think up to 37' ahead of yourself (board + leash + paddle + you). Without a leash, a stand up paddle board loose in the surf is a nightmare waiting to happen. It needn't be like that though. If you know the rules, keep your eyes open to the dangers and show respect in the line-up, everyone can get along just fine.

First things first

Don't venture anywhere near the surf until you have mastered balance and paddling techniques. For your first few sessions choose a gently sloping beach and a very small swell. Avoid high tide and make sure you're aware of the areas you can launch. Paddle away from crowded areas.

You don't need to be sitting on the best peak all the time. Move off and explore different areas of the line-up. If you employ good technique with good safety awareness you and your fellow water users should be able to get along just fine.

Just bear the following points in mind.

You will be riding the biggest board in the line-up.
You look quite imposing to other surfers lying down on their boards.
With your paddle-assisted speed, you can catch pretty much every wave going - so you mustn't.

Lets clarify that last point. The paddle is a powerful propulsion device, both for catching waves and for getting you back out into the line-up real quick, so if you really wanted to, you could starve the whole line-up of good waves for the duration of your session, but that's no way to make friends! You will find that pretty soon you can become an unwelcome addition to the party.

Rules of respect (common sense)

Let some waves pass you by. Don't take a wave from every set. If you're close to other surfers then you can call them into waves - your elevated position means you can see sets coming from a long way off. Don't ever drop in - don't pull onto a wave that other surfers are already riding or trying to paddle into. This rule is the same for everyone, but it's even more important for a stand up paddle surfer.

Wave and beach classification

Photo Steve West / Mallorca Spain

Surfers are by and large, observant, analytical creatures. As part of their surfing lifestyle they are intrinsically connected to the ocean's moods and spend many a pensive hour, gazing out over the ocean to see what's going on. If they're not hanging out on the beach, checking it out, then they may be found glued to the internet observing high and low pressures on the weather charts counting the days until that elusive ocean swell may travel to their doorstep generated by some far away storm. Stress levels in the surfer may reach critical mass during prolonged periods of a glass-off, that travel becomes the only solution; downwind paddlers can also feel this same frustration due to a lack of wind.

In short, as a result of many hours of surf observation, beach study and weather forecasting, many surfers in the absence of any formal study, become highly skilled in interpreting their local areas and of surf in general and the mechanisms at play which go together to produce good surf.

Surf or more precisely waves, can be classified under various types and some basic understanding of classification will help in your gaining of surf knowledge. Importantly, certain wave types are more conducive to learning. Additionally there are differing beach types the geometry of which, greatly affects the nature or type of waves created.

Breaking waves or breakers, form as a wave enters water shallower than half its wave length. Water near the trough of the wave is ultimately influenced by the seabed below and is subsequently retarded by friction, causing the wave to increase in height until becoming too high relative to its motion causing it to fall over into the preceding trough.

Beach classification

The surf zone can be defined as the area commencing from the first breaker 'out the back' to the point of finishing on the beach. Wave-dominated beaches consist of dissipative beaches, at the high-energy end of the spectrum and intermediate beaches and reflective beaches at the low energy end of the spectrum. Tide modified and dominated beaches are associated with areas of high tidal range, usually producing smaller waves with less energy.

Additionally, point breaks are associated with rocky headlands, reef breaks with offshore coral reefs and shore breaks, where the shoreline meets the ocean or even lakeside, the bed of which may be composed of sand, mud, rock or coral. Being that stand up paddle boarding can be practiced on inland waterways, wave types associated with freshwater are more likely to be wind chop or those created by passing craft or small areas of rapids.

There are three basic types of breakers in the surf-zone. The slope of the beach and wave / swell type approaching the surf zone ultimately determines which type of breaker is formed.

Spilling waves

In a spilling breaker, the energy contained within the wave transported over many miles, is released gradually over a considerable distance usually due to the seabed being flat and shallow shelving, the water depth gradually decreasing shoreward. The wave peaks up until it is steep but not vertical, the crest of the wave curling over and descending onto the forward slope of the wave, where it then slides down into the trough. This process is why these waves may look like an advancing line of foam.

Spilling waves provide the ideal stand up paddle surfing wave. While you've seen the double overhead pitching barrels in which some stand up paddle surfers place themselves, this in truth is not where the advantages of having a paddle in your hand qualifies as being optimum.
Rider John Hibbard

These wave types are ideal for the stand up paddler to learn basic stand up paddle surfing skills, as the waves, provided of small size, have limited power and present a safer, mellower learning environment. Paddling back out through the waves, board recovery and falls are more easily manageable.

Plunging / dumping waves

In a plunging breaker, the energy contained within the wave, is released suddenly and sometimes violently downward as a mass of water, the crest of the wave thrown beyond the wave face and trough. Air trapped between the trough and wave face can result in air escaping behind the wave, throwing water high above the surface.

Practising stand up paddle surfing within the shore break on plunging waves, raises the risk of impact injuries and should be avoided. Doing so puts the activity into an 'extreme' category; 'extremely stupid'.

These are the waves we most associate with surfing and the ones advanced surfers generally prefer. Hollow plunging waves are however formidably powerful and even a small wave of 1 or 2' can contain enough power to harm. Consequently, these wave types are often not ideal conditions in which to learn.

Large boards can cause particularly serious impact injury if a fall occurs in shore break. The 'pitch' of the wave can be said to increase the further the lip travels ahead of the trough of the wave, which results in greater amounts of energy release.

Photo Steve West / Mallorca Spain

Surging waves

In surging waves, the wave crest tends to advance faster than the base of the wave, which would suggest the formation of a plunging wave. However, because these waves advance faster than the crest, the plunging is retarded and the breaker surges up the beach as a wall of water, which may or may not be white water. These waves are usually found on beaches with a very steep slope. Longer boards can catch surging waves but may need you to work the paddle to maintain momentum. Wind generated surface waves, are often of a surging type as chased by downwind paddlers.

Photo Steve West / Mallorca Spain

A surging wave rolls into the beach having broken as a plunging wave on a bank.

Rips

A rip current is a strong channel of water flowing seaward from the shoreline, typically associated with surf beaches. Water flowing seaward can vary from 0.5 meters per second (1-2 feet per second) to as much as 2.5 meters per second (8 feet per second) and is typically stronger during high surf or during storms, but can still be present on calm days and therefore

Photo Steve West / Mallorca Spain

more insidious. Rips are usually narrow and located in trenches between sandbars under piers or along jetties.

Essentially a rip forms on account of water needing to recede seaward. Wind and waves push water shoreward, the previous backwash heading seaward, is pushed sideways by these oncoming waves, causing the water to flow along the shoreline until it finds an exit back out to open water. Importantly, rips move back and forth along the shore depending on the state of the tide, high or low water, weather conditions and the sometimes constant changing topography of the sea bed, especially if sandy and unstable.

Rips often appear as unusually calm areas of water within the surf zone, caused by the surface current it creates flowing seaward, dampening oncoming waves and often appearing as a different colour.

While a rip can be useful to the stand up paddler in being pulled seaward in these calmer waters back to the line up, caution must be taken. If you find you need to break free of the rip, paddle parallel to the shoreline until free of the rip's grasp, generally only 30 to 100 ft (9-30 m) wide. Alternatively, floating seaward until the current disperses into deeper waters is another method dealing with a dangerous situation, but it may leave you farther from shore.

Shore break

Shore breaks, are essentially waves which meet the shore line and they do so in a variety of forms, some of which are non threatening and lack power, others more so.

Dumping waves are essentially plunging waves and depending on their size could make leaving or returning to the beach extremely hazardous if not impossible. Small spilling or surging waves should present little problem, but nevertheless, caution should be exercised.

Battle of the Paddle styled events, are centred largely on the ability to manage shore break both ways; outwards and then back. For race directors and safety officials, it's an accident waiting to happen and the shore break need not even be particularly threatening.

I have seen many an accident in OC1, OC2 and OC6 events which occur in the shore break; the most dangerous leg of any ins and outs styled event. This being said, for every day sessions you may well need to learn to negotiate shore break on account of where you live.

The launching process

Wherever there are waves rolling or breaking to the shoreline, then there will

Timing is central to a safe launching from the beach where shore break threatens to spit you back up the beach. Waiting for the larger waves to pass, timing your entry, board placement, pushing with the legs and going prone then to the knees to paddle beyond the shore break, is not a failure on your part, but sometimes a smart option.

443

be a shore break. While Battle of the Paddle styled events do not allow for the luxury of 'timing' your paddle out or return, it's generally accepted that good timing is central to safety.

The paddle out

Having selected a venue where the surf is mellow, you will either have to negotiate paddling over the waves or find a channel or flat-water approach to the waves in order to get behind the waves - the line-up.

In order to meet oncoming waves and power over or through them, it is important to have sufficient speed to do so. Paddling hard and efficiently will not only provide added stability to the board and through to your feet, but will prevent the board stalling as it meets the wave. You want to avoid the board's progression being stalled, or worse being stalled then pushed backwards! If you're stationary, there is every likelihood this will happen if facing into wave.

Beyond the simple requirement of speed, there are three differing stances you can adopt in the paddle out.

Kneeling

Reverting back to using your paddle-kneeling position you can generate added speed and balance by lowering your centre of gravity. Exercise caution if the approaching wave is likely to impact you in the chest as this could wind you or force you off backwards. In the event of this happening, at the last moment, lean into the wave, lowering your head and torso, grasping the paddle with the lower hand, place it parallel alongside the board and grasp the rail as best possible, the free hand grabbing the opposite rail. As soon as the wave passes, resume paddling immediately.

Stand up paddling in a natural stance (feet side by side)

In small spilling waves, if you feel confident with your balance, adopt a natural stance and paddle directly into and through the wave. Keep your knees bent and maintain speed by paddling, rather than stopping. Allow your knees to act as shock-absorbers, so as the board can move upwards and downwards with the passing wave. As soon you pass over the crest of the wave, aim to place your next stroke into the back of the wave to regain any loss of speed and to regain stability. Use the paddle to brace yourself.

Stand up paddling in regular or Goofy foot stance.

If the waves are bordering on plunging and a little larger in size, you can adopt your preferred natural or goofy foot stance. Approach the wave with speed and confidence and as the nose of the board begins to travel up the wave face, transfer your weight to the rear foot, bending your knees to lower your centre of gravity. Anticipate the nose of the board dropping off the back of the wave, reach over the wave crest and plant your next stroke in the back of the wave, transferring wait to the front foot to spread the load once again.

Travis Grant demonstrates negotiating an oncoming wave using a regular (natural) foot placement - commitment here is important. He builds speed, legs already in place, the weight is transferred to the rear foot and as the board veers upwards and over, the leading leg controls board elevation and the weight is transferred forwards to bring stability to the board.

Travis Grant rides a stand up paddle surf board and below trims a 12'6" race board along a clean Gold Coast wave in towards the shoreline. Transferring skills between board types allows you to adjust to differing nuances inherent in the board design. Conditions such as this are ideal for practicing board control and focus while using the paddle out wide to brace and at the ready to engage.

All equipment can pose a risk - a leash is worn ultimately for your convenience and safety, but also the safety of others. Over reliance on your leash as an excuse to fall, selection of an inappropriate design or length for any given day and economising by purchasing a 'cheap' option, can all lead down the path of injury and grief. Some things aren't worth compromising on. Below examples of a coiled leash with knee cuff fitment common to non-surf specific activities and a cord leash which is, featuring ankle cuff fitment, both with quick release pins for added security (for river paddling seek out professional advice).

The paddle back in

Selecting your entry point and wave selection on your way back in, is a learned skill. If racing, you may not have such a luxury, but even so, it may pay to wait and select the wave that's going to pay off the most, not necessarily the biggest. Nose diving is common for longer boards, so the moment you drop in, you will be looking to step back to keep the nose up. While you may be able to trim along the wave for some distance, inevitably you will need to straighten as you approach the shoreline. Time your dismount so as you don't nose dive into the beach or grind your fin. As the water shallows, ensure your knees are well bent, so if you fall, you're already lower to the water. Anticipate the board's run-on when you dismount. Avoid swimmers and others by a healthy margin!

Without practice, even the smallest beach breaks can present a problem. Add to this a race situation and the task becomes even more challenging with others in close proximity. Consider practicing taking on the shore break on smaller, wider stand up paddle surf boards before 'trashing' your race board.

Photo Steve West / Mallorca Spain

447

Travis demonstrates returning to the shoreline in a solid shore break. He uses the paddle to brace himself and transfers weight to the rear foot to sink the tail and stall his run.

KANU
CULTURE
publications since 1994

448

16

Body stresses

Paddling while standing can be a great workout.
The question is why promote it this way when no other paddle
sport gets the same acclaim or attempts to promote itself in this
manner. In addition, can the sport be easy
and a core workout at the same time?

KANU
CULTURE
publications since 1994

Photo Dana Edmunds Rider Travis Grant paddles his signature 12'6" TGIF C4 semi displaced race board.

Photo Dana Edmunds Rider Travis Grant.

This high performance semi-displacement hull design with soft rails, rolls with the punches and therefore you need to learn to roll with it not against it, which places an added requirement to be 'loose' through the hips. This is a true body workout. Tense up for one moment and you're probably going for a swim.

Stand up paddle boarding has widely been promoted as an excellent sport for increasing core-strength on account of the physiological and bio mechanical demands placed on the body in maintaining balance whilst paddling in a standing position.

Before considering this widely promoted virtue of the sport, it may pay to wind things back a bit to consider how the popularisation of core-strength training originated to a point where it is often the catch cry of the sport in the absence of any other virtue.

This is worrying when you consider that surfing, windsurfing, canoeing, kayaking - most any other board or paddle sport founded over the past hundred years, never resorted to promotion in this way, reinforcing the possibility that stand up paddle boarding to some degree, has been hijacked by personal trainers, coaches, yoga instructors, opportunists and a variety

Pilates, Swiss Ball and now stand up paddle board workouts. A 'workout' is exactly that, 'work'. The idea of the sport being promoted this way, puts it into the 'fad' category and debases any soul it may have, which means for those who do it for this reason alone, the chances are they will stay with it until the next fad comes along.

of entrepreneurs as a convenient extension in a long line of core-strength workouts.

Yoga is at the top of the tree so far as providing genuine health benefits. Performed on a board it elevates it to another level, activating stabilising muscles and ultimately core-muscle groups. 'Yoga boarding' as it has been termed, has led to the creation of yoga boards and their being used as part of remedial work, meditation and relaxation.

'The genesis of much of the abdominal work we do these days, probably lies in the work done in an Australian physiotherapy lab during the mid-1990s. Researchers there, hoping to elucidate the underlying cause of back pain, attached electrodes to people's midsections and directed them to rapidly raise and lower their arms. In those with healthy backs, the scientists found, a deep

Photo Mandy West Paddler Mark Slater

abdominal muscle tensed several milliseconds before the arms rose. The brain apparently alerted the muscle, the transversus abdominis, to brace the spine in advance of movement. In those with back pain, however, the transversus abdominis didn't fire early. The spine wasn't ready for the flailing. It wobbled and ached. Perhaps, the researchers theorised, increasing abdominal strength could ease back pain. The lab worked with patients in pain to isolate and strengthen that particular deep muscle, in part by sucking in their guts during exercises. The results, though mixed, showed some promise against sore backs.' *Gretchen Reynolds, New York Times June 18th 2009.*

From that highly technical foray into rehabilitative medicine, a booming industry of fitness classes were born centred on core-strength gains.

Thomas Nesser, an associate professor of physical education at Indiana State University who has studied core-fitness comments, **'The idea leaked into gyms in the form of Pilates classes pushing the belief that core health was all about the transversus abdominis. Personal trainers began directing clients to pull in their belly buttons during crunches on Swiss Balls or to press their backs against the floor during sit-ups, deeply hollowing their stomachs, then curl** up one spinal segment at a time. **People are now spending hours trying to strengthen their deep abdominal muscles'.**

Others such as Mitchell Yass, author of, 'Overpower Pain: The Strength Training Program That Stops Pain Without Drugs Or Surgery', notes that core programs were created, and took hold in the fitness industry, much like step aerobics, spinning and other popular workouts. **'The term and the ideas of the core, seem to have stuck the longest, but that doesn't make them legitimate,'** the physical therapist explains.

There are now literally hundreds of stand up paddle boarding websites and businesses promoting the sport in this same vain, cashing in on the core-strength ideology. The question that the sport has not asked itself, as it continues on its sleigh ride of growth, is to what extent is the hype accurate and furthermore, do we assume that those promoting it in this manner are qualified to endorse such claims or indeed promote correct paddling techniques so as core-muscles are in-fact activated as part of the paddling process.

Many who are using the core-strength tag, are neither exercise physiologists or qualified bio-mechanical experts, let alone fully conversant or skilled in teaching the bio-mechanical requirements of paddling. For the most part, it seems merely a convenient promotional cliché, requiring no more than repeating what is promoted on several hundred other websites as a part of a start-up business central hype, while failing to possibly understand the implications of such claims.

Can stand up paddle boarding be easy and provide a core workout at the same time?

A quality workout on a stand up paddle board is no different than on any other piece of equipment - you will only get out what you put in. You will of heard of the sport promoted as being 'Easy' requiring little or no effort or skill, let alone strength, yet at the same time the banter often professes the sport is a 'Great core workout'. While using core muscles is always the ultimate aim of the elite paddler, it's often an elusive concept to the novice.

Well, to all those promoting this concept, the fact is, you can't have it both ways. Like the 'ab-device' or 'fit-ball' you may purchase on TV, the virtues of the device is only true to the degree of stress or challenge you demand of yourself and the way in which you use it.

Promoting the sport as a workout or a way to develop core- strength, seems unusual and somewhat undermines the very long term key elements which transform a sport from a casual interest into a lifestyle choice and ultimately long term involvement. Something promoted as a workout, generally conjures up an activity which we don't necessarily like, but we do because we know we should. Buying into the sport on this basis, is akin to buying a gym membership or set of weights and we all know how that normally ends up. A workout is associated with work, sweat, toil and strain. Is that really how the sport should be promoted and just how long will that promotional slant work?

All other ocean board and paddle sports are largely promoted for their essential enduring qualities, not something as baseless as simply developing core-strength. In 25 years of outrigger canoeing at the highest levels, I don't recall it every being promoted as a workout or for the benefits it provides to core-strength, yet stand up paddle boarding is somehow perceived as uniquely different to the point of being no more than a form of gym equipment that floats.

It's perfectly possible to paddle a super stable board on flat water with effortless-effort, just so as the board moves along. This is not a workout, nor is your core being activated or strengthened or stabilising muscles being fired into action to assist maintaining balance.

Activating core-muscles is in no way as simple or straight forward as promoted. It involves turning in on oneself so as to tap into these deeper muscles at skeletal level. It involves some degree of breath control, focused application, the source of which many elite canoe and kayak paddlers strive to paddle from and within. Expecting your average sedentary newbie, to instantly tap into this illusive source of strength is pure folly, being as it requires concentrated nurturing and application.

A yoga instructor on her stand up paddle board between First Point and the Malibu Pier California performing amazing moves.

'As a personal trainer and core-strength specialist, I see a lot of triathletes and endurance athletes with weak core muscles and more importantly those who don't know how to activate their deep stabilising muscles, even after doing a Pilates class (i.e. transverse abdominus, multifidus, internal obliques, and pelvic floor muscles). Most people can activate and strengthen their "outer unit" muscles with side planks, front planks etc, but this is not necessarily what is going to improve their core strength. It's the deeper muscles that athletes need to work on and will only learn in a 1-2-1 session.' *Nick de Meyer, Level 3 British triathlon coach and Core Strength expert.*

What this tells us, is that many experienced athletes are not aware of the physiological process required to activate their deep stabilising muscles and subsequently their core-muscle groups. Randomly paddling a board with little concept of what core-strength or stability is, won't help much and even when you do know, be aware that the act of paddling is no guarantee you are developing or using core muscles to the degree the hype suggests.

In short you must ultimately learn to apply yourself ever more physically, while challenging your balance in more testing circumstances in order to realise real gains in core-strength, while being aware of the bio-mechanics required to activate this elusive muscle group.

Core muscles

When we talk in term of core muscles, we are essentially referring to the muscles of the upper torso situated well below the visible outer layer of muscle you can see. The major muscles of the core reside in the area of the belly and the mid and lower back and peripherally include the hips, the shoulders and the neck.

Major muscles included are the pelvic floor muscles, transversus abdominis, multifidus, internal and external obliques, rectus abdominis, erector spinae (sacrospinalis) especially the longissimus thoracis and the diaphragm. Minor core muscles include the latissimus dorsi, gluteus maximus and trapezius. Of these minor core groups, the latissimus dorsi is recognised as an important muscle used in the paddling process. The act of paddling while standing, certainly engages the gluteus maximus, the trapezius used during compression of the stroke.

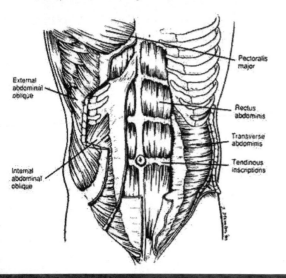

The transversus abdominus muscles are prime power sources for assisting torque and rotation during the power phase of the stroke as are the external and internal obliques, the rectus abdominus providing stability, 'compression' as well as rotation.

Photo Dana Edmunds Rider Travis Grant

The upper body may provide the power, but from the hips downwards, the gearbox. The connectedness and transference of energy from the upper body to the lower body (and to the feet) creates significant amounts of tension especially around the area of the hip flexors, but this needs to be balanced with 'looseness' of the hips, knees and ankles so as to avoid being too rigid in attempting to resist the board's movements, more especially in rough waters.

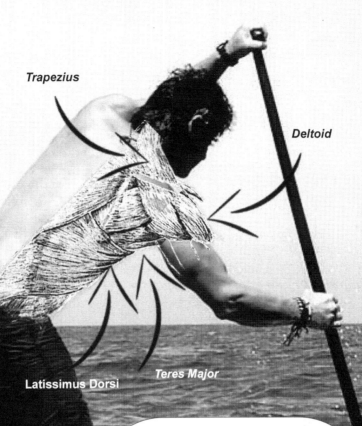

Photo Mandy West

Trapezius

Deltoid

Latissimus Dorsi

Teres Major

Paddling with incorrect technique for several years or more, will ultimately 'sculpt' your body, so as when you attempt to modify this technique in order to create greater efficiencies, the body has to be re-sculpted, new reflexes learned and the body retrained, highlighting the need to ensure you learn sound paddling technique early. Differing 'techniques' whether Hawaiian, Tahitian, Anglo-Polynesian, differing paddle lengths and a multitude of small micro adjustments, will tend to work differing muscle groups harder. In all of this, it's important to keep in mind that the smaller muscles; biceps, triceps in particular are neither as enduring or powerful as the use of larger muscles of the back and abdominals and hence the focus upon engaging the core muscle groups.

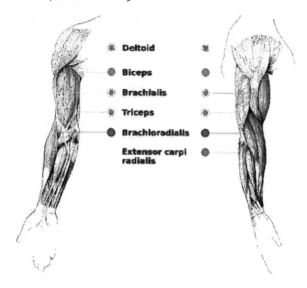

Deltoid

Biceps

Brachialis

Triceps

Brachioradialis

Extensor carpi
radialis

Arm muscles. Transfer of power to core muscles

The smaller muscles of the arm such as the biceps, triceps, forearms, engage predominantly at the catch and power phase of the stroke, together with the latissimus dorsi (minor core muscle).

The greater portion of labour and power is ultimately transferred to the major core muscle groups through torque, activated by the paddler twisting around the spine as the shaft of the paddle nears vertical, using the rotational forces of the oblique muscles. Compression 'over the stroke' is delivered through the trapezium, deltoid, upper back muscles and contraction of the rectus abdominis. This fundamental bio-mechanical technique is well understood by top level canoeists and kayakers worldwide.

Stabiliser muscles

Stand up paddle boarding can make demands of the core muscles early on in the learning phase, more especially if the smaller stabilising muscle groups are triggered. These are activated through nerve impulses, which once activated (contracted) they will in turn serve to support the larger core muscles in promoting balance and of course power to the stroke. This is the same rationale behind the use of a Swiss-Ball or free-weights.

The body has two essential muscle types, movers and stabilisers. Movers are the larger muscles which control and move the body, while the smaller stabiliser muscles hold the parts in place and prevent damage during movement.

'**Stabilising muscle contractions are generally isometric contractions that act to support the trunk, limit movement in a joint, or control balance. These stabilising muscles play a supporting role to the larger muscle groups, but most importantly help prevent injury.**' *The American Council on Exercise.*

Stand up paddle boarding practised correctly with adequate intensity in an environment which effectively challenges some degree of balance, ensures that these core-muscles are activated and that stabilising muscles are triggered into activity and strengthened as a consequence. You will only get out of it, what you put in.

Lower body

What makes the stand up paddling forward stroke unique, are the stresses it places on the lower body on account of the paddler assuming an upright, standing position. The calves, quadriceps and gluteus maximus are all put under tension as are the hip flexors, knees, ankles and feet.

Energy generated from the pull against the blade, ultimately transfers to the feet. When seated in an outrigger canoe, the energy transfers to the paddlers rear and downwards to the feet, dissipating this force between these body contact points, resulting in the canoe moving forward.

In the context of stand up paddle boarding, from the hips downwards to the feet, we could consider the gearbox in the equation of energy transference. The feet in contact with the board, drives this energy, generated at the point of origin, the blade, to the

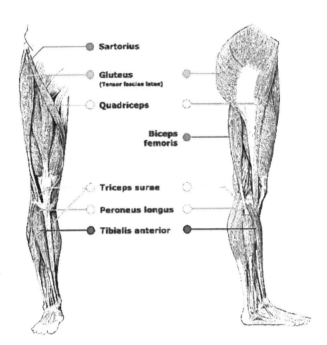

Sartorius

Gluteus
(Tensor fasciae latae)

Quadriceps

Biceps femoris

Triceps surae

Peroneus longus

Tibialis anterior

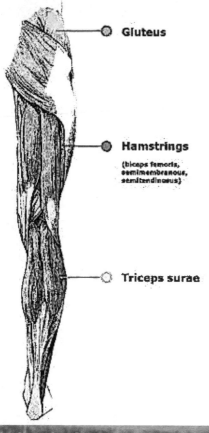

Gluteus

Hamstrings

(biceps femoris,
semimembranous,
semitendinosus)

Triceps surae

Photo Courtesy Ocean Promotions

462

board. The feet therefore, are the essential link which lock in and drive power to the board to move it forward.

The quality of energy transference to the board through the feet relies a great deal on adequate tension being maintained during the power phase (pulling / rotation) of the stroke from the hips. Hip flexors and quadriceps, take substantial strain as the energy is transferred from the blade, downward to the lower legs and to the board.

The most profound point of difference which this sport has over all other paddle sports as a direct result of standing, is the totality of work load (potentially) it brings into play between the upper and lower body. The upper torso and lower body must work together to deliver power to the board. So far as balance is concerned, they will often work independently of each other. Keeping the hips loose enough to permit the board to move with the nuances of your paddling and water movement, while delivering power to the board, is an acquired skill. Paddling with 'loose hips' will permit the board to work with the water's movements, not against - as it will the knees and ankles.

Fast and slow twitch muscles

An erroneous promotional hype we hear, is that the sport will 'improve your fast twitch muscles' - fast twitch muscle is a factor of genetics, not training, though some research suggests that fast-twitch, the speed at which muscles contracts, can be altered by specificity of training, but only marginally. It is a very complex and much debated issue, therefore open statements suggesting that participation will improve (speed up) fast twitch muscle (improve slow twitch muscle rates) contractions, is sweeping to say the least.

Summary

Whether adventure paddling or downwind racing, paddle boarding stand up style, can rapidly change from being an easy go with the flow experience, to an endurance sport where you require these larger, stronger muscles to do the bulk of the work as they will tire less, than the smaller arm muscles.

Consequently, in describing the standing paddle board forward stroke, emphasis must be placed on activating these larger muscle groups. Muscles not involved in actual paddling should be relaxed. Adverse body motion will affect the run of the board, therefore smooth transmission of power in the stroke is essential.

The sheer physicality of downwind paddling in testing conditions, makes it the ultimate testing ground for the stand up paddler. If you did nothing else but downwind paddle most of the time, where it was possible, you would make huge gains in overall paddling fitness, board and paddling skills and best of all, it's a ton of fun.

Photo Karen Baxter Rider Connor Baxter

Like many of my contemporaries who have dedicated a lifetime to ocean paddle sports, having had the good fortune to spend more time on the water than most, the notion of the ocean being the 'blue gym' holds true, where given the choice of time on the water or time in the gym, it's a no brainer. Indeed you would be surprised to learn how few a number of elite ocean paddlers ever touch a set of weights, when it's best to simply move between different ocean craft to work different areas of the body and to work on other skill sets.

KANU CULTURE

Physical conditioning

Stand up paddle board racing can be extremely physical. Entry level paddlers should consider the creation and nurturing of a physical conditioning program in order to fast track 'hardening' of the body required for vigorous paddling. While downwind paddling and paddle surfing are naturally demanding, some individuals will need more off board physical training and conditioning regimes than others. In short however, no matter how fit the individual, all paddlers benefit from cross training and activities specifically aimed at improving the body's ability to paddle at its best.

Skills versus conditioning

In the very first instance, good technique and a high degree of skill must be focused upon. Such skills promote efficiency, reduce injury and focus attention upon the bio-mechanics of the sport beyond any other consideration. Good technique will lead to the development and flexibility of correct muscle groups. In the second instance, physical conditioning must be factored into any training schedule to enhance and improve performance based around five principal factors, of fitness.

If you limit your physical conditioning to on water sessions, you will fall short of addressing some fitness issues which simply cannot be achieved by the act of paddling alone - especially when it comes to cardiovascular fitness. Mountain bike riding works the legs, hip flexors and cardiovascular system in excess of what can be reasonably achieved on your board. Seek out activities that can complement your paddling.

Training to increase speed and strength endurance, involves plenty of sprint work and increasing stroke rates during prolonged paddling sessions. These are best developed through the implementation of on-water interval training sessions, which are characterised by time (mins) x intensity (% of perceived effort) designed to test the body aerobically and anaerobically. In addition skill sets can be developed, such as starting, rounding markers and variance of stroke rates and lengths. Interval training implemented as part of a periodisation plan (see racing chapter) provides the single best means of training for paddle sports.

Endurance - Strength - Flexibility - Speed - Power

Each one of the factors needs careful consideration in the development of physical conditioning of the paddler. While some of these can be gained by paddling alone, in combination with specific drills and set training regimes, others are only acquired off the board to any great degree.

Power

Power training can be identified as being intensive physical work, closely associated with strength training. Power, differs by definition from strength, in as much it is related to time or speed of repetition. Pure strength is concerned for example with one burst of strength, while power relates to repetition.

Resistance training on the board will increase overall power, which can be achieved by paddling into head winds, or wrapping bungee cords around the board to add drag for example. Substantial increase in power can be gained from weight training if required, but time on the water produces better quality, specific power requirements.

Endurance

The ability of the body to endure extended periods of repetitive physical exercise. Stand up paddle boarding is primarily an endurance sport, therefore much of our training must centre around building endurance and an efficient paddling technique. In order to develop endurance, the body (muscles, tendons, ligaments) must develop strength. Isolated muscle groups for paddling, need to develop strength and an ability to handle heavy loads periodically as associated with endurance paddling and certainly some of this can be achieved through the use of weights.

Gradual increases in distances paddled will need to be factored into a training schedule. Depending on what event you are training for and over what distance you will need to prepare for, you can gradually orientate time and distance paddled to suit, keeping in mind that your ultimate goal will be to train over distances greater than the race distance.

Endurance is a very complex issue, which need take into the account the overall physiology of the individual. Some of us are built for endurance whilst others for speed and power in short bursts. Strength of mind and the will to persist are all crucial personality factors within endurance. Cardiovascular fitness (aerobic) plays a major role in endurance paddling and therefore this needs to be improved through cross training to raise heart levels for sustained periods of time. Swimming is an excellent, low impact sport to supplement paddling as is prone paddle boarding.

Strength
Maximum strength
This relates to the maximum force an individual can produce during a given movement of unlimited time i.e. maximum weight they can pull or lift.

Explosive strength
The maximum force an individual can produce in a short amount of time.

Australian paddlers across a variety of ocean paddle sports, have used swimming for many years as a natural extension of their paddling to build cardiovascular strength.

If someone turns up to a race looking like this, have no fear as they will no doubt lack strength endurance (not to mention flexibility) and crash and burn very quickly. Long, lean muscle for the most part, favours the paddler. Your gym work out should not be a body-building regime.

Reactive strength
Relates to the body's ability to absorb heavy impacts.

Sustained strength
Maintaining maximum force over several repeated contractions or throughout a single contraction of long duration.

Strength endurance
Sustaining strength over 5 or 6 minutes of repetitive activity.

Consequently we can see that some elements of strength are more relevant to paddling than others. Power to weight ratio is an important factor for the paddler. While strength is important, we can ascertain that being able to bench press an impressive amount of weight is not as important as strength endurance.

Understanding of the sport's strength requirements, is essential in developing and promoting a successful strength program. The strength demands vary greatly from race to race. Sprint races demand different strength factors than that of distance races, as do flat water races as against downwind paddling.

Sprint races will rely greatly on good explosive and reactive strength, to establish a good start, while distance races will rely more upon strength endurance. Typically, top level paddlers posses a range of all facets of strength, where maximal strength remains the least significant.

468

Improving strength for each of these involves resistance training in a variety of forms. The very act of paddling involves resistance and therefore a variety of training programs will develop each one of these strengths i.e. practice of race starts will improve explosive and reactive strengths, while paddling of a more continuous nature, with burst of maximum power, will nurture both sustained and endurance strength.

Certain resistance training methods can be incorporated. A simple method is to wrap bungee cord or similar around the board to create drag. You can vary the number or thickness of bungee, or you could hole out a tennis ball and slide this along the cord to the centre so as it drags under the board. Be careful to avoid creating injury or aggravating injury.

Flexibility through stretching

Flexibility of the body is essential in order to maximise the full potential that can be gained by additional reach gained in the stroke through twisting of the upper body. Many paddlers remain very short in their reach out front due to being inflexible. Short, tight hip flexors can be a limiting problem. Being inflexible tends to be the result of one's lifestyle postural habits (often work related) along with problems associated with weight training, without the incorporation of stretching routines, so as the muscles are encouraged to shorten, thereby leading to a lack of flexibility. Stretching must be an essential part of any training regime. The benefits associated with stretching and improvement of flexibility include;

Improved range of motion and flexibility
The bio-mechanical needs of paddling are such that any increased range of motion will bring greater fluidity, increase leverage through increased reach, improve overall bio mechanical effectiveness.

Reduction of injury
Improved flexibility results in a greater range of tolerance to which the body can be made to stretch without injury. Flexible muscles and tendons are much less likely to incur strain as again being tight and inflexible.

Increased level of comfort
As a result of paddling and gym work, muscles will tend to increase in size and shorten as they tighten. Stretching helps maintain and increase length and flexibility leading to greater physical comfort while paddling.

Psychological benefits

Associated with team bonding, relaxation, becoming in tune with your body and general preparation. All are important areas of sport. Time out while stretching, allows for these psychological benefits to occur.

Any paddling conditioning program must include stretching. Of all the areas of physical conditioning it is probably the most neglected, yet contributes greatly to improved performance and reduction of injury which need to be considered as paramount. It is not possible to over stretch in terms of frequency and while it should be done prior and after training of any sort, it can also be done at anytime when time and space permit. Stretching to improve flexibility should be done at a separate time to training not simply part of a warm up / cool down. Stretches need to be sustained for over 60 seconds to gain improvement in muscle length.

Tightened (shortened) hamstrings can be a common ailment of the paddler which in turn affects the lower back - stretching the hamstrings using a stretch-band can provide relief.

The stretch band is an extremely safe method of stretching the body while offering up some resistance at the same time. Many paddlers use stretch bands within their exercise regime. Typically, shortened, tight muscles benefit from this form of stretching.

Downwind paddling can be very aerobically demanding. In many ways it replicates interval training, where you're constantly 'on the power' and 'off the power' as your stroke rate varies dramatically in reflecting the boards acceleration and deceleration.

Speed

Training to develop speed, requires a combination of physiological abilities, not least of which is general strength. However issues of fast twitch over slow twitch muscles will essentially dictate an individuals full potential to develop real speed from their muscles than others, however some slow twitch muscles can be trained to marginally increase in responsiveness.

Paddlers rely upon a mix of both muscle types, fast and slow twitch. At the start of a race you will rely upon fast twitch and as time passes, especially during distance paddling you will rely more upon the slow twitch endurance capabilities of your muscles.

Training to increase speed involves plenty of sprint work and increasing stroke rates during prolonged paddling sessions.

Cardiovascular fitness

One interesting physiological factor regarding the act of paddling, is that even at full pace, it is difficult to raise the heart to its maximum rate, as against running up a flight of stairs. What this signifies, is that paddlers need to train off-water in order to raise heart rates beyond that produced by sustained paddling.

Application of training principles

In applying principles of training to any one of these areas of physical conditioning the following concerns need apply;

Specificity

You must isolate the facet of conditioning you are aiming to improve. This will create a goal-orientated approach to training. Implementation of a specific training regime allows for the foundations of general fitness to be achieved first, followed by periods of training and isolating, strength, power, speed and so on, over a given duration as part of your periodisation, planning and preparation.

Progression

Nurturing physical conditioning in a logical sequence so as you first create a base level of fitness, followed by focusing on more specific areas of conditioning, including skill levels. There is no value in missing out a part of the conditioning process, as all must be present to create a balanced result. Naturally, you can prioritise certain aspects on a individual basis.

Individuality

Individuals vary in strength, weaknesses, athleticism, co-ordination, water skill and all manner of abilities. It is therefore important that you recognise these individual differences and cater to them to whatever degree possible. Failure to do so can lead to damaging results primarily by demanding too much of yourself (or others).

Variety of training regimes is not only good in order to keep things interesting, but also ensures the body is experiencing a wider variety of movements and stresses, thereby building up general conditioning at the same time. Boredom must be avoided. By being overly repetitive in ones training formats, paddlers loose some interest.

Overload

In order to improve the body's ability to deal with increased physical effort, it must be exerted progressively harder so as it is essentially overloaded. The body must be stressed or pushed which acts as a catalyst for improved physical abilities in all areas of endurance, strength, flexibility, speed, power and cardiovascular fitness. The result of such effort leads to physical and mental fatigue which must be counter balanced by rest (sleep) and recovery. In time these rest periods will diminish relative to improved physical and mental conditioning.

New paddlers in particular who have never experienced such physical activity, will find that they are essentially overloading even in the early stages of learning to paddle. They may well fatigue quickly and be slow to recover as their bodies adapt to the physical demands of paddling. However continued participation, together with adequate rest periods, will lead ultimately to the bodies adaption to such exertion.

Reversibility

This occurs when fitness or physical condition is lost as a result of too much rest or time away from activity, specific or otherwise. Often this can come about as a result of injury or illness or through an extended off- season period. Off-season training needs to be encouraged to maintain a base level of fitness and some form of activity participated in when injured.

Use of paddling machines (See chapter 17)

Photo Steve West Rider Cristina Rozalen

Use of weights - pulling iron to pull paddle

The use of weights can form a basis for resistance work and increase muscle strength.

The following exercise are commonly used by paddlers. As a general rule, heavy weight training is associated with out of season training, whilst during the season, lighter sessions of less frequency are generally adhered to, if at all.

A periodised strength programme, aligned with the paddling programme, will help achieve training and competition goals.

Enlist the assistance of a strength and conditioning coach to put together an appropriate weights programme. Illustrated are some popular upper body gym exercises used by paddlers. This is by no means complete. Variations exist and it is recommended you research a variety of additional gym exercises which can be used.

Warning!
The potential for
injury is high
when weight
training,
especially
shoulder injury.
Exercise caution.

Twisting motions using an
unweighted bar can improve
flexibility and rotational strength.
Weights could be added. Any oblique
work using medicine balls also forms
a great conditioning exercise for
paddling. Pull down exercises,
behind and in front of the head, work
differing muscle groups of the upper
back and chest. This can also be
practised from a standing position.

Photos Steve West

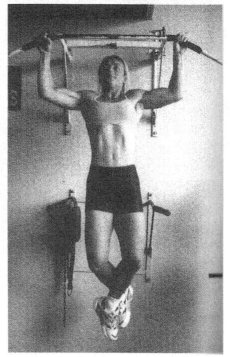

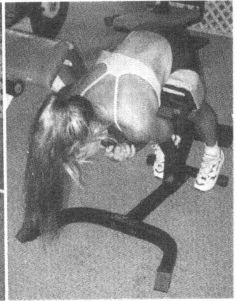
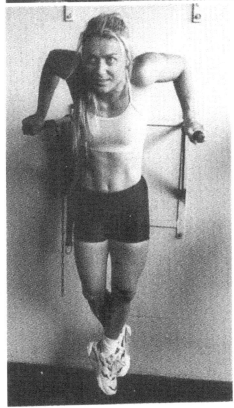

Travis Grant's take on increasing, maintaining and gaining paddling fitness

Chin ups - on account of the sport being a 'pulling exercise' where strength to weight matters. **Boxing** - for a solid cardio-workout. **Outrigger Canoeing** - the synergy between the two sports is amazing! SUP is outrigger canoeing standing up. **Body Surfing** - to connect with the ocean and work the body. **Stretching** - for recovery, injury prevention and improved muscle performance. **Good food** - to fuel your performance. It's the foundation of being a competitive paddler. Eat well all the time as part of your lifestyle. **Surfing** - playing in the waves hones your skills and reminds you to have fun whilst connecting with the ocean. **Downwind paddling** - my favourite thing to do in harnessing nature's energy and for all-round skills development and fitness. **Interval training** - done on the water, paddling hard then backing off to set intervals. Great for BOP training. **Surf ski paddling** - for cross-training and something different again. Great for speed training and working the cardio system. **Sleep** - remember to have plenty of rest and sleep.

Weights generally don't play a large part of the ocean paddler's regime when they can find plenty of water time in! There's no substitute.

478

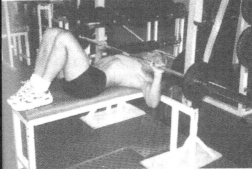

The radiant physical prowess of indigenous Pacific island outrigger canoe paddlers is without equal. Waka Ama (outrigger canoe) crew Aotearoa (New Zealand) National Championship.

Photo Steve West

KANU CULTURE

publications since 1994

OC1 paddling - the best quality cross-training craft for stand up paddle boarding. Travis Grant punching out the miles.

17

Drills, stretches and simulators

Using drills to practice and hone your skills can be very rewarding, but mostly it builds discipline. Stretching with the paddle brings gains in knowing what you're trying to do with it and improving your fine motor skills in managing it, while gaining the benefits associated with stretching. Various simulators are on the market, while other true and tested devices have already found solutions to bolting on accessories to simulate the stroke.

Dry land contortions

Trainers, coaches, instructors often need to be creative in getting their message across with regards to the mechanics of paddling - more importantly the bio-mechanics. Here are a few considerations which I have either evolved, or borrowed over the years.

While most of us get the idea of stretching and flexibility, it has to be said that of all the abilities many of us may gain through regular paddling and elsewhere, universally, flexibility remains often the most over-looked consideration. With the emergence of yoga boarding, there has been more attention on this area of fitness which makes up part of the sum of the whole in pursuing a holistic approach.

Rotate and drop

This simple dry land exercise is hugely affective and one of the simplest ways of replicating and learning the feel of what you are setting out to achieve. Some of the key elements can be considered and performed and in the hands of a coach you can be tweaked into position. This exercise will affirm how flexible you are for paddling.

Whether you're coaching somebody or wishing to figure out a few things for yourself, drills such as this benefit you from the point of view of being able to consider your movements (even if exaggerated) while testing your own levels of flexibility.

Photo Steve West
Cornwall.England
Marie Buchanan demonstrates.

1. The first image demonstrates the importance of rotation of the shoulders and hips as you turn away from the stroke as part of the wind-up phase. If performed correctly, you will feel the need to relax your leading leg relative to which side the paddle will enter.

You soon appreciate, that failing to relax the hips and in turn, the knees and ankles, you are fighting against the body's 'will' or need for you to go with the flow of things not fight it. Turn fully so as your rear and leading hand are near in horizontal alignment, blade face directly forward. You can simply twist back and forth either way as a stretching / warm up exercise. Twisting is the first part of ensuring good reach forward of the blade.

2. The second image takes us to the point of entry and reinforces that this is simply achieved by a lowering of the leading shoulder and 'falling' of the upper body downwards. The angle of the blade stops you falling. Critically this technique ensures the paddler does not commit all of their body weight directly downwards as would be the case if they failed to twist and simply plunged the paddle, downwards with square-on hips. The added benefit is of course improved reach and the torque (rotation) which can now be delivered to the paddle when winding back through the stroke. Note: The leading knee, bends inwards and downwards to accommodate the weight of the torso and added reach.

What we are aiming to replicate on land, is an exaggeration of what it is we aim to do when on the water. Exaggerated twist results in highlighting the gains in reach to be had as well as the degree of torque which can be created during the rotational phase of the stoke. Note also the bending of the leading knee, inwards and downwards to accommodate the hips during the set up phase and how it straightens during the pull through.

Photo Mandy West / Ireland

Taken a step further, this rotational exercise can be practiced when on the water. As eccentric as this might seem, this simple test can demonstrate and fast track fine motor skills in the context of developing your paddle skills in bringing about improvements.

The Pendulum Drill

This drill has been in existence for some years now and has been used by such coaches as Billy Whitford with Offshore Californian outrigger canoe crews and a drill I have used to good effect to promote and highlight the need for fine motor skills to be present as part of sound paddling technique. Designed to test your fine motor co-ordination, this drill immediately separates out those who are co-ordinated and possess fluidity in their movements and control of the blade.

The drill brings home the need to develop awareness of the importance of controlling the paddle's alignment through the upper hand (as the axis point) timing of your rotation, the need to reach, develop balance, poise and discipline. Importantly it also demonstrates how your lower hand must not over work the exit or the follow through, that it must be controlled to be in sync with all other forces. Those who are race training, often spend very little time developing skills devoting all their time to 'smashing' themselves in the pursuit of fitness - skill development is essential.

As the paddle is exited from the water, the paddler begins their recovery, then literally 'throws' the paddle forward from the lower hand in a controlled manner. Too much and the paddle will swing across the body-line. The top hand is the axis point around which the paddle now works and you must work to control the paddle's line of travel. As the paddle swings back toward you, you will be forced to rotate and reach for the shaft.

Photos Mandy West / Bona Ona Mallorca Spain

Photo Mandy West / Ireland

Photo Mandy West / Ireland

Photo Steve West
Bona Ona Mallorca Spain

Photo supXscape / Portugal

Pre on water stretching using the paddle can help reinforce the relationship the paddler forges in terms of moving with it and developing spatial awareness of its proximity to the surrounds. Being able to wield the paddle with the confidence of an experienced swordsman, you will be comfortable with its nuances and how you can literally move it from side to side, over your head, behind your back, with confidence.

Skimming

This simple drill is invaluable in training the paddler to develop a relaxed low swing through during the recovery phase of the stroke. While it's understood that a square, 'up and over' recovery can be used I have already addressed the limitations with this approach; encourages downward drive through the legs rather than a more angled trajectory, negates shoulder rotation and twist of the upper body and if a bracing or correctional stroke is needed during the recovery, this cannot be achieved as fast. Besides these factors, the entire outrigger canoeing community cannot be wrong as this is their primary approach throughout the recovery phase.

Relaxation of the shoulder, rolling of the lower wrist inwards, relaxation of the upper wrist, the body winds back up and the leading shoulder is brought forward again, the blade is 'feathered' as it travels low over the water, keeping the flow of the board smooth, a reflection of the smoothness of recovery. From here the paddler can quickly brace out wide if needs be or bring about a correctional stroke.

Photo Mandy West / Italy

Photo Mandy West

Practice feathering the blade and keeping a low recovery by skimming the blade edge over the water back to the entry. Developing paddle skills through drills can fast track the learning process.

Use of Tanks / Mirrors

Jim Terrells Quickblade 'Flume' tank, has had a good deal of exposure and received a variety of comments as to its efficacy as a training device and alerted new paddlers to the concept. The use of mirrors and a water tank for paddlers to go through the motions is however, not a new concept. The efficacy of such a device resides in understanding its limitations and factoring this in, with regards to what you're feeling as a test pilot or observing as a coach. This is what serves to elevate such a device from novelty, to going concern.

Quickblades device, may offer a taste of the real thing, but in truth the limits would seem obvious and in no way is it being offered up as a substitute for such; you can only paddle on one side, the flow of water created by the paddler causes the paddle to be entered into 'moving' water, flowing not in a laminar direction but circular, when in reality, the water is for the most part stationary; the board would move, not the water, so in this context the reality of the situation is reversed. In addition the water can become heavily aerated and therefore a 'clean' catch not entirely achievable.

492

Jim Terrells 'Flume' in action (C1 paddling)

In 1995 I photographed members of the Outrigger Canoe Club (Hawai`i) ladies crew training under Steve Scott, one of the club's all time most successful coaches, using the club's simulator located in the under-ground car park. Here the paddlers sit in part of a canoe and face a mirror. From watching the girls training, the device was brilliant from the context of ensuring good timing between the girls in 'mirror-imaging' one another and for the coach to micro-manage individual techniques / styles. The blade sizes are downsized in order to bring about some blade slippage, but when added to heavily aerated water, they appeared to move quite freely.

Without the need to build anything per se, a singular plank across a stretch of water (small swimming pool) permits the paddler to paddle on either side and a mirror in front allows some stroke analysis, while using a very small blade area to permit some slippage - even a simple modified shaft and custom made blade area of only several inches width.

Outrigger Canoe Club Hawaii 1995 training in the club purpose built simulator.
Photos Steve West Outrigger Canoe Club Hawai`i

Photo Steve West
Outrigger Canoe Club Hawai'i

Simulators

When the Concept II Rowing Ergo was first created back in 1981, the device revolutionised training methods for many thousands of rowers and found favour with many gyms as standard equipment, used by the paddler and non-paddler alike.

In 1995 Mark McAndrew of Vermont Waterways began work on a paddling adaptor to meet the growing needs of outrigger canoe paddlers (and canoeists in general) and his work led him to Hawai`i to work alongside Todd Bradley. The idea was to create a retro-fitted device which would turn the Concept II from rowing simulator to canoeing simulator.

I had several conversations with Mark and was fortunate enough to road test the device at Todd's home and between us, we realised this was going to be a brilliant bit of kit. The modified set up was a great success and was able to be fitted by home owners and gyms. Now with the growth of stand up paddle boarding, it's no surprise that there is now a paddling adaptor for the Concept II to meet the demand.

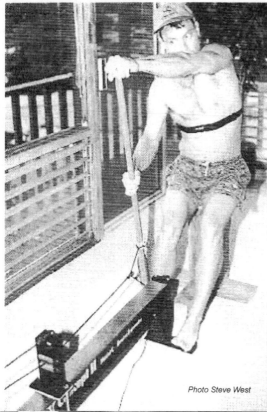

Todd Bradley at home in 1995 training with the prototype paddling adaptor for the Concept II rowing machine.

'With the addition of the SUP kit, the Paddling Adapter becomes a sport-specific trainer for standup paddle board paddlers as well as a cross training tool that improves core strength. When used with the balance platform placed behind the rower, the Paddling Adapter simulates the side-to-side motion of a paddle board. Combined with a longer paddle shaft, the balance platform allows for SUP training strikingly close to an on-water feel.'

Photo Steve West

Photo Mandy West

The Concept II rowing machine now adapted to mimic stand up paddle boarding bio-mechanics.

Greg Long, longtime competitive outrigger and SUP paddler from the Gold Coast of Australia has this to say about the SUP Paddling Adapter:

'To be honest, I had my doubts about how effective it would be in activating your core whilst paddling when you could apply the

Greg Long paddles an OC₁ at Hamilton Island.

full power in your stroke and I've been suitably impressed by the whole thing. It's been really good. The tippy board - balance platform - I think they've pretty much nailed it in terms of tippiness for a Stand Up. It's not over the top but it still makes you activate your core and you can still blade in that power. I think it's awesome.'

KayakPro have produced a from the ground up, purpose made SUP Ergometer and represents the top end of the gene pool so far as stand up paddling simulators go. Danny Ching has been an advocate and it certainly has many features which make it the weapon of choice if you're looking for the complete system and where budget isn't an issue - for a club purchase it makes perfect sense and when there's 6' of snow on the driveway, even more sense.

'The adjustable resistance and adjustable paddle shaft length allows you to train at your preferred resistance level, to best mimic your own board. The "feel-real" stand-on, moving tilting SUP platform provides the board motion that you would expect from a real SUP board, encouraging you to use the small

Danny Ching modelling the KayakPro SUP Ergometer.

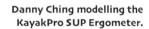

stabilising, and core muscles that also need to be trained in order to give you the full body work out that you would expect from on the water SUP paddling. This "feel real" board motion is essential in order to encourage the relationship and balance between maintaining board stability and intensity of effort - that's how to increase performance and speed on your SUP board.'

There are several other simulators on the market, considerably cheaper, consisting of a balance board, rubber band and / or pulley mechanisms. For balance training, land based balance boards can be of some value and can be easily home made or purchased commercially.

Above: Digital readouts of distance travelled, strokes per minute, distance of each stroke taken are standard calculations with expensive set ups. Below: An old school windsurfing simulator, used to teach the basics of windsurfing can be useful for teaching some of the mechanics of stand up paddle boarding. These were often made from discarded wheel hubs and simply welded with box steel legs and a platform, the board is held in place using rack straps.

Photos Steve West

As subversive as this act may seem, paddling a kayak standing up will test your balance and reinforce the need for smoothness throughout all phases of the stroke; set up, entry, catch, pull, exit and recovery. The rules defining, what is, or what is not, a stand up paddle board do not currently exist and as it stands, you could legally race this alongside any other stand inside 'board' in the Unlimited division and argue your case. It was once told to me a kayak or canoe should fall within a 6:1 ratio and that the use of a single paddle would be, canoeing and the use of a double ended paddle, kayaking. Regrettably and typically Eurocentrically, we use the word canoeing and kayaking literally to mean both things which is a nonsense and disrespects the cultures from which the craft originates.

Acknowledgements

So many to thank and not just over the past 5 years, but back over 25 years and more. But directly and as a constant throughout this publication, my wife Mandy and the assistance from various sectors of the business community as sponsors and supporters.